Trade and b... early modern England

Eric Kerridge

Manchester University Press

Published by Manchester University Press
Oxford Road, Manchester M13 9PL

Distributed exclusively in the USA and Canada
by St. Martin's Press, Inc., 175 Fifth Avenue, New York, NY 10010, USA

British Library cataloguing in publication data
Kerridge, Eric
   Trade and banking in early modern England.
   1. England – Commerce – History
   I. Title
   380.1'0942   HF3515

Library of Congress cataloging in publiction data applied for

ISBN 0 7190 2652 0 *hardback*

Typeset in Great Britain
by Williams Graphics, Abergele, North Wales

Printed and bound in Great Britain by
Biddles Ltd, Guildford and King's Lynn

Contents

Acknowledgements

I am deeply grateful to the Trustees of the Houblon-Norman Fund for the generous grants that made this work possible; to Professor J. R. S. Revell, who gave much help and encouragement; and to Dr C. E. Challis and others who shared their knowledge with me. My debts to Professors M. G. Davies and T. S. Willan and the late N. S. B. Gras will be apparent from the references to their work. Most of all I am indebted to my late wife for her constant help and support, for her unpublished dissertation on Liverpool history, and for her study of the Liverpool probate inventories. I lay exclusive claim to all errors.

To Anna, Jeffrey and Steven

by the same author

Textile manufactures in early modern England
The farmers of old England
Agrarian problems in the sixteenth century and after
The agricultural revolution

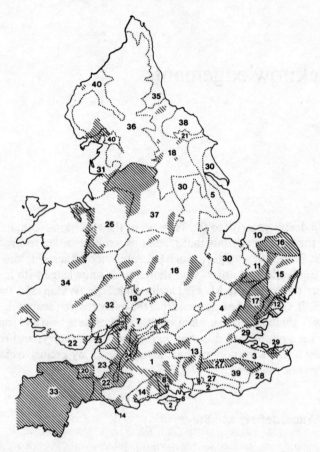

Fig. 1 The farming countries of early modern England, with the textile regions superimposed (shaded).

1 Chalk Country	15 High Suffolk	29 Saltings Country
2 Southdown Country	16 East Norfolk	30 Fen Country
3 Northdown Country	17 Woodland	31 Lancashire Plain
4 Chiltern Country	18 Midland Plain	32 Vales of Hereford
5 Northwold Country	19 Vale of Evesham	33 West Country
6 Oxford Heights Country	20 Vale of Taunton Deane	34 Wales
7 Cotswold Country	21 Vale of Pickering	35 North-eastern Lowlands
8 South Seacoast Country	22 Butter Country	36 North Country
9 Petworth District	23 Western Waterlands	37 Peak-Forest Country
10 Norfolk Heathlands	24 Cheese Country	38 Blackmoors
11 Breckland	25 Vale of Berkeley	39 High Weald
12 Sandlings Country	26 Cheshire Cheese Country	40 North-western Lowlands
13 Blackheath Country	27 Wealden Vales	41 Vale of London
14 Poor Soils Country	28 Romney Marsh	

1
Introductory

In ancient and medieval times, banking sprang from three main sources: merchants who financed foreign and long-distance trade and then took to exchange-banking and high finance; money-changers who acted also as deposit bankers; and public banks, which were concerned with state finances and currency regulation.

The ancient Greeks diffused their private, money-changing type of banking throughout their world, to Italy, Israel, Egypt, India and elsewhere.[1] This kind of business had tenacious roots in the multiplicity of different coinages. We find it still in the twelfth century in Lucca, Genoa and Venice, in the thirteenth in Lille and Douai, in the fourteenth also in Bruges, Barcelona, Milan, Pisa, Palermo, Naples, Constantinople, Strasbourg, and Frankfort-on-the-Main. It took no root in England, simply because ours was the only nation-state and the only large territory with a single, unified coinage. Royal exchangers at the sea-ports provided all the services needed. In other lands money-changing bankers managed current accounts both large and small, effected credit transfers between customers, cleared accounts between each other, worked on a fractional reserve principle, created credit, extended overdrafts to favoured customers, took a few deposit accounts, and invested in trade, industry and state bonds. Being small, local undertakings, and lacking any lender of the last resort, bankers like these succumbed all too easily, especially during the economic depression of the later middle ages.[2]

Public banks were likewise of ancient origin.[3] The Knights Templars and Knights of St John and Jerusalem provided similar services at one time, but from the eleventh century onwards many municipalities had their own banks, the Rialto bank in Venice perhaps being the most famous, and among the more prominent ones in the

seventeenth century those in Amsterdam and Hamburg. Public banks
like these owed their often ephemeral lives to a variety of needs: the
handling of municipal and state debts; the institution of *banco* moneys
of account to regulate the use of diverse and mixed coinages; and the
provision of facilities for payment on bills of exchange, at Rotterdam,
Delft and Hamburg especially for the convenience of the Merchant
Adventurers of England. The Bank of Stockholm also issued bank-
notes in substitution for the impossibly cumbersome Swedish copper
coinage. The capital for these public banks was provided sometimes
by the municipality or state itself, sometimes by its creditors. Banks
like these characteristically accepted deposits, especially safe deposits,
from the general public; made internal transfers; administered
municipal and state debts and loans; collected taxes; lent on easy terms
to the authorities; acted as their paymasters; supervised the coinages
and bullion dealings; and provided facilities for foreign exchange.
They did little or nothing by way of commercial banking or the
financing of trade or industry; had no fractional reserve system; and
created no credit, unless for, or at the behest of, the authorities to
which they were subject; and profits, if any, came almost entirely from
fees and charges. Once again, England was exceptional: she had no
public bank until very modern times and nothing approaching one
until 1694.[4]

Merchant bankers arrived on the scene only when and where
itinerant merchants gave way to sedentary ones who needed bills of
exchange. The negotiating of merchandising exchanges was meat and
drink to the merchant banker. Along all the trade routes that ran
through northern Italy to the Netherlands and England, this commercial revolution occurred in and about the thirteenth century; in
the Baltic and elsewhere it followed somewhat later. In response to
it, merchants in Lucca, Florence or thereabouts invented the bill of
exchange. Sedentary import-export merchants used bills of exchange;
some also dealt in them for others; and a few devoted much or most
of their attention to them. The bills were bought and sold, honoured
or refused and protested, but not discounted, even though they were
mainly *bona fide* trade bills. Italians were the inventors and world
leaders in this kind of banking. The great merchant bankers were for
long mostly Tuscan, especially Lucchese or Florentine: in the fourteenth century the Alberti, Bardi, Peruzzi, Riccardi and Acciaiuoli
firms; in the fifteenth, the Frescobaldi of Florence and Francesco
Datini of Prato; and in the fifteenth and sixteenth, the Strozzi and

the Medici. The sixteenth century, however, saw the rise of the great Augsburg and south German merchant banking firms, notably the Fuggers, the Welsers and the Hochstetters. The earlier banks, the Bardi, Peruzzi and Acciaiuoli for instance, were partnerships of a dozen or so men. Their various branches were managed by salaried employees, who were all too prone to put their own private interests before those of the partners. But the Riccardi London branch may have included one or more partners in the management, and this was the arrangement systematically adopted by most later firms, notably the Datini and Medici. Head partnerships were interlocked with subsidiary partnerships in various cities and countries, each branch being a separate legal entity managed by a junior partner, while some of the head partners were also senior partners in the branch firms. This system made for greater loyalty, but still demanded strict control. As for capital structures, the partners invested their own capital (the *corpo*) and also took deposits (the *sopracorpo*) from outside investors, who were given non-usurious interest payments (*discrezione*) at the discretion of the partners.

The weaknesses of all these merchant banking houses were, that they traded largely on the *sopracorpo*, which could be withdrawn at short notice, and that they tended to build up huge capitals for which it was not always easy to find safe and profitable employment, opportunities in trade and industry being limited. Hence the almost irresistible temptation was to engage in high finance and lend to crowned heads who could repudiate their debts with impunity. The Riccardi and Lucas houses of Lucca, and the Frescobaldi, Bardi and Peruzzi of Florence were all ruined by the repudiation of debts by the first three Edwards, kings of England. The Mannini lent to Richard II, who was deposed, the Medici to Edward IV, likewise deposed, to Charles the Bold of Burgundy, who was killed, and to the Emperor Maximilian, who never lacked a good reason to default. The Fuggers, Hochstetters and Welsers were brought down by loans to Maximilian, Charles V and Philip II. Burlamachi was ruined by James I and Charles I of England. Financier after financier trod this royal road to bankruptcy. As now, beyond a certain point of indebtedness the balance of bargaining power shifted from the financier to the borrower. In a vain endeavour to safeguard what he had already lent, the financier lent more and more, until all hope of repayment or interest was lost, while the borrower sucked the lender dry of loans and then ridded himself of him.

However, by no means all merchant bankers entered into high finance; many were content to continue as they had started, in commodity trade. Yet again, England was an exception; she produced few great merchant bankers and throughout the greater part of our period largely used the services of Italians, Netherlanders, Germans, and, later, Jews. Even in the late sixteenth and seventeenth centuries such names as Horatio Palavicino, Philip Burlamachi, Philip Jacobson, Peter Vanlore and Sir William Courteen overshadowed those of Edward and John Meredith and Sir Sackvile Crow.[5]

In sharp contrast, the specifically English type of banking originated in domestic trade in mainly domestic produce; its roots were not in foreign trade, not in commercial arbitrage between separate markets, as with the generality of import-export merchants throughout the world, but within the home market.

2
The rise of metropolitan markets

Markets are the sum total and upshot of the voluntary, spontaneous, recurrent and mutually profitable exchanges of property at agreed prices between imperfect and infinitely diverse men seeking to satisfy one another's actual and anticipated demands. Markets grow and develop as their participants increase their supplies by concentrating on what they have the greatest comparative advantage in, so widening and deepening the technical, geographical and social divisions of labour.[6]

Every commodity has its own market, which is in turn part of the general market system. Early modern Europe had particular markets in a great variety of goods, and all welded into general markets in which all other commodities were traded against coins of precious or semi-precious metal. In another and stricter sense, a market is an area or region where like things bear like prices at like times, subject only to differences arising from varying transport charges and terms of payment and delivery.

Western Europe had long had small local market areas with their centres in retail, pitched market places in market towns, and some goods were dealt in over larger areas at fairs. In addition, regional markets had made their appearance around such towns as London, Bristol, Norwich, Exeter, and Paris. Regional markets subsumed the local ones within their precincts. Prices were now formed in the regional centre and the old market-places became scenes of wholesale as well as of retail trade. Badgers and similar dealers had formerly conducted arbitrage between local markets; they now did the same for regional ones.

In the sixteenth century England was unique in that she was fashioning a metropolitan market system, with all trade centred on

London, all prices being made there, and regional markets being in their turn subsumed. London merchants started this new development by 'country buying', by going out and buying up existing provincial stocks. The chief characteristics of the mature metropolitan market were: the regular, contracted consignment of wares by producers, factors buying on commission, and other suppliers, to London factors selling on commission; the distribution by London merchants or factors, throughout the market, of a great part of the wares they received; the conduct of trade on credit terms; professional transport services; wholesaling on the basis of samples only; retailing in sale-shops; central banking, insurance and other services; and the extension of the geographical division of labour throughout the metropolitan market area. Pitched markets in agricultural produce often continued, for the sake of regional and local trade, but the badgers and drivers now largely became factors for metropolitan merchants. Fairs went on, but were now frequented by the agents and factors of these merchants. Cross-country trade and transport grew, but only as part of the metropolitan market and according to its prices and practices. Eventually the British Isles had one single market. And then, mainly from London, an extended or extra-metropolitan market was developed through exports oversea. This marked the beginning of the growth of world markets that in due course replaced the infinite succession of arbitrage operations between separate, distinct, and discrete markets that had previously constituted foreign trade.[7]

Metropolitan markets covered areas far wider than the compass of the towns that supplied London. For instance, little or no corn went to London from Bristol, but sellers in, say, Salisbury, could choose to send to either, so prices were uniform, give or take the usual allowances; and Bristol sent corn to South Wales, so people there had to pay prices formed in London, and so too did those in the Lake District when they had to have recourse to outside supplies. A metropolitan market in corn and malt had been established by the middle of the seventeenth century, and so had ones in lean and fat stock, cheese, butter, wool, textiles, hosiery, ironmongery,[8] coal,[9] land,[10] and much else. The strongest and earliest metropolitan and extra-metropolitan markets were in woollen textiles, but others followed.

Chance and accident led to the rise of some pitched markets and the decline of others, but by the sixteenth century the whole English countryside was covered with a close network of market towns, so that a farmer might have up to a dozen market-places where he could buy and sell on different days of the week.[11] There were also numerous fairs for wider trade in livestock, dairy produce, textiles, fish, fineries and many other commodities. Both market-places and fair-grounds were subject to tolls, for instance, of twopence for each beast sold and fourpence for each gelding, half payable by the purchaser and half by the vendor. Tolls like these met the costs of the fair or market and might even bring a modest profit.[12] Other tolls were taken from passengers over many bridges, from boats passing along rivers or through locks, from carts and wagons travelling through a lordship, or, even before turnpike roads became general, from carriages and cattle going along certain highways.[13] Tenants in ancient demesne, the burgesses of some boroughs and the citizens of most cities were quit of all pontage, passage, murrage and other tolls and local customs, and one might furnish oneself with a certificate to this effect before setting out on a business trip,[14] but for less fortunate mortals tolls were a considerable burden and generated some friction, being sometimes regarded as unnecessary interruptions of business and useless taxes on the consumer.[15] But love laughs at locksmiths and inland trade expanded regardless of tolls.

In the hill-farm countries of the north and west, goods had to be moved almost entirely by packhorse, usually in panniers, and almost everywhere packhorses were used for some purposes, especially when the road was bad and speed essential, for then packhorses were cheaper to use than wheeled vehicles. Thus trotting packhorses conveyed fresh fish from the south coast to London. Everything else being equal, however, vehicles were more economical. The roads, as always, left much to be desired. The fat stock of the Midland Plain had to be sold off in autumn not only because the grass stopped growing, but also because they could hardly be moved once the rains set in. Road haulage in the Wealden Vales and the Saltings Country was extremely difficult in winter and not always easy in summer. On warm, light, permeable soils, however, the roads were as good in one season as in another, and as far as possible the main highways had been made on such good bases. The downland ridgeways, in particular, were so much used throughout the year that Weyhill Fair owed its great importance almost entirely to being at the junction of several of them. Road surfaces, then, were not generally as bad as depicted in some tall stories. Moreover, horses and horse-drawn vehicles can go where automobiles, unless tracked or with four-wheel drive, cannot.[16] Furthermore, many writers have ignored the causeys or causeways up to thirty miles long that ran between such places as Aylesbury and Wendover, Warrington Heath and Bewsey Gate, Prescot and Wigan, Sherborne and Shaftesbury, Tiverton and Silverton, Exeter and Chudleigh, Norwich and Wymondham, Beverley and Hull, and Bristol and Gloucester, or out from towns like Norwich, Ely, Nantwich, Gloucester, Bideford, Barnstaple, Nottingham, Oxford, Oundle, Haverfordwest, Cricklade and York. Such causeys were raised above the soil, strengthened at the sides, cambered, guttered, and surfaced, usually with stone, gravel, or iron cinders; and most were wide enough to allow two carts, wagons or coaches to pass.[17]

Two-wheeled carts carrying about 20 cwt, which had been the usual vehicles, hardly sufficed for the increasing volume and weight of goods to be moved, and by about 1600 had generally been replaced by four-wheeled wagons drawn by up to ten or twelve horses and taking loads of 60 or 70 cwt. Wagons were first introduced into England about 1558 and their use spread to most parts before very long. In 1582, for example, Robert Lane was the first man to bring such a vehicle into public service at Ipswich, for which the borough gave him a patent for ten years.[18] Road wagons had shod wheels with cogs protruding an inch above the rim to give purchase on slippery surfaces. This was why they were usually banned from cobbled and paved streets within towns. The use of wagons much facilitated the regular movement of heavy goods. Warminster came to be supplied with Mendip coal, and lead from the Peak-Forest Country went to Bawtry by road en route for Hull and London.[19] But the great increase in heavy traffic caused surfaces to deteriorate and wagons spoiled the roads for all other users, leading to an urgent need for repair and improvement. The surveyors of roads rose to the occasion. Road works became more efficient, especially when, from 1654, wage-workers were used instead of statutory labour. Then, from 1663, turnpike trusts shouldered the financial responsibilities on most major roads. Bridges were also much improved and widened and by 1663 signposts and milestones were being set up. By these means lowland England, which was the part that stood in most need of transport, received roads sufficient for the purpose.[20] Improvements in highways, in vehicles, in draught animals, and in organisation, combined with the relative fall in the price of provender, contained road transport costs in the period 1560–1760, even in the face of the general and almost continuous rise in the prices of most goods in the sixteenth century and first half of the seventeenth. Freight rates between Rochdale and London, for example, hardly varied throughout all these two hundred years.[21]

Road carriers built up a vast and close network. Already by the early seventeenth century, regular services operated for goods, passengers and letters, some daily, some weekly, some twice or thrice a week, between Bristol, Salisbury and Southampton, between the North Country and the east coast, and between London and provincial towns like Wakefield, Preston, Halifax, Chester, Reading, Cambridge, Salisbury, Leicester and Exeter. By 1637 some two hundred towns had at least weekly services to London and some two thousand carriers and wagoners were listed in the handbook that served as a timetable, not to speak of higglers and other 'demi-carriers' who gave some similar facilities. All towns on the main highways were provided with both passenger transport and road haulage. The Shaftesbury carrier, for instance, called at, amongst other places, Devizes, Westbury and Marlborough. Each main line, too, linked up with branch services, so that the London-Exeter wagons had connexions to Newbury, Hungerford and Chippenham. And there were interchanges or junctions at such towns as Leicester, York, Lancaster, Hereford, Worcester, Chester and Exeter. Thus Leicester was the interchange at the junction of the roads from Manchester to London and from Norwich to Birmingham, and here the carriers loaded and unloaded as required. Thus universal consignment was achieved. In short, carriers conveying letters, money and goods of all kinds joined villages and market towns to each other and to the main roads, where they connected with others radiating in all directions from London and cross-country ones between provincial towns and cities.[22] By means of carriers, landed gentlemen near Peterborough and Carlisle bought candles at Huntingdon and Newcastle respectively. A carrier would pay one's bills to tradesmen, or take one's razor to be honed or one's watch to be repaired. In brief, the carriers acted just as do present-day country carriers, who will shop for their customers or higgle for them in the market.[23] Most carriers conducted a general trade, but not all. Specialised glass carriers sprang up in the Weald and one Chalk Country township had twenty-five carriers engaged almost entirely in corn transport, and this was not counting any cadger or loader employed by the local miller to go the rounds of the farms picking up corn and taking back meal.[24] In 1621 there were said to be 150 teams hauling loads every day from the Guildford district to wharves on the Thames.[25] Wagonloads of cloth went regularly to Blackwell Hall in London from Exeter and the West Country, the West-of-England district, Colchester and the Woodland, and from Kendal in the Northwestern Lowlands.[26] Before the River Weaver was fully navigable, salt and cheese from the Cheshire Cheese Country largely went to London by wagon. And wagons supplied the capital with barley from the Norfolk Heathlands.[27]

Until the end of the seventeenth century by no means all road hauliers, any more than transporters on the inland waterways, were common carriers. In law, many were simple bailees and as such had an absolute liability for goods carried, unless they had explicitly disclaimed responsibility for what were Acts of God or hostile actions by the Crown's enemies. In case of loss or damage by fire, the bailee had his remedy in law against the man in whose house the fire first started, and in the event of theft, were the thief not caught by hue and cry, against the hundred within whose precincts the crime had been perpetrated. A common carrier, on the contrary, like a common innkeeper or common farrier, could not make such special exceptions; he was himself liable for all losses, irrespective of any legal remedy against third parties; all goods were carried at his risk. He was a bailee of the first class and was even obliged to carry money at his own risk, entitled only to safeguard himself by demanding a declaration of contents from the consignor. He could charge special rates for carrying money, but all his rates had to be reasonable and were liable to regulation. All carriers, of course, bore some risk and therefore needed to be men of substance, but it should not be thought their risks were exceptionally high in the early modern period. It was a relatively law-abiding society in which they operated. They travelled without armed guards and when extraordinary danger was apprehended, for example, from highwaymen near London, merely formed up in loose columns to minimise possible losses. Badgers and the like were not *ipso facto* common carriers, but became ones if they accepted letters or parcels for delivery from persons otherwise unknown to them. Obviously it would often have been difficult to get a return load without making oneself into a common carrier, unless one adopted the usual course of using an innkeeper as agent for the receipt of letters and parcels. The innkeeper then bore the risks and liabilities. This was why innkeepers' names were omitted from directories of carriers; the names of the inns were given, but the keepers prudently kept their

own names out. Boroughs and cities often took another detour around
the legal difficulties by appointing one or more official carriers who
served only their fellow burgesses or citizens and were thus not
common carriers available to the public at large. Such official carriers
generally had their parcel, letter and money rates regulated by the
appointing authority.[28]

The roads connected with a great and increasing mileage of almost
steadily improving inland navigations. Improvement came partly
from canalisation and the digging of new cuts, partly from the use
of engines, presumably what we now call mud-dredgers, to deepen
river beds. Great Yarmouth, for example, had its own engine, which
in 1643 Norwich decided to borrow. The Thames was made navigable
as far as Lechlade, where a wharf took goods in transit to and from
the hinterland of the river-head. Between London, Maidenhead,
Chertsey and Reading there was even a regular service of passenger
boats by 1637. The Severn and its tributaries provided another and
expanding waterway system. It was in and about the Fen Country that
some of the greatest advances were made in canals, for the same cuts
that carried away floods also floated boats, and Morton's Leam had
been cut primarily as a waterway. Our period saw constant improvement. In 1574, for instance, Woodston township agreed to widen one
of its drains to accommodate the passage of lighters. In 1616 Bardlike
had recently been made navigable for lighters so broad in the beam
that for ten miles on end no boat could pass them. In 1617 the Earl
of Exeter dug the first spit of the work that was to bring navigation
to Stamford. By 1640 New Po Dike in Marshland was navigable for
barges. Seventeenth-century Bottulph Bridge was a junction, complete
with warehouse and wharf, for canal boats plying between Peterborough, Yaxley and Lynn.[29] Water transport was generally much
cheaper than land carriage for heavy or bulky goods like coal, timber,
corn and cheese, perhaps at ratios of 1:16 and 1:12 as against
packhorses and wheeled carriages respectively,[30] but much depended
on the state of the particular roads with which comparisons were
struck. Coal was carried by water wherever possible, and, as coal
consumption rapidly increased, waterborne supplies reached more
and more inland ports, whence they went by wagon to places as remote
from coalfields as Huntingdon.[31] So efficient were the waterways
that they were used to move farm produce that might have been
expected to go by wagon, if only the roads had not been on wet, deep
land. In 1599 wool from Stony Stratford and thereabouts was sent

to Peterborough by road, shipped thence through the fens to the North Sea and so to Norwich and other East Anglian ports.[32] Since farm produce and timber could be transported so readily by water-ways, manors within easy reach of them acquired an extra value, as did Bosley in the Severn valley, Watlington, which was only four miles from the Thames, and Mettingham, just a mile outside Beccles, whence keels and barges of twenty tons burthen could take heavy goods down to the sea.[33]

Finally, the roads and inland navigations were all linked in a great outer circle by the rapidly expanding coastal trade. Coasting vessels, which were being much improved, provided the cheapest freights of all. They also made up for the deficiencies of some of the roads, as in the Saltings Country, where the foulness of the ways necessitated much of the corn being taken to market by coasters. But corn was often shipped in coasters even where the roads were good.[34]

Transport improvements went forward step by step with the general advance in agricultural, manufacturing, extractive and processing industries, and in trade and finance. To enquire which came first, progress in transport or in the economy in general, is to ask the same of the chicken and the egg.

Carriers' services were essential to all branches of trade, not least to retailing. The rise of sale-shops was due to the increasing geographical division of labour and the abandonment of local self-sufficiency, but it was facilitated by advances in transportation. Rural and West End shopkeepers alike could now either buy goods at fairs or order them from London or elsewhere by letter, take delivery of them at their doors, and pay for them through the carrier. They also used carriers to deliver to out-of-town customers. Furthermore, improved road transport encouraged shopkeepers to set up branches and even small chains of shops, all managed from the main seat of business. Thus Bury St Edmunds shopkeepers could have branches in Newmarket, Leigh ones in Ashton-in-Makersfield, Hempton ones in Feckenham, Aldeburgh ones in Saxmundham, Manchester ones in Warrington or Bolton, Leicester ones in Lutterworth and Melton, and Newtown ones in Llanidloes. The man who ran three shops in Rattlesden, Hesset and Elmswell was probably not the only one of his kind. Specialist butchers, drapers, booksellers, ironmongers and others set up in various places; but most provincial shops had a more general trade.[35]

One essential service provided by road carriers was the conveyance and delivery of letters and papers. Masters of coasting ships also undertook this,[36] but most inland correspondence went by road, confided to common, municipal or other carriers. In addition to conveyance between towns, common carriers in a substantial way of business would deliver letters anywhere, even to all parts of London and the suburbs, from the inns where they stopped or terminated, by means of the porters they employed for general delivery, like the porter for the Nottingham carriers at 'The Ram' in Smithfield. Other carriers delivered letters in person. Carriage by wagon was admittedly slow. In 1625 from Chester to London took eight days; in 1630 Prescot to London, ten; in 1617 Barnstaple to London, a fortnight. Many carriers, however, speeded up letters by sending riders on ahead of the wagons. The universities and cities and boroughs employed despatch riders whose services were at the disposal of all their members. These riders were not postmen; they did not travel by way of postage, on post-horses, but went all the way on the same steed. For most business, wagons or riders were 'tymely enough'. For urgent business, there were long-distance runners, often Irish kernes, who could leave the roads to take short cuts and go, for example, from Leicester to London and back in a week. Royal messengers apart, the only horsed postmen were the hackneymen of Canterbury, Sandwich and other towns on the Dover and Sandwich roads. They conveyed letters, via Gravesend, to and from London and the Channel ports of Sandwich and Dover. They rode at a 'Canterbury gallop' or canter, but had the advantage of running a relay-race, not a long-distance one.[37]

The Crown had its own Messengers of the Chamber and other and occasional riders. Henry VIII set up a Master of Posts with power to keep 'standing posts on pay'. These were 'able men well horsed', riding day and night as required. They were accompanied by guides, who were armed with post-horns to tell all passengers to give way, and at each post returned the spent horses at an easy pace to the previous post. The only exception to this general scheme was that until 1594 hackneymen acted as postmen and guides on their own routes and under contract to the Crown. Nearly all the postmasters were keepers both of inns and of livery-stables of post-horses for the travelling public, a business in which they were granted sole rights in their own localities. These postmasters then hired post-boys to do the actual riding, while they themselves became salaried officials who also derived private incomes from purely local parcel and letter delivery services and from the hiring out of horses, not to speak of innkeeping. As long as purveyance lasted, the Crown had power to impress horses at low cost to itself and so its postmasters had an impregnable advantage in the delivery of letters on the growing number of post-roads; and when purveyance ended in 1660, monopoly powers were invoked to replace it in respect of the posting of letters. But from 1635 private people were officially allowed to use the royal posts, 'by-posts' (off post-roads), and 'cross-posts' (between post-roads), sending their letters alongside the official packet. Such letters were registered, timed and dated. High fees were charged, but, then, the posts were swift. A letter went from Chester to London in eight days by carrier, in thirty-six hours by post. Many businessmen and others with urgent correspondence were thus enabled to avail themselves of services that would otherwise have been for the Crown alone, while the Crown, for its part, was able to cut the cost of state business and spare its own coffers and those of the taxpayers. And although no private person was allowed to set up his own public postal service for letters, ordinary riders (or runners) were freely allowed, and carriers were expressly permitted to convey letters and to employ riders for the purpose as long as these preceded the wagons by no more than eight hours.[38] England could thus congratulate itself on an efficient three-tier service for the delivery of letters.

These services, especially those provided by carriers, were of the first importance to domestic trade, both retail and wholesale. The road carriers' chief freights were cloths of all kinds, stockings and other knitwear, leather and leather goods, and hardware, and for these and other trades they provided essential communications. When their right to carry letters by rider was threatened in 1638, the carriers of Norwich, Great Yarmouth and Ipswich protested vigorously and were powerfully supported by the citizens of Norwich. They explained it was vital for letters to do with the city's trade in stuffs and stockings to go by the carriers. 'The merchants', they said, 'imploy great summes of money and hereby are occasioned to write much, large and many letters, bills of exchange, and bills of lading, with patternes of advice.' Since the workmen (i.e. manufacturers) of Norwich and the rest of East Norfolk made their markets in the city on Tuesdays, Fridays and Saturdays, the merchants received letters by the carriers on Thursdays and replied every week by the carriers' riders on Fridays, which was when the week's consignment of goods was due in London. This they did with little or nothing by way of charges, whereas the posts were prohibitively expensive.[39] This is one example of how the carriers, especially road carriers, as well as drovers, made metropolitan markets possible, not merely by the conveyance of goods, but by the invaluable service of providing their customers with commercial intelligence, especially about the goods available and the prices obtaining in London and the provinces. Until a knowledge of current buying and selling prices at both ends of the trade route is shared by, or at least open to, all would-be buyers and sellers, no market is possible. The communication of such intelligence throughout the market area was an essential part of the metropolitan market itself, just as, conversely, it was precisely the lack of this sort of intelligence that made it impossible for remote and barbarous people like the Red Indians to participate in any world market.

Some of the most advanced trades were in textiles and hosiery. The towns that were fulling and finishing centres were naturally important markets and collecting points for the products of local manufacturers. Wholesalers in Norwich, Tiverton, Exeter, Shrewsbury, Kendal, Rochdale, Manchester, Leeds and elsewhere bought semi-finished fabrics or raw webs and sold them wholly finished and often also dyed in the piece. Maidstone, Ipswich, Sudbury and Bury St Edmunds played a rather similar role. Manufacturing and marketing towns carried on a good deal of cross-country trade, not only to the ports through which they transported goods, but also overland from end to end and from side to side of the kingdom. Much wholesale trade was conducted in fairs like the Candlemas, May and St Faith's fairs in Maidstone, Tombland fair in Norwich, Bartholomew fair in West Smithfield, and Stourbridge fair near Cambridge. Another kind of cross-country trade was in the hands of travelling salesmen, notably the 'Manchester men' who went the rounds of provincial sale-shops.

The main stream of trade, however, flowed through the normal channels to London, and all others, save some cross-country ones, were but tributaries of it. Londoners engaged in 'country buying' and provincial merchants found first partners, then factors, in London; and thus metropolitan markets were built. London became the commercial centre chiefly by virtue of her role in distribution throughout the kingdom. All the manufacturing districts specialised in the lines they produced best and all bought each other's products, and all other places bought some of all the lines, through the medium of the metropolitan markets. Irrespective of whether they went in and out of London or across country, all these goods sold at metropolitan prices formed in the self-same market. At Blackwell Hall in Basinghall Street, and at Leadenhall, wholly pitched markets were soon abandoned in favour of consignments contracted on the basis of samples, exemplars of stockings and hosiery, and swatches or scantlings of textiles. Such consignments went straight into warehouses, bypassing the halls, which became textile exchanges and deposits for faulty and unsold goods. Clothiers and provincial merchants simply sent their wares to hall factors to sell on their behalf on commission and to see to all the necessary paperwork. This system of trading was complete in all essentials before the end of the sixteenth century. In the seventeenth we find the factors not only selling on commission, but also supplying a wide range of raw materials to the manufacturers. All business was conducted on credit, chiefly book credit, and the normal tendency was for provincial suppliers to keep credit balances with their factors and for accounts to be settled once a year.

Somewhere about half to three quarters of all English textile and hosiery exports went out of the port of London, and the rest from such ports as Hull, King's Lynn, Great Yarmouth, Ipswich, Colchester, Sandwich, Southampton, Lyme Regis, Weymouth, Bridport, Topsham, Plymouth, Dartmouth, Bristol and Chester. But obviously not all these exports were made by merchants belonging to the ports they went out of. A Norwich merchant might export through Yarmouth, an Ipswich one through Plymouth, and a Taunton one through Topsham. What was even more significant was that much of the export from outports like those we have mentioned, was undertaken by London merchants, who bought and sold and conducted all transactions in them as freely as in their own city. Anyway, once the metropolitan market was established, all exports from it were extra-metropolitan ones.[40]

The greater complexity of markets in raw materials as opposed to finished goods, and the consequently greater difficulty in organising them, is illustrated by the history of the wool trade.

At the outset, most clothiers bought their wool from the nearest available source and made from it what they could, so the system of farm management predetermined the composition of the cloth. The Midland Plain generally used fallow wool from sheep folded on the fallows; Hereford, Leominster and Worcester, Leominster wool; the West of England, Cotswold wool; the Chalk, West, and Peak-Forest countries, their own fleeces; the Cheshire Cheese Country those of

Wales; the Woodland those of the Norfolk Heathlands; East Norfolk those of the Fen Country; and so on.

Then, in the early modern period, as the agricultural revolution was changing the types of wool grown, clothiers in most districts started to look further afield for supplies, choosing fibres they could convert to their greatest profit. The great change they had to adapt to was the fall in the volume and quality of fallow wools, which stemmed from sheep-and-corn husbandry, and the huge increase in the shear of pasture wools. Roughly, they had two options: they might switch to Spanish wools instead of English fallow ones; or they might bring in quite new fabrics made wholly or partly of pasture wool. Some took one course, some the other; either way, the wool trade was transformed.

What fallow wools there were, were now increasingly diverted and drawn off to distant places for inclusion with pasture wools in union cloths like baize and serge. Midland fallow wool, for example, was now being snapped up by factors for the Norwich baizemakers. More important, the flood of pasture wools from the Midland Plain, the Western Waterlands, Romney Marsh, and the Fen, Saltings, Cotswold and Northwold countries, as well as from Ireland, was surging to the Vale of Taunton Deane, East Norfolk, the Woodland, the Breckland, the Vales of Hereford, and the Peak-Forest, Cheshire Cheese, Cheese, Butter, Chalk and West countries and elsewhere, for incorporation both in worsted, jersey and union cloths and in knitwear. Matters were further complicated in that the trade in yarn pursued that in wool, only at a higher level, in that different parts of the fleeces were sorted and earmarked for distinct purposes, and in that wool of all kinds was sold, re-sold, interchanged, blended and redistributed at all hands. Clothiers, fellmongers, glovers, whittawers, parchmentmakers, blanketmakers, woolcombers and others all had a finger in the pie. The upshot was, the places of growing and the places of converting were as far distant as the scope of the kingdom would allow. Moreover, one source of wool, the Iberian peninsula, was far outside the kingdom.

As long as converters used wool from local sheep, their women-folk could readily sort it. It was otherwise when wool was drawn from new and strange sources and was unlike the kind they had been used to. Then it was often preferable to leave the sorting and blending to the wholesaler, from whom the clothier could order the blend he wanted. Woolcombers and yarnmasters had long provided this service for the users of pasture wool; now all clothiers were forced into a similar reliance on the wholesaler. The Merchants of the Staple stepped in to fill the breach. Their export business having collapsed, they turned to the home market and developed this new trade of buying, sorting, blending and selling, employing the services of jobbers, brokers, breakers, sorters and blenders of wool, seeing to the whole business, and selling each blend where it would fetch the best price. At the same time, woolcombers now began to find it more convenient to buy their pasture wool from the Staplers in much the same way and for much the same reasons. As the Staplers conducted their businesses in or through London, which was where the manufacturers sold most of their wares, the latter found it convenient to buy their materials there, especially when this could be done through the self-same factors, some of whom were also Staplers. And manufacturers who used Spanish wool, silk, cotton wool or imported linen yarn, as many now did, had little option but to buy these from London, and usually did so through their factors. Thus it was more and more on London account that wool came to be bought and sold, and so the metropolitan market in wool was established. By about 1630 it was complete in all essentials.[41]

The initial impetus to, and mainspring of, trade in agricultural goods and produce between farming countries was simply the circumstance that the finished product of one was the food or drink stuff, or raw material, or capital, required by another. Trade articulated the various countries. Then the more one farming country concentrated on one line of production, the more others in turn were induced to specialise in others. Once this process had been set in motion between many countries, it went forward under its own momentum. It could hardly have been otherwise when some countries suited corn, some livestock, some mining or manufactures, and so on. Each had its own distinct advantages and disadvantages in natural endowment, and people in one wanted to exchange with those in others.

There had long been some regional specialisation and the interchange of produce was nothing new. Nevertheless, since commonfield agriculture was conducted primarily for the sake of mere housekeeping and subsistence, and only secondarily for the market, the growth of trade was roughly commensurate with the decline of family and dwarf farms in the common fields and the advance of farming in severalty. By this yardstick alone, it is clear that specialisations in the various farming countries were much intensified in the early modern period, and remarkably so in those devoting themselves to fat stock and the dairy, the Midland Plain, the Vale of Pickering and the Cheese Country for instance. Increased specialisation in cereals and stockbreeding was less conspicuous, because achieved simply by neglecting petty dairying and fattening. Meanwhile, by process of innovation, the production of new commodities became localised in particular countries, as hops in the Northdown Country, the Vales of Hereford and the Woodland; turnip butter and cheese in High Suffolk; turnip beef in East Norfolk; turnip mutton in the Northdown, Chiltern, Cotswold and Northwold countries and the Norfolk Heathlands; and cole-seed mutton in the Fen Country. One of the things that most struck the Swedish traveller in England was that every country specialised in a few crops and left others to be grown elsewhere.[42]

The very soil differences gave rise to trade in seeds. Inside half a dozen years Robert Wansborough of Shrewton bought both clay and hill wheat seed from Easterton, Imber, Market Lavington, West Lavington, Corton, Urchfont, Wilsford, Langford, Chalke, Stert, and Salisbury, and barley seed from Salisbury and Milford. Seeds were interchanged between hill and vale, north and south, east and west, between sandy, clay, chalk and fen soils, and between countries producing winter-hardy, late-ripe, middle-ripe, rathe-ripe and hotspur varieties. Seed wheat from the Vale of Taunton Deane and from the Polden Hills amidst the Western Waterlands, was sold through Weyhill to the Chalk and Southdown countries. Hotspur barley and pea seeds from Patney and the Vale of Pewsey in the Chalk Country sold the length and breadth of agricultural England.[43] And then new crops swelled the seed trade. Midland farmers bought turnip seed from Norfolk and the Northdown Country added clover to the wheat and other crops it grew for seed.[44]

Livestock strains were also interchanged. The Spencers of Worm-leighton were the most successful and noted breeders of pedigree pasture sheep for sale to men wishing to improve their flocks; but many lesser-known breeders carried on similar businesses. About the year 1650 selected Midland pasture rams were selling at £10 a head. Midland graziers, for their part, bought marsh tups from the Fen and Saltings countries and Longhorn cows from the Lancashire Plain. In 1615 Sir Robert Drury of Hawstead in the Chiltern Country had a herd of fifty-five Hereford bulls and steers and was apparently in the way of running a stud or selling pedigree cattle.[45]

Cereal, dairy and meat production depended greatly on the livestock trade between different farming countries. Horses were bred in
all countries, but those most needing teams were not always the ones
where heavy horses were best bred and reared, for their colts needed
soft land under their hooves. Punches became the speciality of the
Sandlings Country, where to the advantage of drained marshland was
added that of carrot cultivation. Suffolk punches were sold not only
to High Suffolk, East Norfolk, the Saltings Country, the Woodland,
the Breckland, and the Norfolk Heathlands, but even, in limited
numbers, to the Fen Country.[46] Shire horses bred in the Fen Country,
or to a lesser extent in the Western Waterlands, and reared chiefly
in the Midland Plain, were then sold to farmers in the Chalk, Northdown, Northwold and similar countries, where they were worked
gently, inured to toil, and then sold off again, at about six years, for
heavy road and street work. Before they ended up in knackers' yards,
the horses, in the ordinary course of events, would have passed
through at least three pairs of hands and seen a good deal of various
parts of England. This complex trade was conducted at horse fairs
in Northampton, Leicester, Worcester, Towcester, Rothwell and
elsewhere, as well as in the London and other markets.[47] The
Cleveland district, where the Midland Plain abutted on the
Blackmoors, specialised in breeding and rearing Cleveland bays as
riding and coach horses for distribution to other parts of England
through the fairs at Northallerton, Ripon, York, Penkridge, and other
places, and, of course, through the London Smithfields.[48]

The trade in cattle was even more intricate. Consider what was
needed, say, to put beef on the Londoner's table. Longhorn cattle
were bred in the Craven district of the North Country, reared in the
Lancashire Plain, fatted in the Midland Plain, the Saltings Country
or elsewhere, depastured awhile by a grazing butcher, in the Vale of
London most likely, and then sold to a cutting butcher. Shorthorns
bred in the North Country were reared in the Northeastern Lowlands
and then fatted in the Midland Plain, or in the Fen or Saltings
countries before passing south. Among the other countries that
imported and fatted cattle bred in the North Country and reared in
the Northeastern Lowlands or the Lancashire Plain were the Norfolk
Heathlands, East Norfolk, the Sandlings, Northdown and Cheese
countries, the Woodland, the Wealden Vales, and Romney Marsh.
Cattle bred and reared in the Vales of Hereford were bought by
farmers all across the Midland Plain as far as the Chiltern Country.

From the West Country, store bullocks went to the South Seacoast and Butter countries; from the High Weald, to the Wealden Vales and Romney Marsh, more particularly Pevensey Level; from Wales, to the vales of Berkeley and of London, the Wealden Vales, the Midland Plain, Romney Marsh, and the Butter, Cheese and Saltings countries. Peak-Forest stores sold in the Midland Plain. Dairymen in the Midland Plain and the Cheese and Cheshire Cheese countries bought cows from the Lancashire Plain. Then, in their turn, the dairy farmers sold their surplus calves to graziers. Those from the Cheshire Cheese Country went to the Midland Plain, the Vale of London, the Wealden Vales, Romney Marsh and other places; those from High Suffolk to the Sandlings and Saltings countries; and some from the Midland Plain to the Vale of London.[49] Eventually, the expansion of beef production in England led to the import of lean cattle from Scotland[50] and Ireland.[51]

The trade in sheep was no less complex. In the west of the Midland Plain, March ewes were imported from Wales for the common fields and their lambs later exported to be fattened in the Vale of Evesham and the Cheshire Cheese Country. In the east of the plain, sheep were bought from the Chiltern Country. Lambs bred in Romney Marsh were sold for rearing in the Northwold Country and then resold to be fatted in the marshes. Sheep from the Northdown, Sandlings, Chiltern and Chalk countries and the Norfolk Heathlands, were fatted in the Saltings Country and Romney Marsh. From the Butter Country, house-lamb sheep were exported to the Petworth District, the South Seacoast and Northdown countries and the Vale of London. Almost everywhere sheep bred and reared in hilly and mountainous countries were sold to the neighbouring plains and vales to be fattened. They went from Wales to the Saltings Country and Romney Marsh; from the North Country, to the Northwestern and Northeastern Lowlands and to the Lancashire and Midland plains; from the Peak-Forest Country, to the Lancashire and Midland plains, the Cheshire Cheese Country and even the Woodland; from the Cotswold Country, to the vales of Evesham and Berkeley, the Butter Country, the Midland Plain and the Western Waterlands; and from the Southdown Country some went to the Wealden Vales.[52] Arable sheep from the Chalk Country were sold through such fairs as the ones at Wilton, Chilmark, All Cannings and Devizes, and above all at Weyhill fair, to the Northdown, Chiltern, Cheese and Butter countries and to the common fields of the Vale of London and the Midland Plain. Small wonder that sheep-jobbers were a distinct class of dealers with their own tricks of trade.[53]

Various countries were interdependent also for fodders, fertilisers and, not least, for salt, which grain-growers needed for their seed-steeps, dairymen for their cheese and butter, and all farmers for their stock. Farmers and others in the Midland Plain bought lime from the Northeastern Lowlands and the Peak-Forest Country, in the Butter and Cheese countries from the West Country, in the Cheshire Cheese Country from the North and Peak-Forest countries and from Wales, in the Lancashire Plain from the North Country, and so on. The Wealden Vales and the Saltings Country bought chalk from the Northdown Country, the Butter Country from the Chalk, and the Midland Plain from the Chiltern Country. Farmers in the Chalk, Chiltern and Northdown countries and the Norfolk Heathlands imported soot and other fertilisers from London.[54] In the early part of our period, too, farmers in the Chalk and Cotswold countries imported hay from the Cheese and Butter countries, or, what was tantamount to it, wintered their stock there by agistment.[55]

By their nature and plan of management many farming countries grew little or no wheat or rye and were deficient in bread corn. In the ordinary course of events, the labouring folk of the North and Peak-Forest countries, Wales, the Blackmoors, the High Weald and even the Lancashire Plain, ate oatcakes, porridge and the like; but in bad summers the oats might be fit only for fodder; and the well-to-do people always enjoyed wheaten bread. Thus what in normal times was a steady trickle of wheat to such countries, sometimes turned into a broad stream. The West Country and Wales habitually imported corn from the Chalk Country and the vales of Evesham, Taunton Deane and Hereford; the Peak-Forest Country, from the Midland Plain and beyond; and the North Country and the North-eastern Lowlands, from the Midland Plain, the Norfolk Heathlands, the Fen and Northwold countries and elsewhere.[56] Many farming countries, too, were unable to grow malting barley, and while they did malt oats or bigg, for the best brews barley malt had to be imported. Thus the Northwestern Lowlands bought 'southern', and the Lancashire Plain 'eastern', malt (or occasionally malting barley) through Liverpool, Chester, Derby, Newcastle and Halifax; the Vales of Hereford, from the Vale of Evesham; the Northeastern Lowlands, from the Woodland and the Norfolk Heathlands; and the Peak-Forest Country, from the Midland Plain and the Northwold Country.

As for hops, the Chiltern and Cheshire Cheese countries grew little
or none, but bought them via London from the Northdown Country
and the Woodland, while people in the Western Waterlands and the
Butter Country got theirs from the Vales of Hereford and from the
Chalk and Northdown countries. The last two countries were also
great sources of ale, and Burton-on-Trent supplied beer to the Peak-
Forest Country.[57]

By reason of their plans of management, and the consequential
enclosure of common fields, the vales of Pickering and Berkeley and
the Cheese and Butter countries became increasingly dependent on
grain from outside. Cider was the usual drink in the Butter Country
and the farmers there grew enough wheat for themselves, but spring
corn was deficient, so oats were bought from Wales. The Cheese
Country came to depend on the Cotswold, Chalk and Oxford Heights
countries for wheat, barley and malt. The Vale of Berkeley imported
corn from the Cotswold Country and elsewhere, and even High
Suffolk, which was an arable-dairy country, took some grain from
East Norfolk and the Norfolk Heathlands.[58]

Conversely, the corngrowing and stockbreeding countries, many of
them, relied more and more on imported cheese and butter, for every
cow spared from the dairy meant more stock for sale or more sheep to
fold on the cornfields. Different types of cheese were sold all over the
kingdom to suit all purses and palates, manual workers eating it for
nourishment and gentlefolk for digestion. The Western Waterlands
produced perhaps the finest, in the form of Cheddar, but Cheshire and
the Gloucester Cheese from the Cheese Country and the Vale of
Berkeley commanded the widest sale. The West and Chalk countries
bought butter and cheese from the Butter and Cheese Countries and the
Vale of Berkeley; the Northdown Country, the Wealden Vales and the
Northwestern Lowlands, from High Suffolk, the vales of Pickering
and Evesham and the Cheshire Cheese Country; the Midland Plain,
from the Cheshire Cheese Country; the Northwold Country, from the
Vale of Pickering and the Fen Country; the West Country, from the
Cheese and Butter countries; and the North and Peak-Forest countries,
from the Midland Plain, the Cheshire Cheese Country and the Vale of
Pickering. Moreover, the dairy countries themselves interchanged
their produce. The vales of Evesham and Berkeley had butter from the
Butter Country, and the Butter and Cheese Countries bought from
each other, the trade in butter and cheese between the two being
mostly in the hands of the self-same dealers.[59]

Much the same sort of exchange developed between some of the meat-producing and corngrowing countries. The Midland Plain and the Wealden Vales were self-sufficient in corn, but Romney Marsh had to import from the Northdown Country. Both the Cheese and Butter countries sold beeves to the Chalk and Cotswold ones. Even the Woodland and High Suffolk imported some muttons from the Midland Plain. Furthermore, different meat-producing countries specialised largely in either winter or in summer grass meat, so the Cotswold Country had good reason to export winter and import summer mutton, and East Norfolk to import grass beeves and export corned or turniped ones.[60]

The Northwestern Lowlands imported small, the Vale of London huge amounts, of farm goods and produce, but neither exported any of its own growth to speak of. Many countries sold solely or mainly producers's goods, chiefly in the form of store sheep or cattle. These were the North, Peak-Forest and West countries, Wales, the High Weald, the Blackmoors, and Northeastern Lowlands and the Lancashire Plain. The Vales of Hereford, too, relied heavily on sales of wool and store cattle. Still other countries sold many stores, even though their other produce was more valuable. The horses of the Midland Plain and the Fen and Sandlings countries and the sheep of the Chalk and Butter countries may be mentioned.[61]

Thanks to specialisation, a complete range of foods was put on the market. Grass cheese came from the Cheese and Cheshire Cheese countries, the vales of Berkeley and Evesham, High Suffolk, the Western Waterlands, and the Midland Plain; hay cheese from the Cheese Country; winter cheese from High Suffolk; grass butter from the Western Waterlands, the Butter and Fen countries, the Vale of Pickering, the Midland Plain and High Suffolk; turnip butter from High Suffolk; grass beef and mutton from the Midland Plain, the Wealden Vales, the Fen, Saltings, South Seacoast, Cheese and Butter countries, Romney Marsh and the Western Waterlands; lamb from the South Seacoast Country and the Petworth District; veal from the Saltings Country; winter beef from East Norfolk and High Suffolk; coleseed mutton from the Fen and Saltings countries; turnip mutton from the Northdown, Chiltern and Cotswold countries and the Norfolk Heathlands; wheat from the Woodland, the South Seacoast and the Saltings countries and the Vale of Taunton Deane; and barley from the Norfolk Heathlands and the Chiltern and Chalk countries.[62]

Other comestibles were provided by the table fruit of the North-down and Chiltern countries and the Vale of Evesham; the hares and coneys of the Chalk and Northwold countries, the Norfolk Heath-lands and the Breckland; the fresh-water fish of the Blackheath Country and sea-fish from all the coasts; the wild fowl of the Fen and Saltings countries and the Western Waterlands; the mustard of the Fen and Saltings countries and the Vale of Evesham; the liquorice of Pontefract and Worksop; the saffron of the Chiltern Country; the geese of the Western Waterlands and the Fen Country; the turkeys of High Suffolk, East Norfolk and the Sandlings Country; and the bacon and pork of the Cheese and Poor Soils countries, the Midland Plain, the Vale of Pickering and High Suffolk. Drinks were furnished by the ale and beer of Burton and the Midland Plain, the ales of the Northdown, Chiltern, Sandlings, Southdown and Chalk countries, especially Salisbury bottled ales, and the perry and cider of the Vales of Hereford and the West Country. By 1619 pipe-tobacco had become a speciality of the Vale of Evesham.[63]

Improvements in the husbandries of the various countries mostly tended towards increased specialisation and greater interdependence. The floating of catchwork meadows increased the output of Hereford cattle. Flowing meadows boosted barley and fat-lamb production. Marling, liming, draining, fertilising, up-and-down husbandry, and the introduction of root crops and clover and 'seeds' mixtures, resulted in more meat, dairy produce, grain and wool being marketed.[64] Occasionally, improvements led to the opposite tendency. Greater tillage, the extinction of common fields, and other developments,. enabled more winter corn to be grown and tended to diminish the dependency of Wales and the West and Peak-Forest countries on imported grain; but this tendency was countervailed by the growing division of labour between agricultural, extractive, processing, transportation and manufacturing industries. The expansion of textile manufactures in the Cheese and Peak-Forest countries, for instance, drew in swelling imports of farm produce from elsewhere.[65] Coal mined in the Peak-Forest Country, the Northeastern Lowlands and the Mendips was increasingly exchanged for corn from the Midland Plain and the Chalk and Northwold countries.[66] Industrial expansion was also accompanied by the wider cultivation of industrial crops such as flax, hemp, woad, weld, madder and cole-seed in the Midland Plain, High Suffolk, the Norfolk Heathlands, the Fen, Butter, Cheese, Chiltern, Northdown and other countries.[67]

Greater productivity on the farm permitted a widening division of labour between agriculture and other pursuits, and consequently a growth in urban and industrial centres, concentrating an increasing proportion of the demand for farm produce in certain localities. A like effect was produced by so much of the rising income drawn from the countryside in the form of rent being disbursed not in rural areas, but in the boroughs and cities. Oxford butchers, for instance, were amongst the chief buyers of beeves in the Cheese Country.[68] A similar demand was created by military establishments and by the growing coasting trade, mercantile marine and royal navy. Plymouth provided an outlet for the produce of the West Country. High Suffolk, the Woodland and the Sandlings Country served ships' husbands, and High Suffolk supplied the Berwick garrison with cheese and butter. The Chalk Country furnished corn to naval contingents at Bristol and Ringwood. Fat stock from Romney Marsh and North-down and Southdown grain and malt were sold in Rye, Hyde, Romney and Dover.[69]

For the most part, however, it is impossible to distinguish between urban, naval and industrial outlets, because many urban centres were also ports and seats of industry; or between rural and industrial ones because much industry was itself rural. What we know is, a number of great urban and industrial districts emerged, each of which was deficient in food and drink stuffs and the focal point for regional trade. With the growth of manufactures in and around Birmingham, this town became one such point.[70] With the rise of the coal, salt, glass and shipping industries, Tyneside and Wearside attracted corn from the Northwold Country and from King's Lynn.[71] The Peak-Forest Country became another such centre, drawing corn from the Northwold Country, corn and fat stock from the Midland Plain, cheese from the Cheshire Cheese Country and the Midland Plain, and oats, butter and bacon from the Vale of Pickering.[72] Bristol, whose population trebled or quadrupled between 1500 and 1800, had by 1600 become the centre of an area of deficiency that included Bath and the West-of-England clothing districts and had supply routes extending eastwards to Salisbury Plain, northwards to the Cheshire Cheese Country and southwards to the Vale of Taunton Deane. Bristol herself drew barley, malt and wheat (including white wheat for ships' biscuits) from the Chalk Country through pitched markets at Warminster, Hindon, Market Lavington and Devizes; corn and fruit from the Vales of Hereford and the Vale of Evesham; butter from the Butter Country and the Western Waterlands; cheese from the Western Waterlands, the vales of Berkeley and Evesham and the Cheshire Cheese Country; corn from the Vale of Taunton Deane; and fat stock from the Vale of Berkeley and the Butter Country.[73]

By far the most important deficiency area was that composed of London, Westminster, Southwark, their suburbs and liberties, and the Vale of London as a whole. The three towns had long been the largest conurbation in the kingdom. Between 1500 and 1650 its population increased about tenfold and rose from around one fiftieth to around one fifteenth of that of all England, and the vale's demand for imported produce grew even faster than the population, for more and more farmland was taken over for dwellings and warehouses, work and sale shops, breweries, market gardens, stables, cow-sheds, butchers' grounds, accommodation closes, hay, suckling and cramming farms, and the like.[74]

London buyers drew more and more wheat and wheat meal from the Woodland and the Saltings Country, which were the two largest suppliers, and from the Chalk, Cotswold, Northdown, Southdown, Chiltern and South Seacoast countries, the Petworth District, East Norfolk and the more accessible parts of the Midland Plain. More and more malt was imported from East Norfolk, the Norfolk Heathlands, the Woodland, the Midland Plain, and the Chalk, Chiltern and Northdown countries. Barley from these countries was chiefly malted either in its place of origin or in towns on the perimeter of the Vale of London itself, and in consequence only modest amounts of malting barley came into the metropolis. Oats and oat meal were brought mainly from the Northdown and Saltings countries, but also from the Fen, Chalk and Northwold ones, the Wealden Vales, the Midland Plain, and even the West Country.[75]

Londoners imported 'Cheshire' cheese, at first mostly by road, and later both via Chester, Parkgate, Frodsham and Liverpool by the 'long sea', and via Burton-on-Trent, Gainsborough and Hull by the 'short sea'. Most 'Gloucester' cheese came to the metropolis from the Cheese Country, often through Tetbury, Marlborough and Highworth and then down the Thames by barge. Later a little came by way of Bristol from the Vale of Berkeley. 'Warwicks' cheese from the Vale of Evesham came down the Avon and the Severn to Bristol, where some was taken off for London. Some Midland cheese arrived by way of Uttoxeter, Burton-on-Trent and the 'short sea', and 'Cheddar' came from the Western Waterlands. High Suffolk was a great source of cheese, which was chiefly shipped from Lowestoft, Southwold, Walberswick, Blythburgh, Dunwich, Aldeburgh, Woodbridge, Ipswich and nearby havens. Some butter came from the Midland Plain and the Fen and Butter countries, but much more from High Suffolk and the Sandlings Country, and, later, from the Vale of Pickering.[76]

Londoners bought grass beef from the Midland Plain, the Cheese, Butter and Fen countries, the Western Waterlands, the Wealden Vales, the Vale of Berkeley, Romney Marsh and the Woodland. Both beef and veal came from the Saltings and Sandlings countries. Later on, winter beef came from East Norfolk and to a lesser extent from High Suffolk. Grass mutton was imported from the Wealden Vales, Romney Marsh and the Midland Plain. Earlier some grass mutton, and later large supplies of turnip mutton, were bought in the Chiltern, Northdown and Cotswold countries and in the Norfolk Heathlands. Coleseed mutton came from the Fen Country and house-lamb from the Petworth District.[77]

Hay was supplied chiefly by the Vale of London, but some was later imported from the nearer parts of the Midland Plain.[78] In addition, London dealers bought table poultry from the Wealden Vales; wild fowl from the Fen Country; turkeys from East Norfolk and the Sandlings Country; ducks from Aylesbury and elsewhere; rabbits and hares from the Chalk, Northwold and Chiltern countries, the Breckland and the Norfolk Heathlands; bacon from the Vale of Pickering, and both porkers and baconers from High Suffolk; fresh fruit from the Northdown and Chiltern countries; hops from the Northdown Country, the Woodland, and the Vales of Hereford; cider, after 1670 if not before, from the Vales of Hereford; and also sea-fish, fresh from the Thames estuary, Rye and Lyme Regis, and preserved from fishing ports all the way from Berwick round to Chester. Lastly, horses of various kinds were purchased, directly and indirectly, from the Midland Plain, the Vale of Pickering and else-where, largely at the numerous horse fairs. By 1640, for instance, the chief buyers at Penkridge fair were London Smithfield dealers.[79]

As local markets were overridden by regional ones, and regional by metropolitan, the organisation of marketing was for a long period in a state of almost continuous change. One sign of rupture in previously existing arrangements came in times of dearth, when centres of consumption felt compelled to send out purveyors to scour the country around. In 1608, for example, in the Cheese Country, Trowbridge and Bradford-on-Avon claimed they needed their own

purveyors of corn and grain; Melksham was licensed to have one
to buy corn in the Chalk Country, to which the Calne bakers had
already resorted; and Bath wanted one purveyor to buy wheat and
barley from the Chalk Country for baking and another to fetch
malt for brewing for visitors who came to take the waters.[80] In more
normal times seemingly ubiquitous badgers, licensed or unlicensed,
bought in one market to sell in another. The justices of peace took
recognizances from them in droves. In the years 1651–5 Cheshire
licensed scores of swalers (mealmen) and badgers of corn, malt,
butter and cheese. In the course of fifteen years Wiltshire licensed
nearly two hundred.[81] No less essential were the kidders, who bought
on the farm to sell in the market; the higglers, who sold there on behalf
of others; and the laders, who bought for transit to wharves and ports.
The birth of metropolitan markets, as always, was marked by 'country
buying' by London merchants, or their factors and agents, either at
the farmhouses, or in the inns lining the market-squares, or from
badgers, laders, carriers and kidders who switched their operations
to the new lines of demand.[82] Carriers, tranters and others, seizing
their opportunities, became traders on others' or their own accounts.
As the markets grew, the dealers multiplied astonishingly. Local
consumers complained in vain, 'Badgers, loders, and common carriers
of corn, doo not onlie buie up all, but give above the price to be served of great quantities.' Dealers bought wheat and barley on the
ground, a hundred acres or more at a time, and farmers sold by the
mow, the stack, the acre or the ridge.[83] Under such influences, pitched corn markets might expand enormously, as did those of
Warminster and Farnham, or, more often, would turn into sample
markets or corn exchanges, all transactions being on the basis of
samples, while the corn itself was stored on the farm or by tranters
at inns and houses in the market towns. Then all the business could
be settled over a tankard in an inn, the seller merely producing a small
bag of corn for approval. The badger just said, 'Let me see it, what
shall I give you, knit it up, I will have it, go carie it to such a
chamber.'[84] This is how a Northwold farmer describes his sales at
Bridlington: 'Wee sende a sample of our wheate to the shipmasters
(by the salters that goe thither), and alsoe the price of our corne; and
then if wee can agree, they sett downe a day and wee sende our corne
to that key or other place assigned. This wheate is carryed by shippinge
to Newe-castle and Sunderland.'[85]

The fatstock and meat trades also became better organised.

Farmers sold their fat stock, either directly, or through markets like those at St Ives, Ely, Melton Mowbray, Market Harborough, Northampton and Thame, largely to drovers and jobbers who acted for, or resold to, the dealers and brokers at the London Smithfields or other market places. These men sold to the grazing and carcass butchers, who in turn supplied the cutting butchers. The grazing butchers kept the fat stock in preserved pastures until the cutting butchers took it off their hands in the course of the winter. Grazing butchers were very numerous in the Vale of London, but a few were found in most provincial towns of any size, John Freake of Leicester being a typical example. Drovers and jobbers performed essential functions, for not only did they relieve the farmer of driving his own stock through unfamiliar country, they also secured him better prices than he could have got for himself. Anyway, an inexperienced countryman would have been out of his depth trying to sell fat stock in Smithfield.[86]

Professional dealers played the most highly active part in the extension of commerce. Provincial corn merchants displayed great skill and resource in buying up wheat and barley on distant farms, and their ears were always cocked for the merest whisper of a surplus in some market town or other. In the end, the bulk of the cereal trade came into the hands of shippers and others who sold through one of the dozen or so London corn factors.[87] At one time local factors were wont to travel from farm to farm in the Woodland buying up hops on the ground.[88] London dealers made the rounds of capital farms in the south of the Midland Plain to purchase livestock. They then left their own drovers to move it along Watling Street, stopping by night in one of a chain of lodgings with accommodation closes nearby. Dealers also toured markets like those at Ashford, Enfield and Romford, and staging camps like the one at Brook Street near Brentwood, where the owner of the pastures also provided the services of drovers and salesmen.[89] Housewives in the Vale of London who sold their fruit in the city met some of the demand, but wholesale fruiterers sprang up to barge supplies along the Thames from the Northdown and Chiltern countries.[90] London cheese-mongers employed the services of factors at, among other places, Reading, Newbury, Abingdon, Marlborough and Tetbury for the Cheese Country; Uttoxeter for the Midland Plain; Chester, Frodsham, Nantwich and Whitchurch for the Cheshire Cheese Country; Gloucester for the vales of Evesham and Berkeley; and Cretingham,

Heveningham, Dunwich, Woodbridge and Ipswich for High Suffolk. The factor contracted with farmers for deliveries of butter and cheese, and might lay out hundreds of pounds a day in the purchase of cheese alone.[91] Such transactions swiftly engulfed regional markets and replaced them by metropolitan ones.

It is impossible to delineate exact boundaries for the metropolitan markets in particular foods and foodstuffs. They were most far-flung for store cattle, corn and cheese and least for fresh fish and table fruit.

That London took half the production of Cheshire cheese in the second half of the seventeenth century, seems feasible.[92] In 1534 the conurbation consumed perhaps 150,000 quarters of corn; in 1605 about 500,000; in 1661 about 1,150,000. Little can be argued from the port books about the extent to which coastwise traffic increased. Anyway, much or most of the supplies came by road and inland navigation.[93] Some were from the Vale of London itself, but to distinguish between these and those from elsewhere is impossible, simply because all were milled in the same towns on the perimeter of the vale. Farmers throughout the vale sold their wheat to meal-men at Croydon, Uxbridge, Enfield, Watford, Hertford, Ware, Brentford and other market towns where it was milled and passed to the city bakers; and these towns were the very ones, along with others like Henley, Reading and Caversham, through which London imported grain by road and river.[94] Thus wheat meal brought to London from, say, Ware, could equally well have originated in the Vale of London or in the Chiltern Country, the Midland Plain or elsewhere. It would be hard to tell what the vale's imports were, unless, perhaps, by deducting its production from the city's consumption, which would be to subtract a guess from a far-derived estimate. If the vale was largely self-sufficient before 1534, it certainly did not stay so for long.

But it was not only for itself that London imported foodstuffs. Goods moved to the metropolis not merely for consumption there and in the vale, but also for distribution to much more distant parts of the metropolitan market, not to speak of exports oversea. In the period 1460–1585 London sent oversea little or no corn and, if anything, had an adverse balance in the foreign trade in grain. Between 1600 and 1660, however, the port of London began to send corn abroad on a large scale and by 1662–70 had established a clear lead in this business. Overseas exports rose steeply and appear to have gone on rising throughout two thirds of the next century.[95]

Moreover, as is well known, London grew partly by taking over trade from merchants in other towns, particularly seaports. Londoners themselves exported much from provincial ports; it was often unnecessary for the merchandise to make the journey in and out of London.[96] England was already exporting corn oversea in the early sixteenth century, but London handled hardly any of this trade. Yet once the metropolitan market was fully established, Londoners emerged as leading exporters of corn, and beer and other processed farm produce. This position had been reached already by 1639. London had become far more than a centre of consumption. Her merchants had made themselves distributors.[97]

Much the same may be said for the cheese and butter markets. In the early sixteenth century High Suffolk already exported dairy produce to the Continent.[98] London's cheese purchases increased enormously, but by no means all this cheese was consumed in the city. The cheese and butter the London cheesemongers imported from High Suffolk, the Cheese and Cheshire Cheese countries, the Midland Plain, and the vales of Evesham, Pickering and Berkeley, was largely distributed throughout the length and breadth of the Vale of London, as far afield as the south coast, and even to High Suffolk and the Fen and other countries. And then, of course, not all the cheese and butter Londoners traded in actually passed through London; some went across country. Once the demands of London and the home market were met, Londoners exported dairy produce oversea. By the middle of the seventeenth century, Londoners were selling butter and cheese from High Suffolk and other countries to Germany, France, Spain and elsewhere.[99]

Londoners became the great distributors for many other products also, for bacon from the Vale of Pickering,[100] for woad from the Midland Plain,[101] for hops and for corn and grass seeds from the Northdown and other countries,[102] for horses and store cattle, which were redistributed from Smithfield to Romney Marsh graziers and others,[103] and for cured sea-fish like herrings.[104] London's other imports and re-exports are more difficult to trace. We can only see such things as bacon, eggs and poultry coming into the city from the Vale of London, the Midland Plain and elsewhere.[105]

What is as clear as crystal is that London imported not simply for herself, but for the British Isles, the Continent, and even Africa, Asia and America.

3

Commercial credit

The crucial event in the history of inland trade in early modern England was the rise of metropolitan markets.[106] Their organisational essence was the regular consignment of wares by suppliers to London factors working on commission.[107]

In the ordinary course of wholesale trade, in all kinds of markets, it had long been the usual practice for sellers to give credit to buyers, so, naturally, when selling to or in London, suppliers accumulated credit balances on the books of their merchants or factors, and a single supplier often had such dealings with two or more firms. Credit accounts like these were held in London by weavers, clothiers, yarn-masters, lacemen, grazing and wholesale butchers, and provincial corn, cheese, coal, fish and other factors and dealers.[108] These accounts were complemented by those held with merchants in Chester, Liverpool, Newcastle, Bristol, Norwich, Portsmouth, Bolton, Rochdale and elsewhere.[109] Domestic commerce ran on credit and gave rise to a whole range of credit instruments, arrangements and facilities. The seller gave 'day' or credit to the buyer, perhaps charging slightly more than he would have done had he been paid on the nail, making allowance for the time between the contracted dates of delivery and payment. Conversely, when, more rarely, the buyer gave day to the seller, the price might be reduced accordingly. Payment was rarely made on the nail, but one clear instance has been found. William Herrick notes in his accounts, 'Paid Mr Greene the 17 of July 1614 the 100*li*. I aught him uppon a bill to be paid the 16 of July 1615 and because I paid him so lonnge befoure his day I took 8 pounds of him, so I paid 92*li*. −00.' Since giving and taking day was normal and paying on the nail unusual, the ordinary price was the one for sales on credit, with discount allowed in the event of payment on the nail.[110]

No loans being given or taken, these credit arrangements normally involved no interest, still less usury. Usury and interest were clean different, but are nowadays so often confused that our argument will be clarified by a short digression on these subjects.

Usury was the taking of payment merely and solely for a loan. Since money, of itself, was barren, and could not beget money, Christians condemned usury as ungodly, immoral, unproductive and a grave impediment to economic advance. Anyone who received back more than he lent by way of *mutuum* or loan in the full sense, where the borrower bore all the risk, was committing the sin of usury. 'Usury', says Blaxton, 'is mutuation or lending for gaine ... The contract of usury is nothing else but illiberal mutuation.' Liberal mutuation, in contrast, was where the borrower made a gift of his own free will, unsought and uncovenanted for, merely out of gratitude; it was a rare act of friendship. The usurer lent not merely for gain, but for certain and assured gain; he took no risk. As Miles Mosse points out, 'The usurer never adventureth or hazardeth the losse of his principall: for he wil have all sufficient securitie for the repaiment and restoring of it backe againe to himselfe.'[111] Interest was another matter. It was the gain that accrued to a man for his interest in a transaction, and could arise in a number of ways. A sleeping partner, who put up money for a venture in which he ran the risk of losing all or part of his investment, was no usurer, and his gain was not usury, but interest, under the title of *periculum sortis*. He who lent charitably to someone in need what he could otherwise have used profitably in industry or commerce, was permitted reasonable compensation for his opportunity lost, under the title of *lucrum cessans* or cessant gain. He who by lending incurred expenses he would not otherwise have borne, such as the transport of coins, covering loans necessitated by the extension of credit, the keeping of accounts, scrivener's fees, and insurance premiums, had a right to compensation, under the title of *damnum emergens*. (Incidentally, any prince who took forced loans from his subjects was in duty bound to pay interest to them for any cessant gain or emergent loss). He who lent and was not repaid on the agreed day, might claim interest for the delay, *titulus morae*, under title of *mora*. When the contract of loan itself stipulated a penalty for such delay, interest might be charged, under title of *poena conventionalis*. In both cases the lender had to forbear suing for recovery of his loan, and the interest he received was in return for this forbearance. Lawful gains might also be made from ordinary transactions on genuine outland bills of exchange, because of the slight but real risk of loss of part or all of the money advanced and the uncertain amount of any possible gain, due to fluctuations in the exchanges. Sudden debasements of the coinage were the greatest risk in such bill business. Interest payments were thus freely allowed wherever lenders were entitled to them.[112]

Misunderstandings arose from the confusion, now all but universal and in former times not wholly unknown, between interest and usury, especially in relation to forbearance. Mosse explains this well:

Note by the way for the better discoverie of the usurers evill dealing, that howsoever hee, to glose with the world is wont to confound the names of interest and usurie – and men are woont to say, that they take interest, and lend upon interest, when indeed they take usurie and lend upon usurie – yet that there are two manifest and essentiall differences between usurie and interest, which doe so distinguish the one from the other, as that they cannot possibly be confounded. One difference is this: usurie is an overplus or gaine taken more than was lent; interest is never gaine or overplus above the principall, but a recompense demaunded and due for the damage that is taken, or the gaine that is hindered, through lending. Another difference is this: usurie accrueth and groweth due by lending, from the day of borrowing unto the appointed time of payment; interest is never due but from the appointed day of payment forward, and for so long as I forbeare my goods after the day in which I did covenant to receive them againe. So that, if once I have lent freely unto a certaine day, I shall not demaunde interest for any damage susteined or gaine hindered during that tearme of time for which I have lent unto another. But if at the covenanted time I receive not mine owne againe, then what harme soever do betide me after that day, for the forbearing thereof, reason will that it be recompenced of the borrower.[113]

Ordinary commercial credit, then, entailed little by way of interest, for default in due payment was unusual, since any tradesman or merchant worth his salt coveted the name of a good payer. Even if, by giving day, the seller had been enforced to take day in transactions where he was the purchaser, the reward for forbearance would not have been usury, but interest under the title of *damnum emergens*. Since buyers were also sellers, and vice versa, once a chain of credit transactions had been established, the enhancement of sellers' prices would have resulted not in usury but in interest. Obviously, interest and usury in such transactions were divided by the narrowest of lines, so even apparently ordinary commercial credit could be used as cloak for usury. In Mosse's example, 'I sell wares, I give three moneths day of payment, and, for that I am to forbeare my money so long, I sell above mine ordinarie price and above a reasonable gaine: herein (no question) I commit usurie.'[114] For an instance of an unconscious confusion of interest and usury in this kind of transaction, we may cite the alleged victim of a Marlborough usurer artlessly describing him as a man 'who did usually lend mony for interest.'[115]

Throughout our period, in England, usury was, in a greater or lesser degree, unlawful, with the sole exception made for courts of orphans in boroughs and cities where the usury was solely for the benefit of the orphans and the good was widely considered to outweigh the evil. Interest, on the other hand, was always lawful. Respectable businessmen, merchants and others, earned interest, largely by true forbearance. This was expressly allowed in the very same Acts that were intended to suppress all, and especially surreptitious, usury. The 1496 Act had a proviso 'savyng laufull penaltees for nounpaiment of the same money lent.' The 1552 Act forbade only spurious and usurious forbearance:

No parson ... shall ... by anny corrupt, colourable or disceitful conveyaunce, sleight or engyne or by anny waye or meane ... lende, give, sett owte, delyver, or forbeare anny somme or sommes of money ... to or for anny manner of usurie, encreace, lucre, gayne or interest to be had, receyved or hoped for.

And even Acts of Parliament that regulated the taking of interest, left all usury punishable not only by the ecclesiastical courts, but also by the royal ones. The 1571 Act, like that of 1545, limited legitimate interest arising from loans to ten per cent., but, 'forasmuch as all usurie being forbydden by the lawe of God is synne and detestable', enacted

That all usurie, loane and forbearing of monye or gevyng dayes for forbearing of monye by waye of loane, chevysaunce, shyftes, sale of wares, contracts or other doynges whatsoever for gayne ... whereuppon is not reserved or taken or covenaunted to be reserved, payde or geven to the lender, contracter, shyfter, forbearer or deliverer, above the summe of tenne pounds for the loane or forbearinge of a hundred poundes for one yere ... shalbe punished [by forfeiture of] so muche as shalbe reseived by way of usurie above the principall for any money so to be lent or forborne ... and ... further ... that the sayd statute ... shalbe most largely and strongly construed for the repressing of usurie.

Once again, corrupt bargains were especially aimed at. One reason why the 1545 Act allowed up to ten per cent. was simply that, largely due to the debasement of the coinage (inflation), many prices were rising at ten per cent. or more per annum, so limiting the rate to ten per cent. was tantamount to prohibiting usury altogether, the real gain at that rate being nothing or less than nothing. The Act of 1552 could forbid all usury only because debasement had stopped and prices were fluctuating normally. In 1563 a Bill to revive the Act of 1545 passed the Commons, but failed to be enacted. The 1545 Act recognised that previous legislation had 'bene of so litle force or effect that by reason therof litle or no punyshment hath ensued to thoffendors ... but rather hath encouraged them to use the same.' The 1571 Act said the 1552 one had 'not done so muche good as was hoped it shoulde, but rather the said vyce of usurye, and specially by waye of sale of wares and shiftes of interest, hathe much more excedingly abounded.'

Both the 1545 and 1571 Acts, while denying the usurer any remedy in law to recover more than his bare principal, realistically recognised the sheer impossibility of suppressing all usury whatsoever, and both effectually tolerated it up to ten per cent. when frankly and openly taken, and, explicitly in 1571, only on condition the borrower actively willed the transaction. What was unique about the 1571 Act was, first, that it was passed at a time when inflation had ceased and ten years after its demise had been marked by the recoinage of 1561; and, secondly, that while all usury was forbidden, the usurer who took no more than the statutory rate was allowed a remedy in law to recover his bare principal. This Act was a response not to inflation but to rising prices and a strong demand for loans, some it seems at rates of over ten per cent. This development was accompanied or followed by a shift of opinion on the ethics of usury. Man being imperfect and having to live by the sweat of his brow, the necessity of usury for productive purposes, what we would now call productive interest, was acknowledged by a wide range of men, including John Calvin and Francis Bacon. If great minds now started to think alike on this question, it was because they were all now confronted with the same new reality, namely, a great upsurge of prosperity and consequently a steady and prolonged rise in most prices. Under such circumstances the charges for productive loans could be moderated by tolerating limited usury, for this very toleration removed most of the risk from loan transactions: once the lender knew he could recover up to ten per cent., he could afford to lend at lower rates than when he operated under the constant fear of remediless default. The consensus now became, that usury was allowable on productive loans, while biting and unconscionable usury, especially on consumers' loans, above all those to the poor, should be strictly and rigorously suppressed;

and this was the effectual result of the 1571 Act. Subsequent Acts merely lowered the tolerated rate of usury as the demand for, and price of, usurious loans fell away during the recession and depression of the period after 1619. In 1624 the rate was brought down to eight per cent., in 1651 to six, in 1713 to five. No one of all these Acts so much as mentioned compound interest, so presumably the maxima were in simple terms.[116]

One result of the 1571 Act and its successors was that there was normally no need of corrupt bargains to evade the usury laws, except perhaps when the commercial rate greatly exceeded the statutory, apparently a rare occurrence, partly because the statutory maximum rate was sometimes excessively high, pending legislation to reduce it, and partly because the maximum rates for usury were rather like our maximum speed limits for the roads in that they were mostly enforced only when greatly exceeded. Almost all recorded rates of usury were at or below the legal limit, and this seems to correspond to reality. Another result of these new usury laws was that bills of exchange might be discounted with impunity, even though such discounting remained usurious.[117] A further and more general result was that moderate usury became almost respectable and was practised ever more widely. William Harrison relates that usury was still condemned by old men in his village, but was 'now perfectlie practised by almost everie Christian and so commonlie that he is accompted but for a foole that dooth lend his monie for nothing.' As George Wither put it,

> To make of griping usury their trade,
> Among the rich, no scruple now is made
> In any place. For every country village
> Hath now some usury, as well as tillage.

Nevertheless, as Harrison said, there were still merchants and businessmen to whom usury was 'a hell to a good conscience'.[118] All the same, usury within the statutory rate became more and more to be regarded as interest and only gains above the rate as usury.[119] Later still, such excessive gains came to be called excessive interest, all notion of usury having been lost.

As long as ecclesiastical courts maintained their general jurisdiction, they continued to try cases of usury and punish offenders, even when no more than the statutory rate had been taken. But ecclesiastical courts had solely ecclesiastical sanctions at their disposal, and the typical punishment meted out for petty usury was no more than a compulsory payment into the poor box, lesser and greater excommunication being seldom resorted to for this particular sin.[120] Helped by the promptings of common informers, the lay courts went on enforcing the usury laws, but, in practice, after 1571, only excessive usury was usually punished.[121]

Obviously, there never was such a thing as a legal limit to the rate of interest, and no more than now was there such a thing as a single, general rate of interest. Any interest charged had to be at a reasonable rate, but what was a reasonable rate depended on the degree of risk run by the lender. The false notion of so-called 'excess profit' had not yet been concocted. The Court of Chancery could be depended upon the disallow all harsh and unconscionable usury, but freely allowed thirty or more per cent. compound interest where reasonable. Although an Act of Parliament in 1833 exempted bills of exchange and promissory notes with less than three months to run from the usury laws, the legal concept of excessive interest and harsh and unconscionable transactions on account of gross excess of interest arose only after the repeal of the usury laws in 1854 and merely continued the provisions of those laws under other names and titles. Then harsh and unconscionable usury became harsh and unconscionable interest, but, still, whether a rate of interest was conscionable or unconscionable depended on the degree of risk borne by the lender, and risk may be almost infinite. As Lord Bramwell put it, 'Suppose you were asked to lend a mutton chop to a ravenous dog, upon what terms would you lend it?'[122]

Now we may return to our main theme: commercial credit and credit instruments.

The bill obligatory, bill of debt or bond was the usual way of combining an acknowledgment of debt with an undertaking to settle it at a certain date or dates, usually one, three, six or twelve months hence. A formal English bill obligatory typically contained the names of the parties, the amount of the debt, the date or dates for payment, and the date on which the bill was sealed, for it was a sealed document, distinguished by its seal and invalid without it. No consideration need be stated, but the bill might have clauses covering this and stipulating the place, medium and mode of payment, e.g. a house in Cheapside, good and lawful money of England, three instalments. Moreover, the obligation might be made contingent upon certain conditions being met, e.g. the delivery of goods as agreed, so transforming the obligation simple into an obligation conditional. A simple bill, in payment for farm goods, might run like this:

Memorandum that I Thomas Everingham of Beal in the County of York yeoman do owe unto Henry Best of Elmswell in the same county gent. the sum of 3*li*. 10*s*. of lawful money of England to be paid unto the said Henry Best his heirs executors or assigns at the now dwelling house of Thwaites Foxe of Beverley the 8 April 1626. Unto the true and faithful payment whereof I bind me my heirs executors or assigns by these presents. In witness whereof I have hereunto set my hand. – Thomas Everingam his mark. Witness Jane Laurance her mark.

Over and above the bill obligatory, for the greater assurance of payment, the debtor might enter into a penal bond, which was a special form of the obligation conditional: in the event of non-payment on the original bill obligatory, the debtor obliged himself to the penalty of paying more than the original debt, commonly twice as much. Such a penal bond ensured immediate judgment to pay in case of default. The debt then became a 'judgment debt' and the debtor a 'judgment debtor', and further default led swiftly and inexorably to outlawry. With the penal bond we are not immediately concerned except as an instrument of credit. The bill obligatory was a specialty drawn up and written by a scrivener, a contract or covenant under seal, the highest form of documentary evidence. The discharge of such an obligation could be proved by nothing less than a special and equally formal acquittance, or, much more commonly, by the return, slashing or destruction of the original bill. This remained true even when stipulated instalments were, on payment, endorsed off, i.e. 'writen and indorsed to be paide upon the backeside of the said bill of debt.'[123]

Englishmen habitually made or set over their debts; creditors regularly assigned sealed bills obligatory. This often facilitated the collection of the debt itself, just as the use of a credit factor does today. But more usually debts were assigned primarily as a means of settling other and counter debts, enabling payment without coin. Men went on setting over debts one against another until they encountered someone able and willing to pay cash and so end the credit chain. In this bill traffic, two points had to be regarded: the sum specified and the date it was due. The first involved no more than addition and subtraction, but the second was dealt with by discounting, the price of the goods being adjusted accordingly. By the strict letter of the law, a sealed bill obligtory could not be assigned by endorsement, only by the first creditor and then by a deed of attorney creating an attorney to whom the debt could be assigned. Furthermore, even this legal allowance of assignment was limited by the requirement of the law that no assignment be made without the consent of the existing debtor. This was to safeguard the debtor against assignment to an enemy who might take unfair advantage. While this consent was commonly requested and then usually given, it was probably more often taken for granted, leaving it to the debtor to raise any objection he might have when confronted by the creditor by assignment. In practice, these legal requirements were far from being insuperable obstacles to the transference of bills obligatory from party to party, provided only these parties were prepared to forego strict legal assurance. Anyway, it was up to the assignee to ensure the debtor had no objection, for otherwise he might not be paid. Since nothing but an acquittance or the return or slashing of the bill was taken as proof of payment, most debtors made sure to pay nothing and no one except in return for the bill itself, and preferably all under the supervision of a scrivener. The bill once returned and slashed, it mattered not whether the attorney or attorneys, assign or assigns had been formally and legally constituted or not. Conversely, creditors saw their way to taking bills they felt confident would be honoured. Thus bills obligatory, though not negotiable in law, were in fact assigned and passed from hand to hand until the due date.[124] No usury was entailed in the discounting of bills obligatory by traders, for no money changed hands and no loan had been made. In any case, even if this practice had been usurious, it would have been tolerated by the Act of 1571.[125] This being so, formal, sealed bills were often unnecessary; informal, unsealed ones would do. These were the 'bills', 'bills of hand' or promissory notes that 'everie man of credit and reputation giveth of his owne handwriting, or made by his servant, and by him subscribed, without any seale or witnesse thereunto.' Whether formal or informal, such obligations had been used for ages in western Europe. It was said in 1622,

The most usuall buying and selling of commodities beyond the seas, in the course of trafficke, is for bills of debt, or obligations, called billes obligatorie, which one merchant giveth unto another, for commodities bought or sold, which is altogether used by the Merchants Adventurors ... beyond the seas at Middleborough, Amsterdam, Antwerp, Hamborough, and other places ... For when they have sold their clothes unto other merchants, or others, payable at 4, 6, 8, or more months, they generally transferre and set over these billes (so received for the payment of their clothes) unto other merchants, and take for them other commodities ... to make returne of the provenue of theirs; and so selling those forraine commodities here in England.

Bearer bonds of this kind were often used in commodity transactions in Antwerp from the early sixteenth century onward, and were readily discounted there. Bills of exchange were thus so much the less required. In England, too, informal bills obligatory were much used and such bills were often made out to payee or bearer and were freely assigned, even though they lacked the full force of law until 1705.[126] So it is that we find sealed bills, some payable to XYZ and his certain attorney, heirs, executors and assigns, and unsealed ones, some payable to XYZ or bearer. Bearer clauses could not confer legal negotiability, but, then, their absence in no way prevented bills passing from hand to hand; they were freely transferred. In any event, people tended to avoid bearer clauses whenever possible, because of the danger of bearer bills getting into wrong hands. (Incidentally, and it goes without saying, bank-notes, when they came, were simply promissory notes from goldsmith-bankers payable to bearer).[127] Setting over debts was second nature to English businessmen[128] and bills obligatory, sealed or not, were currency among them. Sealed bills were used when occasion demanded, when cast-iron legality was the first consideration, for example, by clothiers' factors in London when making out bills of debt to executors or to clients in remote parts.[129] Otherwise, informal bills sufficed. As one clothier explained, 'In dealings between the clothier and the draper in delivery of cloths upon credit from one fortnight to another, they do not take specialties, but from time to time upon delivery of new cloths receive money for the old upon account.'[130]

Informal bills were couched in some such terms as these:

Memorandum that we Richard Kirby and Mathewe Morden of Helperthorpe do owe and confess ourselves and either of us to be indebted the sum of 2*li*. 1*s*. of lawful money of England to be paid to Henry Best of Elmswell or his assigns at or upon 24 June next ensuing the date hereof. In witness whereof we have both hereunto set our hands this 6 May 1626. – Richard Kirby. Mathew Mording.

4th March 1641. I doe hereby promise to pay unto Rachell Browne of Yorke or her assignes in London by the hands of Mr Isacke Knipe factor in Blackwell Hall the some of One hundreth pounds upon the 20th day of Aprill next. Witnes my hand the day and yeare above written. – Edward Firth.

These are examples of what are nowadays called promissory notes, i.e. unconditional promises in writing made by one person to another, signed by the maker, engaging to pay, on demand or at a fixed or determinable future time, a sum certain in money, to, or to the order of, a specified person, or to bearer. The first bill concerned a simple, the second a more complex transaction. Rachel Browne's London factor or agent showed this to Knipe, who wrote his acceptance upon it: 'Accepted this xvjth of March 1641 per me Isacke Knipe for the usse of Mr Edward Firth.' It now only remained for one factor to pay the other, or, rather, for them to adjust their clients' accounts accordingly and to render them statements of account. An informal bill obligatory could thus be much like a postdated cheque or a bill of exchange at thirty days sight, and even be open to acceptance or refusal and perhaps protest just as a bill of exchange was. If Knipe had found Firth's account in debit and had not wanted to make him a sufficient advance, to allow him to go into the red for so much, he would have refused the bill informally and have referred Rachel Browne to the drawer; in modern colloquial parlance, the bill would have been endorsed 'RD'; it would have 'bounced'. However, what we have hypothesised about refusal was of rare occurrence; all the bills recorded in this manuscript were accepted as usual. For further instance, on 24th February 1641 Firth received from Edmund Kay £100, which he then promised and bound himself to pay over at London on 20th March, through Knipe, to John Owen at the 'Three Anchors' in Lawrence Lane, which turns off north from the east end of Cheapside. Knipe accepted this bill on 14th March and on 23rd March, on the last of the normal three days of grace, Richard Brown gave a receipt for the £100 on behalf of his master, John Owen.[131]

Evidence of the extensive and habitual use of bills obligatory in England throughout our period abounds at all hands.[132] We can see their various forms being used in a variety of ways. In the 1580s William Leonard of Taunton was trading with far-away Suffolk clothiers. John Winterfloode of Edwardstone gave his bill for £47 12*s*, 'which bill was lefte by Richarde Leonarde in John Davyes hande clotheworker in London − the place wher his house is learne of William Morris the factor', notes William Leonard. His brother Richard appears to have received the bill on William's behalf and to have left it for acceptance by Winterfloode's factor. Possibly the bill had no clause specifying the exact or correct place of payment, thus leaving it payable, strictly speaking, at the factor's place of business.

Davye, of course, frequented the sale hall, but his seat of business was his residence. William wanted to find out where this was and naturally assumed his factor would know. Another entry in this account book reminds Leonard that 'Richard Symons my brother is to accompte for too bills delivered to one Mr Cardinall myne attorney against George Manle of Stoke Nayland in Suffolk, for which bills I have judgement against the said Manle for 57*li*. and he standeth owtlawed uppon a judgement, wherof my brother Symons can declare.' Here we see formal, sealed penal bonds payable to an attorney, with letters of attorney duly made, and a judgment debtor outlawed. Cardinall was another clothier in Stoke Nayland, and one Leonard had many dealings with. It would seem that Cardinall had taken the bills in settlement of a balance due from Leonard, the bills having been delivered by Leonard's brother-in-law.[133]

We can also see bills obligatory being used in response to long terms of credit. John Newcombe, a West Country clothier, accounts on 28th April 1599 for £24 17*s* due from William Jenyns, citizen and cloth-worker of London, 'to be payd at iiijor monethes per his bill', and notes, on 22nd September, 'Thomas Woode cittizen and haberdasher of London oweth unto me John Newcombe the some of thirtye nyne pounds which ys to be payd by his bill at six moneths.' These were extended credits, especially when one considers the relative substance of clothiers and merchants. Long lists of similar debts follow in the same document; they are to be paid by London wholesalers at three, four, five or six months and often by instalments.[134] At least one of these debts had been made over: 'Henry Francs bill but Walter Morrels debt'.[135] On 10th January 1634 another businessman in those parts, named John Hayne, entered into his accounts the £189 owed by John Henley of Leigh-upon-Mendip, 'being for a debt of Mr John Hill merchant of Dorchester whose four bylls I tooke from Mr Bartlet, being all paiable to severall men the 18th past, and all had the same witnesses, viz. Giles Greene and John Crewkerne.' Henley and others gave bills to Hill, who discounted them with Bartlet, who in turn passed them to Hayne. Here we see the bill as currency.[136]

4

The rise of the inland bill of exchange

A bill obligatory, then, originated as an undertaking to pay an acknowledged debt, and was thus quite distinct from a bill of exchange, which was an order to pay. But, as we have seen, by 1641 hybrid bills had come into use, bills that combined a promise to pay with an order to pay. For example, when we read in Isaac Knipe's accounts a transcript of a writing from Edward Firth, 'Received the 4th of March 1641 of Mr Edmund Kay the som of One hundreth pounds which I promyse by these presents to pay to Mr John Owen att 3 Anckers in Laurence Lane the first day of Aprill next by Mr Isaac Knipe facter in Blackwell Hall, I say received', we are confronted with a receipt plus a promissory note. Then this writing was 'accepted this xiiij of March 1641 per me Isacke Knipe', who obviously regarded the receipt as an order to pay. When Thomas Walton gives a receipt for the money, it is in the following terms: 'Received the 6th of Aprill anno 1642 the some of One hundred pounds in full of this bill of exchange of Mr Isacke Knipe and is for the use of my master John Owen.' The writing drawn by Firth and superscribed by Knipe is described as 'this bill of exchange'. It was a hybrid instrument, a receipt-cum-order to pay, or, in common parlance, a bill of exchange. A similar receipt from Firth dated 24th February 1641 for £100 from Kay, in which Firth promised and bound himself to return to Owen at the 'Three Anchors' through Knipe, was accepted by the latter on 14th March, and the payment was receipted by Brown for Owen on 23rd March. These proceedings appear to have been commonplace and unremarkable. Similar practices had obtained for more than a score of years before this time. Thus we find a London factor giving a receipt for payment in which he undertook to pay the money over to a third party. The self-same little writs served as receipts, promissory notes and bills of exchange.[137] And this helps to explain how lawyers in the late seventeenth century were almost splitting hairs when distinguishing between bills obligatory and bills of exchange, especially as by then the latter often had such long tenors (usances, currencies, *échéances*) as to be substitutes for bills obligatory in credit sales.[138]

Suppliers who built up balances on their accounts with factors and merchants in London often purchased raw materials and other goods there and paid for them by deductions from their accounts. If the purchase were carried out by or through the factor, he could without ado deduct his outlay and commission. If the purchase were made independently, the buyer usually settled his account with the seller by ordering his factor to make the necessary transfer from his own account to that of the seller (or to him and his assigns or to his order), just as debts from third parties were settled by transference to the supplier's account.[139]

It sometimes happened that an account went into debit, paying usury at rates within the legal limits, and overdrafts were allowed, and even expressly created, as a means of extending credit. There thus arose businessmen who were bankers in all but name. By 1615 the Brownings and Gurneys were veritable bankers in Norwich and London, lending, receiving, drawing drafts on London, selling bills on London, and carrying on all banking transactions. Francis himself operated in London, while his father-in-law Browning saw to the Norwich end of the business. At this time, then, the Gurney banking firm was already essentially the same as it was in the first half of the eighteenth century, when it has earned greater fame. In 1615 or thereabouts the factor usd by Mr Hooke of Bristol was paying 3½ per cent. per annum on a fifteen-day conditional deposit, while in 1620 Henry Blois of Ipswich was paying a man called Leke, his London factor, 8 per cent. per annum on a three-month overdraft.[140]

In 1603 Sir Thomas Temple of Stowe, a noted landowner and sheepmaster, had an account in London with Thomas Farrington, merchant and banker. Farrington made payments from the account as instructed both by word of mouth and 'by order of your letter', and received payments from Temple's tenants and from graziers, woolmen and others to whom he had sold produce. Farrington also lent out, at legal rates, at 9 or 10 per cent., a fraction of the balances remaining in the bank, mostly to London businessmen, e.g. Benjamin Ducros of the Muscovy Company and William Courteen, the merchant banker and company promoter.[141] As early as 1576 similar current accounts were provided by some of the London scriveners, who received payments on behalf of their clients, disbursed moneys as authorised, paid usury on deposits, and on occasion allowed overdrafts.[142] Such disbursements were nothing novel. Accountants and receivers to the Crown and others had been acting in this way for ages, making payments on the order of their principals out of money received on their behalf.[143] Most bankers, however, were factors or merchants or both. They were bankers in nature, though not in name. Banking was still without 'bankers' so called. In England, 'banker' came to mean someone largely engaged in 'discounting bills of exchange, promissory notes and ... in drawing or remitting money from one inland trading city to another' in England, Scotland and Ireland, in contrast to 'remitters' who negotiated foreign bills of exchange and of whom there were as yet relatively few over here and then largely Italians and Netherlanders.[144] Just like their modern counterparts, English bankers presented statements at regular intervals, often yearly, or on request, or when the account became overdrawn. When Richard Bradshaw has one of his bills refused by Owen Hughes of Chester, he protests 'that this three yeares past he had no notice of the areare of his accompte'.[145] Abraham and John Rodes of Rochdale copied several of their factor's statements of account into their own books. One factor's original statement has been preserved: the 'Account for Mr William Pratt Junior to the 30th of Januarie 1653'. Since 26th November 1652 twenty-four of his cloths had been sold for the sum of £264 8s. Carriage cost £7 4s and the hallage and porterage of five pieces 6s 3d. On 4th April £50 had been 'paid Thomas Hussie per Bill of Exchange'. Total outgoings amounted to £133 3s 3d, leaving Pratt £131 4s 9d in credit.[146]

This was the banking system used in England by merchants, traders, suppliers and manufacturers as their principal means of payment. Since they all had accounts in London, they paid each other by transference from one account to another, by the Bill on London.[147] Funds could also be drafted by the same system from London to Portsmouth and other provincial towns, through the banking facilities offered by merchants in various commercial and industrial centres. Thus on 10th March 1645 the Rodes paid Joseph Ryder, who also lived in the Rochdale district, £100 that a Mr Worall had paid their factor, William Ryder, in London. Similarly, on 19th April 1646 the Rodes paid out £100 to Thomas Lancashyre 'by the apoyntment of Mr William Ryder ... which money Mr William Ryder

received in London'. The Rodes, who were wholesale drapers, also
paid their suppliers in Rochdale and district through Ryder. In 1646,
for instance, Ryder was ordered to pay John Sharples for his Rochdale
baizes. Almost everything was done 'by Exchange'.[148] In 1582
Richard Martin in London had to pay £300 to a Mr Blande in Bristol,
and said, 'It may stay while I send my letters to Bristol to have so
much provided there'.[149] In 1584 the Norwich Dutch elders wrote to
their London opposite numbers, 'As regards the money laid out for
us, please draw for it on one of our merchants, Jacob Bufken or
Maeliaert Ryckewaert'.[150] In 1593 Thomas Radcliffe of Cockerton
in Darlington received 'one letter of James Dale for 5*li.*' and 'one
letter of William Wormeley for 52*s*'.[151] In 1600 Robert Delaval of
Seaton Delaval wrote to his son Ralph about a debt outstanding from
one Lyon and his partners for two shiploads of salt amounting to fifty-
four weys, saying, 'But I do heare that they have assigned a
fishmonger of London to paye me xviij*li.* this next weeke, which wyll
discharge for the xxxij wayes'. Delaval sold salt to London salters,
who, it seems, had dealings with a fishmonger, who had, perhaps,
to pay for fish bought from a northeastern port and so could transfer
to Delaval what he owed to the salters. A financial link had been
forged between Seaton and London. In 1613, Francis Delaval was
receiving his annuity from Sir Ralph by means of letters to Sir William
Slingsby.[152] A wholesale hosier's accounts in 1612 show credit transactions of the kind we speak of, for instance, £3 'paid to one Francis
Turner att Cambridge with a letter', £140 'paid to Mr Johnson in
Watlinge Street for Mr Lambton', £20 'paid to Mr Huchinson vintner
for one Huchinson of Swadell', £15 'paid to Mr St Albons for Mr
Dawson of Rippon', £6 10*s* 'paid to Mr Richinson hosier for Mr
Jamson of Newarke'.[153] Robert Gray, of Bread Street in London,
used to ride the rounds of provincial fairs to buy cloths, which he
then finished and dyed. In 1616 he wrote to his wife from Bristol,
somewhat irritably, 'My man George wrights me that Mrs Walker
of Hull appoynted me xxiij*li.*, so because he could not com to her
bill, he could not have the mony. I showed you the mornynge before
I came awaye wher you should have all the biles; this is some
hendrance that the bill was not looked for, so God knowes howe longe
I shalbe without my mony.'[154]

Henry Blois was immersed in inland credit transfers. In 1617 there
was 'dew unto Mr Leke the which hee payed unto Mr John Bond
fyshmonger of Lonndon for Mr Gros of Yarmoth and the owners

100*li.*, being in part of 150*li.* the which John Baker charged him with, I saye dew to him 100*li.*' Other funds were received by Leke for Blois 'of Mr Burnell by the apointment of Mr Mathew Brownbryg'; 'dew more in that letter the which you recheaved of Anthony Dyngham by the apointment of Mr Benham 50*li.*'; and £33 6*s* 8*d* 'dew to Mr Leke as in hys of the 23 July 1619 the which hee had payed unto Mr John Brook of Lonndon marchant by the apointment of John Baker'. A sum of £90 was to fall due from Leke 'for so mutch the which is to bee payed from Mr Grandish of Norwich by a note sent him upe in myne of the 29 July 1619 by Mr Jennyngs his man and this note is to bee payed the 20 August 1619 by Joseph Scottowe at the George'. (Perhaps this was 'The George' in Lombard Street where Thomas Rowe later had his banking shop.) Next there was 'dew from Mr Leke as in hys of the 4th February for 8*li.* the which Capten Parker dooeth wryt that Mr Abreham Colmar is to paye at 6 dayes; of this Mr Leke is to have ¼ part of also of the 18-06-08 formarly resayved; to charg now the somme of 8*li.*' Leke also owed £26 which he received on 5th January 1619 'from Mr John Rany by the apointment of Mr John Ackton' and £100 received 'of Mr John Revet by Mr Barron his order and was by John Baker his order to Mr Leke'. Another sum received by Blois was the £16 11*s* 'as in a letter from Anthony Dyngham to Mr Benham ... the which was payed unto him by Mr John Revet by the apointment of Capten Lovell'. As yet another example, Blois notes 'in myn to Mr Lek of the fyrst August 1620 I wyshed hym to wryt Mr Thomas Fownes that I had apointed hym to paye the 23 August next 158-10-02½ with the alowance for 3 moonthes after 8 per cent.', i.e. £161 13*s* 6*d*. Finally, we may instance 'the drafts made by Mr Morse for the company of the sewgar house' on behalf of Blois, who was a shareholder in that concern.[155]

The Rodes sold their cloths in London through their factor and paid their debts through their account with him, e.g. there was 'charghed of Mr Ryder ... by severall men at severall tymes by severall bills from the 26th June 1648 to the 20th June 1649 ... 2748*li.*01.08'. Ryder settled their debts in London, Leicester, Coventry, Wellingborough and elsewhere and received what was due to them from Norwich and other towns.[156] We can see William Gaby of Netherstreet, clothier and general dealer, settling his debts in 1663 by drawing on his factor, Richard Scott, and Whitby people who supplied fish and butter to London, drawing bills on fish and cheesemongers in East Smithfield, Old Fish Street, New Fish Street, Fetter

Lane, Stradwell, Billingsgate, Queenhithe and other parts of the city.[157] William Leonard of Taunton notes how he bought twenty cloths from John Browne of Edwardstone at £7 10s each, the £150 to be paid in three equal instalments. All three were 'paid him by William Morris of London my factor'. Leonard had many other debts paid by Morris and some 'by John Davye of London clothworker'.[158] William Browne, citizen of Norwich, settled his debts the same way. Between 1600 and 1605 John Newcombe of Exeter received payments 'of Nicholas Firmage by order of Mr Browne' or 'of Mr William Browne per Mr Firmage'. Newcombe received other sums 'of Nicholas Firmage by order of William Greene', citizen and draper of Norwich, 'of James Stocke in parte for Richard Owen', 'of Mr William Ritche by the appointment of Mrs Smethurste', and 'of Henry Wallington for Richard Owen', a member of the Ironmongers' Company. Needless to say, Newcombe settled his own debts by similar means.[159] Edward Firth of York sold ten packs of wool for a sum to be paid in four instalments. He 'received this x[th] day of June 1641 the some of eight poundes eight shillings per Isaack Knipe per the appoyntment of Mr Edward Firth and for his use', as were later the other payments.[160]

Understandably, not all payments could be made through the credit network. Even after clearance, some balances remained outstanding. These were normally settled by transporting specie, which might be entrusted to a common carrier, perhaps concealed in bales of ordinary goods.[161] In later times some payments were made by posting Exchequer bills, but most payees preferred coin.[162] And, then, anyone wanting to move large sums in haste had to resort to the carriage of coins. No one could have transferred by a single credit transaction the £13,500 Sir William Cavendish wanted moved from Derbyshire to London in 1602.[163]

Another shortcoming of this, as of every credit network based on bills of exchange, was that each increase in the amounts in circulation by bill, by diminishing the resources of the market, made the negotiation of further bills more difficult. In particular, cyclical shortages of bills could be occasioned by seasonal fluctuations in trade and payments. In the Midland Plain, grass beeves and muttons were sold to London during the summer months, but not after the grass had stopped growing and when the roads had become wet and bad. Thus it was on 19th October 1611 that Robert Herrick of Leicester wrote to William, his brother and factor in London, 'About Harborow fare, here was greate store of monye to be returned, and now I cannot heare of anye ... I sent up and downe on Saterday, and have spoken with divers, but cannot have anie promise'. When the London butchers or their buyers or factors were at Market Harborough at the height of the sales, the district was awash with their bills; but at other times, with the end of the selling season, they were in short supply. Similarly, on 8th May 1616, before the selling season was properly under way, Robert wrote to William to ask him to get his man 'to try soom of the bootchers in Estcheape or ellswheare yf anny of them that coom downe to Rowell fayre will leave you 150*li.* or what you can return of them, for I cannot return anny.' Rothwell fair was due to start soon and the hope was that some butchers would buy bills in antici-pation of their purchases there. The same problem had arisen on 10 May 1614 and on 5 November 1613, when Robert wrote, 'I have spoke and sent to all that be lykly in the market this day and cannot fynd one to return untell the 17 of this present, then soon go to Northampton fayre.' Moreover, when the opportunity came to transfer funds to Town, it came in a rush, and the Country demand for bills was rapidly sated, so that it then became temporarily difficult to raise money there by selling bills on London, as royal agents found in Chester in May and June 1581, though here, admittedly, the difficulties were com-pounded by competition from the drovers and by many of the local merchants being away on business in the capital.[164] Similar diffi-culties arose in Wales. In autumn, store cattle were sold to the drovers who took them for sale in London, but in springtime there were no such sales and no bills to be had, so there was nothing for it but to transport coin.[165]

Another, though minor, difficulty was an occasional lack of information by a debtor as to who the creditor's banker was. Thus in 1707 Michael Reynolds wrote from Banbury to Thomas Dickson in Bristol, 'These are to desire thee to lett me know to what person I may pay twelve pounds to in London for thy use.'[166]

Obviously, not everyone was a part of the credit network; only a minority had bank accounts. As today, 'the great unbanked' were a numerous throng. Still, not having a bank account of one's own by no means excluded one from any use at all of the banking system. A debt could be discharged by making payment in coin to the creditor's banker to the use of the creditor.

One important group of outsiders needing a limited use of the banking system consisted of those who collected in the provinces money they wished to convey to London. Many landowners (if not also merchants, graciers or suppliers to London) were in this position, as often as not because they were going to stay in Town for the term or season and needed spending money there. How landowners in the Midlands and thereabouts went about this business after 1651 has been thoroughly looked into and well described. They, like other outsiders, paid (or promised to pay) their money to cheese factors, ironmongers, grazing or wholesale butchers, wool staplers, lacemen and others in market towns like Chester, Nantwich, Whitchurch, Stourbridge, Buckingham and Leighton Buzzard, and in return received, either gratis or for a small fee, written orders to present to London factors. Armed with such an order, the payee, or his bearer in the person of a servant or agent, could repair to the factor's place of business, near one of the Smithfields or elsewhere, and receive payment in cash on what was tantamount to a traveller's cheque, or, alternatively, if, as was now becoming commoner, he had an account in London, he could have the money accredited to him there, and then he need only endorse the order, telling the factor to pay the money into his account and post the order off. The landowner, like Sir Justinian Isham of Lamport, 'paid here to have it again in London'.[167] Midland landowners entered into almost exactly the same kinds of arrangements well before 1651, at latest by 1595, and, both before and after, so did those in the Norfolk Heathlands, the West, North and Peak-Forest countries, the Northeastern and Northwestern lowlands, the Vale of Pickering, and other parts of the kingdom.[168]

Nicholas Herrick (or Heyricke), son of John Herrick of Leicester, having been apprenticed to a London goldsmith, opened shop in Westcheap at the sign of 'The Grasshopper'. Later, his younger brother William served him as an apprentice, before setting up for himself, about 1590, first at 'The Rose' in Cheapside, later in Wood Street, which runs north from Cheapside. William prospered greatly, bought the Beaumanor estate near Leicester, was burgess for the borough in the parliaments of 1601 and 1608, served the Crown, was knighted, and eventually retired to Beaumanor about 1623. Meanwhile, Robert, the eldest brother, had taken over the family business by the market place in Leicester, dealing in ironmongery and hosiery amongst other things. Robert and William were business as well as fraternal correspondents, and William sold Robert's hose for him in London. In 1594 Robert wrote to William, 'This is to desyar you to pay unto this bringer, Mr Richard Barwell, the soom of six skore

thirteen pounde vj s viij d as soone as you may after the sight hereof –
Your loving brother Robert Heyricke in Leicester the xij of November
1594.' This inland bill of exchange was subscribed, 'Receved of Mr
William Heyricke six skore thirteen pound vj s viij d accordinge to
this letter, by – Richard Barwell'. On 15th November 1595 Robert
'receaved of Edward Smythe, baylive of Lougborow, by the appointment of the Right Honorable Earle of Huntingdon, which is to be
returned to my brother Willyem Heyricke of London, for his own
use, the soome of One hundrithe forskore pounds, ten shillings'. The
earl paid money in Leicester to have it again in London. Again, Robert
writes,

The 19th of October 1611. – And this daye Clement Fouldes hath brought
me 60*li.* to retorne to you, which I would very willinglye had him return
himselfe, but he could not ... My Lorde Graye hath a greate deale to returne,
and others, but cannot at this tyme returne it; wherfore if you can by anie
means in Smithfeild or otherwise take up soe much, I had rather it weare with
you then with me.

Yet again, on 8th May 1616, Robert writes to William, 'Many come
to me of the other side to leave money with me to have it in London'.
(Rothwell was just on the other side of the county boundary, in
Northamptonshire.) This was ordinary business for the Herricks. On
12th October 1613 Robert writes,

My man comyng from Woostyarshyre yestarnyght brought me a lettar from
cosen Kynersley that he woold willingly have mooney in London of Monday
the 25 of this present: I doe accompt that 20*li.* or theraboute doothe make
mete owre formore reconynge. With the first hundrithe pound that my Lord
Grey sent mee, which you are to pay to one Mr Thomas his man, and that
21*li.* 10*s* I will take of Clement Folldes, which as yet I have not sene since
you went. Then, that recconyng being clered, there is in youre hands a bare
700*li.*, wherof I have receved of my lords man, Mr Tomas, 100*li.*, so if I
receve I will take but one hundrith from you, and leave 5 still.

On the 25th Robert writes again, saying,

For owre recconyng, I have sent you the same up by Whatton which I did
bring you to Bowmannor, and I received one from you in youre last lettar.
And we doe agre. Then I pray you pay to my Lord Grays solistar two hundrith
pound, wherof one of them is alowed you in this formor recconyng; the othar
is i of the seven: I pray you pay unto my cosin Kynnersley one hundrith pound,
so remaynethe in youre hand but 500*li.*

Here we see great and small landowners, and apparently tradesmen
also, latching on to the credit network.

Evidence from the other end of the banking axis is just as abundant. William's accounts from 1610 show such items as the following:

Receved of Mr Halfords man from my brother 68*li*. ... receved of Mr Hampton for my brother the 26 November 013*li*. 10*s* ... paid to Mr Jarfeeld for my lord of Huntingdon 040-00-0 ... receved of Thomas Jackson for my brother the 21 February 73-00-0 ... receved of William Ashby the 15 of Aprill in paymente of a debt deu by John Allne 47-00-0 ... receved of Mr Watts the 17 of Aprill 1611 the some of 110*li*. in paymente of Sir Hewe Carmichells debtes ... paid my Lord Compton by Mr Harve 27-6-0 ... paid Mr Corselles for Lord Compton 48-0-0 ... paid to Mr Harvey in full payment of a bill to Lord Compton 27-13-4 ... received by the appointment of John Dellin 40-00-0 ... paid Mr Huxley for Robert Joysey 20-00-0 ... paid to Sir Baptiste Hicks for Mrs Aston for the lottery 05-0-0 ... paid Mr Morley for Mr Hueson 10-00-0 ... payd to Mr Watson in full payment of my Lord Comptons bond the some of − the 20 June − 200-0-0 ... paid Mr Massam for Mr Richardson 50-00-0 ... payd to Mr Wren by his sonnes appointment from Oxenford the ferst July 1613 − 6-7-4 ... paid Mr Boyle the 27 July for to pay my Lady Romney 10-0-0 ... paid Mr Boyle for Sir Thomas Curtellis 15*li*. ... receved by Richard the 7 of February 1613 from Stamfor[d] for the Lord Chamberlaine 749*li*. 1*s*. 5*d*. ... paid to Mr Ferris for my Lord Graye 50*li*. ... paid to Boyle for Sebright 10-0-0 ... receved of Mr Garraway the 19 of October 1614 for Mrs Aston the some of ij*C li*. ... receved the 15 of January 1614 of Mr Perry for Sir Arther Gorge 71*li*. 7*s*. ... receved of Mr Garraway for Mrs Aston 100*li*. ... receved of Mr Woolrich the 5 of May from Sir Edwine Riche 1180*li*. ... paid the 8 of June 1615 to Mr Fardinand by Mr Bingley his appointment 324-5-0 ... receved of Haris forom the Countis of Killdayre the 9 November 1616 5-0-0 ... 25 September 1616 paid unto Mr Betts for Sir Edmond Whiller this day 50*li*. ... paid Mr Burlymakee the 22 October for Mr Hueson 152-6-8 ... receved the 21 February 1616 of Mr Vanlore for a debt of my Lord of Mountgonery 280*li*. ... paid to Mr Melishe for Lady Allet to Mr Emery 70*li*. 5-0 ... paid Mr Emery the 10 of February for Mr Melishe 100-00-0 ... receved of Mr Harris from the Countis of Killdar 05-00-0 ...

Clearly William Herrick, with Robert as his agent, was banker to many people, including Sir Roger and Mrs Aston, Sir William Craven, the Lords Compton and Grey, Lady Romney, the Earl of Huntingdon, and the Countess of Kildare. As a goldsmith, Herrick was very much a banker to country landowners; and as a jeweller, he had dealings with colleagues and financiers like Baptist Hicks, Peter Vanlore, Sir John Spillman, and Philip Burlamachi.[169]

Browning and Gurney acted as bankers to Sir Hamon Le Strange of Hunstanton Hall. For example, on 22nd November 1615 Le Strange paid £30 to Browning in Norwich which Gurney in London was to pay to a certain Mr Lock. Several other similar transactions were made. In 1619, 1621 and 1622 the firm transferred funds from Le

Strange in Hunstanton to a Laurence Michael in London and he in
turn paid it to the treasurer of the East India Company in settlement
of the purchase of shares.[170] By a similar arrangement in 1612 a
factor had £100 'paid to Mr Nicholas of the Temple for my Lord
Bruse'.[171] It was by the same sort of transfer that the Earl of
Bedford's West Country rents were returned to him in London.[172]

Provincial tax and revenue collectors were in much the same
position as landowners when it came to sending money to Westminster, and from 1590 or earlier they were using the same methods.
In 1601 Thomas Wilkinson, deputy bailiff of part of the barony of
Kendal 'having delivered parte of his said colleccion into the hands
of certen clothiers of Kendall to be repaid unto him here att London'
to perfect his account, was disappointed by their delay and found
himself temporarily in default.[173] Ship-money was returned from
Shropshire through the Shrewsbury drapers and their Blackwell Hall
factors, and from Devon and Cheshire by bills drawn on London by
merchants in Plymouth, Exeter, and Manchester. In the early
eighteenth century taxes went from Whitehaven to London by bills
obtained in Manchester, Lancaster, Leeds, and Newcastle. As late
as about 1670 Sir Edward Dering was lamenting the fact that taxes
from Kent still went to London in specie, whereas from Devonshire,
Lancashire, Yorkshire and Northumberland they were transferred by
instruments of credit.[174] The Crown, too, had occasion to use the
same instruments.[175] So did ecclesiastics. As early as 1584 the
Norwich Dutch were paying the London Dutch this way. In 1603 the
Norwich Dutch transferred £15 10s to the London Dutch by means
of a bill drawn on London by a member of the one congregation on
one of the other.[176] In 1582, Richard Martin, an active goldsmith
and master-worker at the Mint, wanting to transfer £300 to Bristol,
was either going to use his own letters 'or else agree with some trusty
merchant of London to take of me here and answer so much there
again at sight'.[177]

Obviously, even businessmen who had their own factors and were
accustomed to settling debts by three-party bills, had from time to
time to use four-party ones, that is, pay someone to make the transfer
for them. About 1583 James Bankes, a London goldsmith accused
of being backward in completion of full payment, pleaded that, 'the
most parte of the resydue was paide by his ... brother in Lancashyre
to be paide to this defendante in London'.[178] In 1623 Francis Delaval
had occasion to write to Sir Ralph asking for his annuity payment

to be sent up to Town, adding, 'If you cannot have the meanes to retorne it, that then I have written to my brother Robert that if you will please to pay it to hime that he would get it retorned unto me.'[179] In 1612 a merchant accounts for £116 'paid to Mr Pemblbery and Mr Lambe for Michaell Hood the which Henry Skayff gave me over to give my bill for'.[180] In Henry Blois's accounts we find £100 paid 'to Mr Leke by Robert Ewer ... and is by a resayt to bee payed heer unto my cosen Blumfyld'.[181] On 14th May 1621 George Hartnoll of Tiverton 'received of Mr John Trobridge of Taunton to be paid Mr John Dunster by Mr Petter Dubois' £200, Dubois being Hartnoll's London factor. On 26 April 1631 Hartnoll 'received of Mr Henry Nute junior to repay in London' £14.[182] In 1635 John Hayne notes that John Henley, a merchant of Leigh (presumably upon Mendip) owed him £189, 'which I paid for him to Mr William Bartlett ... This I payd at the request of Mr John Henley upon his letters received.'[183] Many other references are to be found at all hands of credit transactions of much the same kind, even though their exact nature is not always clear.[184]

All this is easily understood. Even today persons without a bank account, especially young ones, will pay the equivalent in cash to a friend or relative for a cheque needed to buy something by mail order. By providing facilities for transferring funds to London or elsewhere, suppliers of goods brought their proceeds home, and so the system was completed.

Before about 1650 the system was far from perfect. Its shortcomings were felt most acutely by those, especially non-commercial outsiders, who needed to transfer funds from London to the provinces, for they had to find men with accounts in London who wished to transfer funds from the provinces to the metropolis, which not many did with any regularity. For the Irish campaigns in the 1580s Lord Burghley usually had little difficulty in transferring funds to Chester by selling bills on London to merchants in Chester and Liverpool; but in May 1581 the Chester merchants happened to have no need of any further money in London, and consideration was therefore given to the expedient of sending money down with a consignment of hops. Even Alderman Richard Martin experienced some difficulty in such transfers. He thought he might have to write specially to Bristol to find out if anyone there was expecting to receive money he wanted paid in in London 'and in such sort to be answered them their money here in London'. Otherwise, he feared he might have to send coin to Bristol by carrier, which would entail greater risk and expense.[185] In 1604 Exchequer officials had difficulty in transferring funds from London to Plymouth and Exeter to pay the sailors there.[186] Another shortcoming in earlier times was the difficulty in hooking on to the network experienced by people who lived some way from the main commercial arteries. It was not until the 1650s that credit transfers were arranged for remitting money from the Earl of Bedford's estate at Thorney. In 1687 a landowner in Milton, near Peterborough, was having to have bills fetched from far afield. As late as 1734 a Whitehaven tax collector fetched bills from Leeds, Manchester, and Lancaster.[187]

It must be borne in mind, too, that the greater the distance involved, the greater the advantage of the credit network over the carriage of coin, so places nearest to London were often the last to adopt the new arrangements. Hence Sir Edward Dering's complaint from Kent:

Taxes, subsidies, poll money, and the standing payments of excise and hearth money are still carried up to London in specie, from whence it never returnes, whereas from the remoter parts of the kingdome it is returned by billes of exchange. Which I conceive to be one reason why Devonshire, Lancashire, Yorkshire and Northumberland hold up at this day much better then the counties nearer London.[188]

The principal financial instrument used in the inland banking system was the inland bill of exchange, as it is now called. A bill of exchange is an unconditional order in writing, addressed by one person or firm to another, signed by the person giving it, requiring the person to whom it is addressed to pay on demand or at a fixed or determinable future time a sum certain in money to or to the order of a specified person or to the bearer. An inland bill is one that is or purports to be both drawn and payable within the British Isles. Inland bills were highly flexible instruments, admirably suited to the most various business needs. One frequent form of inland bill of exchange nowadays is, after place and date, 'Three months after date pay to E.F. (or to E.F. or order) the sum of £x, value received.' signed A.B. and addressed to C.D. But no precise form of words is necessary. In particular, a bill is equally good without the words 'value received', or without the date, or without the place of drawing or payment. This is now the position in law, and it always was the position in fact, the former being merely the recognition of the latter. Various verbal forms were used in these inland bills of exchange. Some specimens have survived and are shown below:

London the 23th March 1645 – At 12 dayes sight I pray pay unto Mr George Student or Mr John Mathews the sume of Two hundred pounds, for the like vallew received here of Mr John Davis. I pray be pleased to give them content herein and place itt to the Account of Your Thomas Browne. – To Mr John Harvy in Chester.

Mathews was a Liverpool merchant and Student presumably his partner. When presented, this bill was refused (and protested), but only because Harvy had died before he could pay out.[189] Another and vitally different form was the order bill, as

Norwich. June 1, 1697. – At four days sight pay unto Mr M.M. or his order One hundred and thirty-two pounds, value received of E.E., and place it to Account as per advice of Your humble servant D.D. – To Mr P.P.[190]

Different again was the bill drawn by Sir Ralph Verney in 1675:

Mr Fowles, I pray pay to the bearer hereof my servant Grosvenor the sum of Five and twenty pounds and put it to the Account of Your assured friend. Take no acquitance but this note.

Verney was in London at the time and had sent his servant round to the bank to draw some ready money, just as a man today might send his servant round with a cheque.[191] A common form of written instruction was along these lines: 'Mr Farington, pray pay to A.B. the sum of X pounds and be pleased to place it to the Account of your friend and servant – R.T.' Payments were then made 'by order of your letter'.[192] A four-party bill might be much more formal than a three-party one drawn on the same account, as will be seen from the two below:

Laus Deo, the 15th December Anno Domini 1641. – Lovinge frend Isacke Knipe, I praye you paye unto Mr John Owen drogiste in St Laurence lane the thirteenth daye of Januarye 1641 the some of One hundreth poundes of corrant Englishe money for the vallewe heare received of Edmund Kay of Yorke grocer. Att the day I praye you make him good payment, and putt itt to Accompt as per Advice, and so God keepe you, Restinge, Edward Firth. – To his loving frend Mr Isacke Knipe leger att Blackwell Haule, lodged att Mr Loves house, packer in Basinge Haule.

Somewhat belatedly, on 21st January, Thomas Walton, evidently Owen's cashier, gave Knipe a receipt for the £100, 'beeinge for thaccompt of Mr Edward Kay of Yorke and is for the use of John Owen'.[193] The next example is much different; being a three-party bill, it simply says,

Mr Knipe, Upon the 20th of February next I praye you pay to Mr John Owen att the 3 Ankers in Laurence Lane the som of One Hundreth pounds: make good payment and putt it to Accompt as per Advice, so resting, Yor Loving Frend, Edward Firth. – January 22th 1641. – Accepted this the 14th of February 1641 per me Isacke Knipe.

With a three-party bill, the drawer had received no value, and consequently needed no receipt specifying on whose account the payment was to be made, and Walton's receipt was correspondingly simple.[194]

A note, letter, or instruction in writing like the one immediately above, differed from a cheque only in that it was all handwritten and had neither serial number nor counterfoil or check. The cheque properly so called was not invented until the late seventeenth century and then in the form of an Exchequer bill with one or two counterfoils. A banker's cheque with a counterfoil was mentioned only in 1715, but orders such as the one above served all the same purposes, except for the stub. But, then, nowadays, in common parlance, a cheque means any such order to pay. In England, which has its share of eccentrics, we read of farmers writing 'cheques' on the sides of cows and driving them to the bank, but nothing of any vellum counterfoils. A cheque is a form of inland bill of exchange and many inland bills of exchange served as cheques and resembled them so closely as to cause some historians to fall into the error of calling them early cheques. [195] But some inland bills of exchange served the same purpose as postdated cheques or bills obligatory, in that they were long-dated, with usances of twenty or thirty days, and so could be endorsed over (and perhaps discounted) by a succession of persons. By 1651, perhaps by 1610, it had become common to endorse and assign long-dated bills, especially those drawn 'payee or order'. One such bill reads,

1 April 1726. – Thirty days after date pay to Thomas Coplestone or order Seventy-two pounds ten shillings, value received of him.,

The bill bears a special endorsement, reading 'Pay unto John Harding', followed by the successive signatures of Thomas Coplestone, John Harding, Henry Smith, W. Fell, and finally Francis Child Esq., who was the banker who eventually paid out, and all in such a form that 'Pay unto' applied to the whole run from Harding onwards, so having the effect of successive special endorsements. This bill is one of a clutch of twenty-nine, all drawn in Exeter for Messrs Cosserat and

D'Orville and payable thirty days after date by John Tolet at the
premises of 'Mr Coussirat' in Laurence Pountney Lane, which runs
south from the Eastcheap end of Cannon Street. Like all bills of
exchange, these were holographs, the hallmark of authenticity being
the handwriting rather than the signature. Some were made out to
payee only, but by far the majority had multiple endorsements, with
up to half-a-dozen names, so, allowing for the post, which was hardly
faster then than now, a bill like this might change hands on average
every four or five days.[196] Some orders to pay are found that can
hardly be described as bills of exchange, not at least in the eyes of
the law. Joseph Churchill of Steeple Claydon, a local businessman
who often returned Sir Ralph Verney's money to London for him,
once drew a bill on London in these words: 'Thomas Rayle, pray pay
what money you have to Mr William Denton by order of your friend
Joseph Churchill and for the use of Sir Ralph Verney and take a
receipt.' Modern lawyers would not consider this a true bill of
exchange, for the sum payable was not certainly stated; but the bill
served its purpose and £18 was paid over.[197] Probably even more
weird and wonderful bills of exchange were used on occasion.

Transfers by means of the banking system were often called
'exchanges' or 'returns' and the instruments themselves 'bills', 'bills
of exchange', 'belles of returne', or 'letters'. The terms 'return up'
and 'return down' were commonly applied to the remittance of funds
to and from London, usually by three-party bills. In 1654, we find
an account of 'the hundred pounds returned to my father Sir John
Pole by Mr Thomas Bradshaw; it was delivered him June the 10th
and returned August 3rd upon Mr Walter Radcliffe in Abchurch
Lane'.[198] The term 'bill of exchange' was used less frequently than
might have been expected. For long, people felt uneasy about it. They
were accustomed to regard as bills of exchange only those whereby
one currency was changed into another. At the same time, they often
called 'bills of exchange' what were hybrid instruments rather unlike
the normal conception of such bills.[199] Therefore just because a
writing was called a bill of exchange and recorded as such, we cannot
know if it really was one in the modern legal sense. We can only be
sure when we see either the bill itself or a notary's true copy of it,
and extant bills or copies from the earlier part of the period are rare.
And even if we rashly guessed what was called a bill of exchange was
truly one in the modern legal sense, we still could not know whether
it were an inland or an outland one. The term 'inland bill of exchange'

hardly occurs before about 1655;[200] previously no clear verbal distinction was made. Moreover, outland bills, bills of exchange in the full meaning of the term and payable in London or elsewhere in England, sometimes passed from hand to hand over here. Henry Blois accounts for a bill of exchange his factor Leke 'recheaved of one Mr Hyll of Lonndon made over from Marzelsa and this was payed unto Thomas Sullom for 100*li*; hee payed unto John Baker at Ipswich and now this whole 100*li*. is to be charged to this account'. Outland bills of exchange were readily negotiated by English merchants within England and were often endorsed three or four times.[201] Nor can inland and outland bills always be distinguished by their tenor or currency. By the 1640s long-dated bills, with usances of between one and two months, were being increasingly used as convenient substitutes for bills obligatory plus short-dated bills of exchange, which in earlier times were mostly payable 'upon sight', 'upon demand', or between two and fourteen days after sight.[202] It was much the same with bills between Chester and Dublin, which ranked as inland ones, even though the Irish pound was worth less than sterling.[203] Outland bills, unlike inland ones, had to go on hazardous journeys, were usually sent, at intervals, in duplicate or triplicate, and needed usances of more than a few days.

As for the idea that a formal was distinguished from an informal bill of exchange by the presence or absence of the formality of acceptance, there is nothing in it, first because there are no essential formalities of acceptance for bills of exchange, and secondly because even informal bills needed acceptance and sometimes received all the formalities. Written acceptance was never necessary; it sufficed to give it by word of mouth or by a nod of the head or by eloquent silence and payment. An Englishman's word is, or ought to be, his bond, and between all merchants 'their word is, or ought to be, as binding as their writing'. In England a verbal contract is as valid as a written one, and so with an acceptance. Moreover, before 1698 there was no legal requirement for inland bills of exchange to undergo any of the formalities, neither acceptance (written or parole), nor advice, nor protestation against non-acceptance or non-payment. Even in 1698 formal protest became necessary only for inland bills of the value of £5 or more, and from 1705, only for bills of £20 or more accepted in writing.[204] And, then, obviously, when shown the most informal of inland bills of exchange, the banker had either to accept or refuse it, either in writing or by word of mouth or somehow, just as now he has either to pay on a cheque or return it marked 'R.D.', 'Refer to Drawer', or, if unsigned, to present it for signature.

In short, in earlier times, notions of formality or informality hardly applied to inland bills of exchange. Anyway, it is difficult to see how anything could have been more informal than some of these bills actually were and still perform the functions required of them. Informality could, indeed, go further: the whole exchange could be conducted by word of mouth. Early bankers preferred to receive orders to pay by word of mouth in person on their premises rather than by written order, for writings could be forged more easily than people could be impersonated.[205] Drovers or carcass butchers could take money from those with payments to make in London, leave it at home or spend it on the journey, and then make payments for, or into the accounts of, their clients in London out of the proceeds of sales there. Thus Chester merchants planning business trips to London sometimes delivered money to the drovers and received it back in Town. It was a simple and mutually satisfactory arrangement. Provided the parties trusted each other, no writing was needed, not even so much as a receipt. Graziers, however, rarely drove their own stock to London. They usually sold to carcass butchers at the farm gate or at the local cattle market, and these carcass butchers employed drovers to take charge of the stock on their leisurely drift to London. Graziers or butchers were obviously better financial agents than were drovers. Stockbreeders in remote parts often used the services of drovers, but then these were drovers of a different kind, who mostly bought store cattle and sheep in hill-farm countries and sold them in London.[206]

In the early records of inland trade and finance, the term 'inland bill of exchange' occurs hardly at all, and 'bill of exchange' infrequently. Even if we add references simply to 'exchange', the total incidence is remarkably small. In 1577, when the Earl of Northumberland wanted money moved south for use in London and Petworth, his receiver advised him to 'fynd meanes to gett your money which is to be sent hence to be delivered by exchange that I may pay yt at Berwyck or here in the country'.[207] During the 1580s royal agents in Chester raised loans that were 'received of the marchauntes heere upon like bills of exchange' on London. In 1603 the Norwich Dutch sent money to London '*door cracht des wisselbriefs hier in geleyt, van Sieur Jan Van Soldt*'.[208] On 6 December 1606 Robert Gray wrote to his wife from Exeter, 'Here is a bill of exchange to Mr Colmore for x*li*. I pray

let Trustron receve yt and paye such monyes as I welled hem to paye.'
On 28th July 1610 he wrote from Bristol, 'I wrought you a letter per
Umphrey Sydnam wherin I sent five bills of Exchange: the which I
would have Gorge to receive in the monyes for them.'[209] In 1612
a London wholesale hosier noted two payments made to a Mr
Broughton, each 'by a bill of exchange'. Shortly afterwards he
received money through John Dickson 'by bills of exchange or
otherwise'.[210] Henry Blois entered in his accounts,

Dew from Mr Leke as in his of 9th December 1617 theese sommes following
being payed over at Plewmoth and the bylls delyvered unto him by my cosen
Huntyng the 7th of January 1617, and is fyrst uppon a byll from Mr Foynes
to Mr Leke the some of 100*li*. ... One byll of 200*li*. being payed unto Abreham
Jennyngs the 27 December to paye Mr Ambers Jennyngs 3 dayes after syte
the which will be the 9th January ... More one other byll unto him at the
leeke tymes for the payment of 12*li*. ... More one byll from Mr Robert
Trewlanes for 35*li*. 10*s* to paye the last January 1617 ... Summe of theese
exchanges 347.10.00 ... Payd more unto him [Leke] the which he recheaved
of Mr John Baker at my being ther and is to bee charged to this account the
some of 000-00-00 – this must be dyscharged for that hee charg the whole
byll exchang.

Another £130 was due to Baker, which he had paid to Mr Richard
Ewer 'uppon Mr Leke his byll exchang', and yet £100 more 'which
was made done from Mr Leke to my cosen Maddock', i.e. was made
down from London to Ipswich, 'made down' being to inland transfers
from London what 'made over' was for those from places oversea
to England.[211] Another entry concerns £33 'Dew as in Mr Lekes of
the 13 November 1618 wherin hee wryt hee payed a byll of exchange
from John Baker dated at Plewmoth the 30 of October last.' In 1621
Blois debits Leke 'for 10*li*. the which hee have overpayd unto Mr
Rychard Ewer being for the fysh and payed unto one John Lamperell
uppon Mr Morhouse his byll exchang and by Mr Leke his apointment
was repayed unto hym by Mrs Ales Wadden at Plewmoth'.[212]

On 23rd February 1620 George Hartnoll of Tiverton received £20
from each of two men: 'Received of Mr Jonathan Maddock for a byll
of exchang', 'Received of Mr John Coggan for a byll of exchang.'[213]
In 1626 Francis Delaval wrote to Sir Ralph, 'Dear brother, I have
receaved a bill of exchainge from my brother Robert unto Mr Bennet
of London glazier.'[214] About 1633 Sir Richard Temple's steward was
reminiscing of the days when 'Sir Thomas his allowance was for
exchange of any money for him at the markets where I sold my cattle
to be paid in London; the which I did many times with the said

butchers.' It was by 'bills of exchange' that Sir Thomas Danby of Masham was paying money into the Court of Wards in 1636 and to other London recipients in the succeeding years.[215] In 1638 the Privy Council sent for Henry Head of London, merchant, for not paying into the Treasury of the Navy £190 returned to him by the mayor of Plymouth 'upon a bill of exchange'. Other ship-money collectors also used bills of exchange.[216] In that same year it emerged that Norwich merchants sent 'bills of exchange' to, and received others from, London.[217] On 8th March 1641 Thomas Walton received of Isaac Knipe 'in full of this bill of exchange the some of One hundred pounds for the use of Mr John Owen'. In this same year bills of exchange were used to supply pay for the troops in York.[218] It was in 1645 that Thomas Browne drew his bill of exchange on John Harvy in Chester. In 1653 William Pratt's factor 'paid Thomas Hussie per bill of exchange'.[219] In 1650 a debt of £30 owed by a Londoner to a Lancashire supplier was settled 'by exchange from Lecester'. Next year Thomas Cromwell of Staughton (near St Neots) found himself owed £20 on a bill of exchange, obviously an inland one.[220]

In the years 1644–46 the Rodes of Rochdale used many instruments that were inland bills of exchange both in name and in nature. What they meant by bills of exchange may be seen from their accounts, where they occasionally receive particular mention. Thus in 1646 '17th Aprill sent Mr Ryder a bill of exchange of Two hundred poundes to bee paid to hime by Joseph Hunton at 3 days affter sight which money I paid here to Mr Wrigley'; and '25 October 1647 sent to Mr Ryder a bill of exchange upon himselfe by Joseph Ryder containing the some of one hundred poundes which money I paid here to Joseph'.[221]

Thomas Ledgard, the Newcastle colliery owner, was drawing bills of exchange on London in 1649. In 1666 Sir Martin Noell, a London 'money scrivener', owed several debts on 'bills of exchange'. In 1670, 1671, and 1684, Bristol Corporation was settling debts in Chester and elsewhere through bills of exchange drawn on London. In 1675 a Rochdale clothier received a payment by 'bill of exchange'. In 1683 Sir Richard Temple's steward got from a Bicester woolman a bill of exchange that had originated in a sale of malt by another Bicester man.[222] About 1685, whenever Sir Ralph Verney was sending a quarterly allowance to his brother he always remitted by what he called a bill of exchange.[223] In the second half of the seventeenth

century and the first few years of the eighteenth, of all the returns
mentioned in the Temple archives only some half a dozen are
designated 'bills of exchange', and of all those in the Fitzwilliam
archives perhaps as many as a round dozen. Much the same is
true of the Verney archives.[224]

One slight clue to this apparent mystery, that so few instruments
of transfer were called bills of exchange, even though all of them
were in the nature of such bills, is provided by the knowledge
that the remittances Verney made to his brother were by four-
party bills of exchange obtained from drawers in London and
drawn upon drawees either in Ireland or Scotland or in remote
parts of England; they were either outland bills bought from export-
import merchants or formal inland bills fetched from goldsmiths
and others with the necessary correspondents and contacts. Similarly,
what the Lowthers of Whitehaven seem to have regarded as bills
of exchange properly so called were the ones bought in their home
town or fetched from Newcastle, Tallentire or elsewhere. A second
clue lies in the further distinction sometimes explicitly drawn between
four-party returns made with and without bills of exchange so
called. Returners often refused to give a formal bill of exchange,
because it tied them to paying out on a specified date or after
the expiry of a specified number of days after sight. Instead they
gave an informal bill promising to pay out in due course and before
long. Thus ship-money collectors, though they usually tried to
get bills of exchange, often had to content themselves with informal
bills of return, the Shrewsbury drapers and others being unwilling
to enter into stricter commitments. This was the real difference
between an inland bill of exchange and a bill of return.[225] Throughout most of the seventeenth century, as we have seen, the habit
persisted of restricting the term 'bill of exchange' to outland and
to formal four-party inland ones, which had usually to be bought
or fetched from someone outside one's immediate business circle.
The Rodes of Rochdale and their factor William Ryder confined
the term to such four-party bills. The Earl of Northumberland's
steward would have fetched bills from Berwick and Newcastle. Gray
bought bills from drawers all over the place.

Looking through the inland bills of exchange, as we would now
call them, in use up to 1651, we find a banking network that included
London, Ipswich, Norwich, Great Yarmouth, Hull, York, Wakefield,
Halifax, Ripon, Darlington, Seaton, Newcastle, and Berwick;

Portsmouth, Bristol, Taunton, Tiverton, Exeter, Plymouth and Dartmouth; Oxford, Coventry, Shrewsbury, Chester, Dublin, Manchester, Rochdale, and Kendal; and Cambridge, Wellingborough, Leicester, and Newark. Marius in 1651 mentions as parts of this network London and Southampton, and in 1655 also York, Bristol, Exeter, Plymouth, and Dover, as well as Edinburgh, which had now been recognised as part of the commonwealth of England. By this time, and apparently for some decades before, the network covered the whole island, coinciding with the combined extent of the over-lapping metropolitan markets in various commodities. Confirmation of this is provided by Malynes in 1622, for he says letters missive (letters of credit) were in use between London, Exeter, Plymouth, Great Yarmouth and many other towns;[226] and letters of credit presuppose credit accounts and credit transfers. Remembering how slight is our total volume of evidence on inland trade and how few relevant account books are extant, it is impossible not to fear some parts of the network remain unrevealed. Perhaps it is not too rash to hazard the guess that by 1651 Barnstaple, Northampton, Nottingham, Sheffield, Bury St Edmunds, Whitby, King's Lynn, and Warrington were already part of it. Some of these banking towns were industrial and commercial centres. Oxford and Cambridge, like London, had many temporary residents who needed to be financed from home.

In the middle of the seventeenth century this credit network was further strengthened by links forged with the goldsmith-bankers. Hitherto even the London goldsmith-bankers had mostly participated in credit transfers only as customers of bankers of the kind we have described above. To this rule William Herrick was a notable exception, and there were no doubt others.[227] Some of the London goldsmiths, like Thomas Vyner and James Bankes, had long been bankers, taking deposits and making loans. In 1616 William Herrick would take a deposit of £150 and pay nine per cent. per annum calculated once a year. This was less than an investor could get by mortgage, but bank deposits were far more liquid. Herrick's rates on deposits varied between eight and ten per cent., and he was a great deposit taker. On 31st October 1611, for example, Lady Warburton deposited £30 'to keep for her till the last of this month' (November). Sir William Craven and Sir John Kay were other notable depositors with Herrick. He also dealt in annuities, payable half-yearly, and made substantial loans to Lords Compton and Dunbar, Robert Joysey, Peter Vanlore, Sir Arthur Gorges and others. Furthermore, he was a teller in the Exchequer of Receipt, which helped to extend his private business. Thus he 'paid Sir Baptis Hicks for Mr Treswell wich I receved at the Recete for him the 26 March 1617 – 13-5-6'. In his time, in the 1590s, Nicholas Herrick had conducted a not dissimilar business. He took deposits, made loans, and, incidentally, kept the funds of his parish of St Fosters. Indeed, William seems to have inherited some of his best customers from Nicholas, for instance, the Lords Compton and the Hawes family. The kind of forbearance money Herrick, Bankes and others of their kind took for their loans appears to have been less *titulus morae* than *poena conventionalis*, less with unstipulated than with stipulated penalties for delay, but rarely tainted with usury. Even when they lent on the security of bills obligatory and penal bonds, it was seldom in the expectation that the due dates would not be met, which would have been usurious in intent. Indeed, it was the usual practice to enquire of one of the scriveners or brokers who specialised in compiling credit-ratings as to the credit-worthiness of the prospective customer and to refuse loans to those found wanting. When this system failed, it was probably because, as revealed by Francis Bacon, (who, as Chancellor, was intimately concerned with these matters), it was not unknown for such experts to 'value unsound men to serve their own turn'.[228] Money scriveners, like John Milton the elder, engaged in money-lending, partly as brokers and intermediaries, on behalf of clients, partly as principals, with their own capital and, on a fractional reserve system, with interest-bearing deposits left with them.[229] Provincial towns also had their moneylenders. In a big industrial city like Norwich, and in many smaller towns, they were styled 'gentlemen', and were generally retired merchants or clothiers. Rich widows, too, were frequently money-lenders.[230]

A harbinger of future events was the emergence, seemingly as early as by 1599, indubitably by about 1622, of a new group of 'goldsmiths about the Cittie Exchanges' and of 'a new kind of trade sprung lately up among them'. These exchanging goldsmiths took to discounting and selling inland bills of exchange, as well as some outland ones and bills obligatory, besides taking deposits and carrying on the usual banking business. This bill business much encouraged an extension of the credit system.[231]

Assigned and endorsed bearer bills obligatory were common in England and Antwerp in the sixteenth century and earlier. Merchants everywhere habitually set over such bills one with another until the chain was eventually completed. Bearer bills of exchange were not entirely unknown; they allowed servants or factors to receive payment in lieu of their masters or customers. In 1544, for instance, Roelof Harlessen of Antwerp refused to accept a bill of exchange drawn in London and payable '*to Johan Van Kasteren oft tom brynger der billen*'. But up until the turn of the sixteenth and seventeenth centuries, neither in Antwerp nor in Italy, were such bearer bills, or bills drawn to payee or order, fully assignable, far less negotiable, only one transfer being allowed. A payee might specially endorse over an order bill to A. N. Other as his agent, but A. N. Other was unable to transfer the bill further, for the endorsement had been to him alone, not to A. N. Other or his assigns or to A. N. Other or order. It was only round about the middle of the seventeenth century that we find English merchants trading in Spain, Pisa and Leghorn taking to the successive assignment and multiple endorsement of outland bills of exchange. Similarly, the discounting of bills obligatory (and occasionally of bills of exchange) was by no means unknown in Antwerp in the mid-sixteenth century, and was certainly not first invented by the exchanging goldsmiths of London; but this was discounting in the old sense, where a man might occasionally agree to take a bill in payment only with a rebate or discount for the interest on the unexpired portion of the term, or, rarely, offer to pay in coin on the nail, instead of by bill obligatory, or even, perhaps, be willing to pay out prematurely on a long-dated bill of exchange only with a similar rebate or allowance deducted. Although it had been conceded in Antwerp in 1580–81, that the bearer might bring a suit in his own name, a considerable time elapsed before full legal negotiability was conferred on foreign or outland bills of exchange. It was not until about 1650 that English courts allowed that the endorsee might be the agent not for the payee but in respect of his own property in the bill and as *procurator aut adjectus in rem suam*. The same legal status was granted in Amsterdam in 1651 and generally throughout Holland by 1677, in Frankfort-on-the-Main in 1666, in France in 1673, and in the kingdom of Naples at much the same time. The development of these commercial and legal practices admits of still more research, but is not our immediate concern, being inessential to our argument. It was, we insist, the rise of metropolitan markets and their accompanying credit accounts that laid the foundation on which was built the peculiarly English system of banking and its discounting of *bona fide* commercial paper consisting mainly of bills on London and largely of inland bills of exchange. What the exchanging goldsmiths were first in the field with was the specialised, systematic discounting of bills of exchange, particularly inland ones, now increasingly long-dated, with a view to holding them until maturity or until required by regular customers of the bank for their own purposes.[232]

The next turning point was the seizure by Charles I in 1640 of the £200,000 or so of coin and bullion confided by London dealers for safekeeping in the Mint vaults in the Tower. This cost the repository its reputation and led to the deposit of such coin and bullion with the goldsmiths,[233] very likely on the initiative of merchants' cashiers, for it was the established practice for merchants to leave their money to the charge of a servant or senior apprentice, and such cashiers already made some deposits with goldsmith-bankers.[234] According to a memoir published in 1676, the next step was,

About thirty years since, the Civil War giving opportunity to apprentices to leave their masters at will, and the old way having been for merchants to trust their cash in one of their servants custody, many cashiers left their masters in the lurch and went into the army, and merchants knew not how to confide in their apprentices; then did some merchants begin to put their cash into goldsmiths hands to receive and pay for them, (thinking it more secure), and the trade of plate being then of little worth, most of the nobility and gentry, and others, melting down their old plate rather than buying new, and few daring to use or own plate, the goldsmiths sought to be the merchants cash-keepers to receive and pay for nothing. [They arranged] with all mens servants who continued to keep any cash, to bring their moneys to them to be culled, and to remain with them at four pence the day interest per centum without the masters privity.

Landed gentry, too, began to confide to these goldsmith-bankers rents and other receipts returned to London. Demand deposits and fractional reserve systems became the order of the day. Such bankers became deeply involved in the bill market, for being cashier to a factor or merchant largely entailed drawing and accepting bills of exchange and discounting bills obligatory as well as bills of exchange that had enough days. Inland bills, if at about thirty days sight, and if not drawn 'payee only', could be, and often were, endorsed 'pay unto', and then might pass through several hands before final payment. Such bills could equally well be bought and sold by goldsmith-bankers.[235] As members of the Goldsmiths' Company they were well placed to engage in this trade. Theirs was a nationwide organisation. Representatives of the provincial goldsmiths had to come to the London company to obtain authority for touch and puncheon and it was then and there that they bought touchstones and punches. The Londoners, too, exercised rights of search and assay over all wrought gold and silver in provincial fairs, cities, boroughs and towns. All provincial goldsmiths had to take an oath to observe the ordinances of the London company and pay them a fee at oathtaking. Accordingly, the London wardens habitually toured the provincial towns where goldsmiths resided, even unto the far north and west of the kingdom. Thus all goldsmiths everywhere were more or less known to each other.[236]

Before long these upstart cashier-bankers were providing services to all kinds and conditions of London and provincial businessmen, from Newcastle coal merchants to West of England clothiers, and to the nobility and landed gentry of all parts, drawing, discounting and accumulating inland bills of exchange, and supplying their customers with bills on correspondents and agents in all the main towns.[237] The new goldsmith-bankers filled a gap in credit transference. Their role is well illustrated in Courtenay Pole's accounts for 1650–58, at a time when he was returning money to his father in London from his West Country estate. Some money was returned by Thomas Bradshaw upon Walter Radcliffe in Abchurch Lane, some by Paul Bole of Exeter upon Daniel Farington in St Nicholas Lane near Lombard Street, and so on; but twenty of the sixty-five bills were returned by either Ralph Hermon (Herman) or Edward Anthony upon Nathaniel Potter, goldsmith, at 'The Bunch of Grapes' in Cheapside. Anthony was an Exeter goldsmith and perhaps Hermon was also, for he was an even more regular and long-standing correspondent of Potter's. Another pair of correspondents Pole used were George Shapcote in Exeter and Richard Warren and his partner John Marshall on the Cornhill. A typical entry in the accounts reads, 'returned of William Searles money by Mr Anthonie of Exeter goldsmith upon Mr Nathaniel Potter goldsmith at The Bunch of Grapes in Cheapside by bill dated September 16th'. Indeed, much of the money was returned by bills drawn by other Exeter or Tiverton men on various London merchants or Blackwell Hall factors and then assigned to Hermon or Anthony for transfer.[238] Further illustration of the connexion between London goldsmith-bankers and provincial remitters is found in the dealings the two London bankers, Edward Backwell and Gilbert Whitehall, had severally with Thomas Smith the Nottingham banker and revenue-remitter who in 1672 had accounts with them both.[239] Over and above this, successful London goldsmith-bankers often

acquired landed estates and could act as remitters for their friends
and neighbours. After Sir William Herrick retired to his country estate
at Beaumanor, he still continued his business in London and acted
as a Town and Country banker.[240]

The new credit and banking arrangements we have described
received the recognition and blessing of the law. Englishmen assigned
bills obligatory and inland bills of exchange from one to another
without apparent let or hindrance. Yet these bills were for long not
negotiable, at least not in the eyes of the law, and since not all the
negotiators could rely on legal protection, full negotiability had not
been achieved.

Assignability is not negotiability. Assignability only puts the
assignee in the shoes of the assignor, whereas negotiability allows
financial instruments to pass from hand to hand as currency, as
though they were money, despite the fact that they are far from that
and are not even fiduciary media, for endorsement and acceptance
are purely discretionary, depending on the perceived credit-worthiness
of the names. Where such an instrument is transferable in this way
and is also capable of being sued upon by due course of law by the
pro tempore holder for value, then it is a negotiable instrument. Thus
the essential difference between a negotiable instrument and one
merely assignable is that the holder for value for the time being of
the former may have an even better right than the original payee. For
example, a man who innocently takes a stolen bank-note in payment
of a lawful debt can nevertheless demand and obtain payment on it
at the bank of issue. To be fully negotiable a credit instrument must,
first, be transferable as by the custom of merchants, i.e. it must be
recognised as transferable in the ordinary course of business and
simply by delivery or by endorsement and delivery; and, secondly,
it must be capable of being sued upon by the holder for the time being.
The *bona fide* transferee for value of a fully negotiable instrument
acquires the property in it and the right to sue on it, even though,
to take an extreme case, it may have originally been procured by fraud,
and even though the person from whom he gets it has and had no
title to it.

At common law *choses in action* like debts were not in general
assignable even when the parties contracted expressly for themselves
and assigns; but, in particular, bills obligatory and bills of exchange
were excepted from this general rule, because they were recognised
as assignable by law merchant, which was the highly efficient custom

of merchants, created by the merchants themselves in much earlier times; and custom, when general, was *ipso facto* common law, and if particular and reasonable, was received by it. As Hobart, C.J., said, in 1622, 'the custome of merchants is part of the common law of this kingdome of which the judges ought to take notice: and if any doubt arise to them about there custome, they may send for the merchants to know there custome'. Coke was repeating Hobart when he declared in 1628, the law merchant '(as hath beene said), is part of the lawes of this realme'.[241] In 1613 it had been decided in King's Bench that the acceptance of a bill of exchange for value received amounted by the law merchant to a promise to pay on it, provided the drawee was stated to be a merchant at the time he accepted. Moreover, in 1667 it was declared that 'the law of merchants is the law of the land, and the custome is good enough generally for any man, without naming him merchant'. It sufficed to plead the bill was drawn *secundum usum et consuetudinem mercatorum.*[242] Thus the law merchant was extended to anyone wanting to use inland bills of exchange.[243]

At the outset of our period, the Court of Admiralty still had jurisdiction over bills of exchange, but by 1564 this was being disputed by the Westminster courts. Despite an agreement in 1575, this contest still remained unsettled until 1632, when the Privy Council decreed that Admiralty have jurisdiction over contracts made beyond the sea and the Westminster courts over those made in this country. This, however, seems to have left in doubt the position regarding many outland bills. Finally, in 1648, the Lords and Commons forbade the Court of Admiralty to hold pleas or admit actions upon any bills of exchange or on accounts between merchant and merchant or their respective factors.[244]

Meanwhile, as unsealed bills obligatory came into increasing use in English business circles, litigation arose from them in the common law courts. Already in the second half of the sixteenth century their books of entries contain pleadings for this purpose. *Assumpsit* already allowed a plaintiff to sue for damages sustained through non-payment of a debt. Now the *indebitatus* count, *indebitatus assumpsit*, came in to provide a new remedy for the non-payment itself. In 1566 occurred the first case so far discovered of *assumpsit* brought on an outland bill of exchange, and in 1602 the first case of *assumpsit* on a bill to be reported. Previously actions for debt could be brought only in the Common Pleas; but by the action of *indebitatus assumpsit* the King's Bench sought to entertain pleas of debt. As King's Bench was also a cheaper and swifter court than Common Pleas, much business was momentarily captured, but at first all such cases were reversed by the Court of Exchequer Chamber. 'This unseemly situation', Plucknett tells us, 'lasted for almost a generation, until the question was finally referred to that other assembly, also called the Exchequer Chamber, consisting of all the judges of all three courts assembled for discussion, in *Slade's case* (1602)'. From this assembly the case was then referred to a conference of judges at Serjeants' Inn, with Coke, the attorney-general, for the plaintiff, and Bacon for the defendant. The final resolution was that *indebitatus assumpsit* was an alternative to an action of debt, at the election of the plaintiff. This being so, unsealed bills could be sued upon by the ordinary course of the common law, without pleading the custom of merchants, but only if a *quid pro quo* could be proved.[245] In other words, even unsealed bills were legally valid, provided they were for value, i.e., if consideration had been given for them.

In cases upon inland bills of exchange, no special difficulty was met in pleading in terms of the common law. The general practice was to rest such cases on the custom of merchants, by which bills passed from hand to hand as if currency. By pleading this custom, the assignability of inland bills could be established in law. Thus in 1664, in *Edgar versus Chute*, a butcher had bought cattle from the plaintiff and got a person to draw a bill on J.S. in the plaintiff's favour in payment for them. But the butcher became insolvent before he had paid the said person, who then instructed J.S. not to pay. The plaintiff brought a case upon the custom of merchants and succeeded.[246] But in order to have this remedy one had, as late as 1632, to be styled a merchant, for it was ruled in the King's Bench, upon a bill of exchange, between party and party who were not merchants, there could not be a declaration upon the law of merchants, though there might be upon the *assumpsit*, giving the acceptance of the bill as evidence of the acknowledgement of the debt. Thus an action on the case upon the custom was not always as satisfactory as an action for debt. To ensure the possibility of an action for debt, all one had to do was to have inserted in the bill a value-received clause, for 'if the drawer mention "for value received", then he is chargeable at common law; but if no such mention, then you must come upon the custom of merchants only'. In 1667 a plaintiff based his case on the custom and law of the realm, that if any man write a bill to another, that then if he to whom the bill is directed, do not pay for the value

received by the maker, that then the maker of such bill should pay.
Verdict was given for the plaintiff, for 'by the common law a man
may resort to him who received the money, if he to whom the bill
was directed, refuse'. The holder for value was thus doubly protected,
by the law merchant and by *indebitatus assumpsit*.[247]

None of this, however, established the legal negotiability of inland
bills of exchange by the ordinary course of law as opposed to custom.
Such negotiability only came in 1696 with an *obiter dictum* from Holt,
C.J., that such a bill, drawn to order, could be transferred by
endorsement and delivery, that the title of a *bona fide* holder for value
was not invalidated by defects in the title of the man who transferred
to him, and that value-received should be presumed and taken as said.
This rule was taken over by the Court of Chancery in 1697. Next year
this negotiability of inland bills was established by statute, without
any need to plead the custom, provided they were date bills, not sight
or after-sight ones, but specifying payment on a particular date, which
at this time was usually set so that, allowing for delivery, it fell about
twenty days after sight, this being now a common usance for mere
transfers of funds by four-party bills as distinct from the payment
of commercial debts. There was then also a requirement for protestation, which was to be either before a public notary, as with outland
bills, or in default of such a notary, before some other substantial
person in the presence of two or more credible witnesses. In 1705
inland bills of less than £20 were excused formal protestation and bills
accepted in writing could be protested by the payee's servant, agent
or assign. Full negotiability had finally arrived.[248]

Bills obligatory were a different kettle of fish. They were not on
the same footing as bills of exchange, as Holt found in 1702, when
he refused to allow an endorsee to sue on a promissory note. Sealed
notes were good in law if payable to bearer, but not if payable to order
and endorsed; and unsealed bills were not negotiable even if payable
to bearer. The first common-law case recognising the claim of a *bona
fide* holder for value of a promissory note occurred in 1699, but it
remained for the Act of 1704 to confer full negotiability on bills
obligatory of all kinds.[249]

It should always be remembered that these legal niceties were
immaterial to the great majority of transactions, where the trust
was mutual and where no party had any thought of instituting
litigation. Nevertheless, these developments, amounting to the full
legal recognition of ordinary commercial practice, are evidence

that this practice was already firmly established, and they in turn reinforced it.

In fine, it is manifest that English inland trade in the period 1560–1660 was already conducted on credit and that the financial instruments chiefly employed were the old-established bills obligatory and the newly invented bills of exchange, the majority of both being informal until the legal developments of the second half of the seventeenth century.

5

The Bill on London

The inland bill of exchange formed the financial foundation of the English banking system that eventually served a large part of the world. By the middle of the seventeenth century the metropolitan markets had mostly extended themselves oversea, and nowhere more markedly than in textiles, hosiery, corn and cheese. English overseas merchants were now employing agents and factors in all the major foreign seaports, and as the names of English merchants and bankers became universally known and trusted, so the Bill on London gradually became the chief negotiable instrument in the financing of world trade.[250]

The goldsmith-bankers proliferated mightily[251] and many developed their businesses further by issuing bank-notes, initially 'running cash notes', which were made out in variable denominations, the amount on them being written or endorsed off as encashments were made. The earliest extant goldsmith-banker's bank-note dates from 1665; but notes were issued before that, probably as early as about 1650. Working on a fractional reserve system, sometimes of one in ten, the bankers issued notes with aggregate face values well in excess of deposits and capital. Their depositors grew ever more numerous, varied, and far-flung. No less a man than Oliver Cromwell had an account at Hoare's. These bankers accepted written assignments, orders to pay, or three-party bills, and that the first extant specimen dates only from the 1670s is due solely to fortuitous circumstances. The bankers also made loans to the Crown and to monarchs personally. They acted, too, as fiscal agents, farming customs, excise and other taxes in repayment for loans, and making payments on behalf of the Exchequer directly from these revenues. Backwell was engaged in such activities very early on, ever since 1642, when he was a receiver of the 'assessments' imposed by the Two Houses. Some goldsmith-bankers, moreover, became bankers' bankers, akin to the Suffolk Bank of Boston and other 'City' banks in America later. Backwell and Whitehall were prominent in this, holding deposit accounts for other London goldsmith-bankers and for provincial bankers like Smith of Nottingham. Combining all these and other functions, Backwell's 'Unicorn' Bank was a prototype of the Bank of England. And the bankers in Town had their counterparts and correspondents in the Country, where many banks developed from amidst the ranks of merchants, factors, goldsmiths, scriveners, tax-collectors, manufacturers and merchant-employers, for example, Newcastle coal merchants, Manchester fustian dealers, and Nottingham hosiery wholesalers. Gurneys, the famous Norwich bankers, like the Oakes of Bury St Edmunds, were also yarnmasters. Country bankers like these dealt in inland bills of exchange, discounted bills on London for clothiers and others, took deposits, worked on fractional reserve systems, allowed overdrafts, issued bank-notes, remitted funds, collected rents and taxes and returned them to London if and when required, ran insurance agencies, and supplied all financial services in their localities. In Town and Country alike, England had 'High Street' banks. The most significant of these important developments was that of discounting with bank-notes, for the demand for money was made less than otherwise it would have been.[252]

Thus both Town and Country banks developed as general banking businesses. Earlier on, specialist provincial banking-shops arose in but a small number of towns, and even then were still often, and probably best, run by men also busied in their original occupations. We believe that during the depression of the 1720s no more than about eight country banks failed, and that by the end of the depression not above a dozen survived, and so may infer that country banking was still mainly unspecialised. Town banks, too, continued to develop along their original lines, slowly shedding their non-banking business, and extending their services to such things as buying stocks and shares and collecting dividends. Their own capital they invested partly in trade and in joint-stock companies, largely in relatively liquid securities like Exchequer bills and East India Company bonds.

Town banks fell into two more or less distinct groups: West End and City banks. City banks were situated in and around Lombard Street and the Exchange. Discounting *bona fide* trade bills was the pivot of their business, though they could not altogether avoid accepting finance bills, and when they made advances to merchants it was by way of discounting. But they still left the negotiation of bills of exchange to the City merchants whose bankers they were and from whose ranks they recruited. As part of their inland-bill work, they acted as agents, bankers and lenders of the last resort to country bankers. The West End banks sprang up in and around Westminster and the Strand to serve landowners, lawyers, officials, parliament-men and others. Understandably, then, some, like Sir Francis Child, continued to trade in jewellery. These bankers received rents for landowners from tenants in London and the home counties, as well as returns of funds from landowners and others against the time when they would be in Town; had correspondents among the country bankers; acted as intermediaries and brokers for mortgages, so competing with the scriveners; and themselves lent, with discrimination, on mortgages and bonds, to creditworthy customers. West End bankers discounted few bills, and usually then only as a favour to valued depositors and as part of a whole range of services that included the buying and selling of stocks and shares and the issue of traveller's cheques, these last being a speciality of Herries' Bank. As their customers were not given to withdrawing large sums suddenly, West End banks could make do with comparatively small cash reserves and had large amounts to lend to City merchants on the security of Exchequer bills and East India, Bank of England and other company shares. West End banks tended to keep aloof from City ones and as late as 1773 refused to join in a clearing house with them, preferring to clear amongst themselves by means of peripatetic clerks. In the eighteenth century all these Town banks took to issuing printed bank-notes at standard denominations, printed cheques, and, later, books of cheques. At the same time, however, there was a growing tendency for them to substitute Bank of England notes for their own.

Over the years, then, private banking made great progress along the lines laid down in the preceding two hundred years, with the City banks concentrating more on the ordinary commercial work and trade bills, the West End ones taking on the transference of funds for persons outside the normal credit network for commodity trade, and the country ones carrying on as before, only on a larger scale and with somewhat more specialisation.[253]

This huge credit structure, an essential component of England's mighty production and trade, soon acquired a governing head. The

'Stop' of the Exchequer in 1672 put an end to private banks being bankers to the Crown. In 1660 Exchequer tallies had for the first time been authorised to bear interest and were then always accompanied by repayment orders, which were assignable by endorsement and so tantamount to negotiable securities. But from 1667 to 1671 this arrangement was abused by the issue of so-called repayment orders not tied to specific taxes, merely in anticipation of hoped-for future revenues, and so were really nothing but unbacked paper currency. The 'Stop' suspended all these fictitious repayments, which were resumed only in 1677, and even then at a lower rate. These five years more or less ruined many of the Crown's chief creditors, like Sir Robert Vyner, Alderman Backwell, and Gilbert Whitehall. Most goldsmith-bankers were little affected, but all took fright of lending much to the Crown, lest they should not be repaid. With the Crown still in this parlous financial situation, there came a great and pressing need for large loans to sustain the life-and-death struggle under William of Orange against French despotism, increased taxes being neither enough nor ready enough for the purpose. But what no number of goldsmith-bankers would undertake as individuals was successfully accomplished by a consortium, which lent £1,200,000, mostly in sealed bills and running cash notes. These arrangements for a temporary bank for the duration of the emergency were formalised by an Act of Parliament creating, and providing for the chartering of, the Bank of England. Shares in the Bank were bought not only by many London businessmen, including six goldsmiths, but also by William and Mary, the dukes of Marlborough, Leeds, and Devonshire, the earls of Pembroke and Portland, and other peers, and likewise by Dutch noblemen and landowners, as well as by bodies like the city of Utrecht orphans court, the hospital in Geneva, and the hospital, city and canton of Berne. The Bank was thus the financial counterpart in the Protestant coalition of the armies raised from among English, Dutch, Flemish, Danish, French and Swiss Protestants. The Bank, in short, was open to the charge of being a 'Whig finance company' (Bagehot). 'The infant Bank of England was not a copy of a Continental model. Its chief original function was that of a bank of issue, whereas the banks on the Continent were essentially banks of deposit and exchange.' (Richards). Like many European public banks, however, the Bank was initially a temporary wartime device, the tunnage and other taxes on which the loan was secured being voted only for four years in the first instance and the

charter itself being valid only for ten. But the titanic war raged on
and off for a century and a quarter, so fresh charters were granted
time and time again, and, as so often happens, what was intended
to be temporary became permanent. From time to time the stock was
increased. In 1697 the tallies were grafted on to it, and short-term
floating debts were progressively turned into permanent stock. By
1715 the Bank's capital had mounted to £10 million.

Unlike contemporary public banks, however, the Bank was 'only
an ordinary banking concern on a large scale' (Lord Overstone 1857);
it was a giant 'Unicorn', but with joint stock and limited liability:
it came to undertake everything the goldsmith-bankers did or had
done. Like them, it lent to the Crown, and, eventually, as the East
India Company and others dropped out of the business, became the
sole such lender. Like the old 'Unicorn', the Bank made all the
Crown's oversea payments. Just as Backwell had seen to the pay of
our garrison in Dunkirk in 1657, so Michael Godfrey of the Bank saw
to that of our troops besieging Namur in 1695. Like some of the
goldsmiths before it, the Bank shouldered the Crown's domestic
financial business. It discounted Exchequer bills and tallies, and,
following in the footsteps of goldsmith-bankers like William Herrick,
gradually came to transact most of the money business of the
Exchequer. Like the goldsmith-bankers, it dealt in bullion. Like them,
it discounted bills obligatory and bills of exchange, largely inland
ones, always endeavouring to confine itself to self-liquidating trade
bills and eschew finance ones, and, fittingly, to large bills, spurning
inland ones under £50, and always with prudence, only on endorsement by known and trusted London merchants. Like them, it issued
bank-notes of suitably high denomination. Like them, it transferred
between accounts both internally and externally, allowing transfer by
written order and by cheque. Like them, and with equal circumspec-
tion, it made advances on mortgage and on pawns of merchandise.
Like them, it took deposits at usury, and kept the accounts of, and
allowed overdrafts to, a variety of firms, though only fittingly large
ones like the Russia, East India, Exchange Assurance, Brass Wire,
Mercers', and Hudson's Bay companies, great London merchant
houses, provincial tax-collectors, London private bankers and Scottish
joint-stock banks. Subject, as the goldsmith-bankers were, to the
usury laws, the Bank responded to fluctuations in market rates of
usury by being either more or less discriminating in regard to the
quality of the bills it discounted. Like some goldsmith-bankers,

notably Backwell and Whitehall, the Bank also acted as a bankers' bank, which it did for both London private banks and Scottish joint-stock ones, and since Town banks performed the same function in respect of country ones, the Bank assumed its position at the apex of the financial pyramid. So placed, the Bank became increasingly aware of its responsibilities and its true interest in ensuring the continued progress of the nation at large. It restrained its discounting in normal times, but rose to the occasion at times of financial stress, freely discounting for threatened but fundamentally sound banks, and so guarding against avoidable damage to trade and industry; the Bank became the nation's *dernier ressort*, her head bank, but not a central bank in the modern sense of a state-run or state-owned affair. In fine, the Bank was a unique English institution and was uniquely English in being a scaled-up version of the goldsmith-banks. Like theirs, its foundations were set on the rock of commerce, in discounting bills of exchange, and above all inland bills.[254]

With the economic recovery from 1750 and the subsequent prosperity associated with the 'Industrial Revolution', private banks made great progress, largely by financing industrial innovation and enterprise. The Darbys of Coalbrookdale borrowed from Goldney's of Bristol, the Duke of Bridgwater from Child and Company, Richard Arkwright from Wright's of Nottingham, Jedediah Strutt from Need's of the same town, Samuel Oldknow from Evans and Company of Derby, and so on. Many industrialists, including textile manu-facturers, Robert Peel and Samuel Oldknow for instance, printed their own bearer notes for local use. In transactions between firms, long-dated bills of exchange, often with three months' currency, had mostly replaced bills obligatory. Familiarity with these and other financial instruments made many manufacturers and merchants fit to be bankers, and some set up their own banks, usually in co-operation with men who already had banking connexions. The new generation of country banks consisted typically of partnerships formed by the sort of men whose businesses had previously often developed banking departments, bringing together as partners, say, a manufacturer, a scrivener, a deputy tax-receiver or rent-collector, a merchant, and one or two others perhaps, with the object of running a specialist banking-shop. In this way were formed the banking firms of Arkwright and Company of Wirksworth, Peel, Greaves and Company of Manchester, and Bacon, Cobbold and Company of Ipswich. One way or another, innovators and men of enterprise were well able to obtain

from others or create for themselves the credit needed for revolution-
ising industry. And country banks in previously enriched agricultural
and industrial areas, often having resources in excess of new opportunities for profitable local investment, made deposits at their Town
agents, while others in areas of innovation and expansion looked to
their Town agents for extensions of credit. Inland bills sold by
Lancashire banks, for example, were bought by East Anglian ones. So
great was this kind of business that, after 1797, bills were increasingly
handled by specialist bill-brokers. Country banking was flourishing
as never before. By 1784 there were over a hundred country banks,
by 1796 three hundred, by 1810 more than six hundred. Some country
banks, like Jones and Company of Manchester, set up London
branches; others entered into interlocking partnerships with Town
banks; and many opened branches in neighbouring towns. Every
market town came to have either a bank or a branch or an agency.
Gurney's of Norwich earlier had agents in Bungay, Brinton, Aylsham,
Great Yarmouth, Wymondham, Diss, Swaffham, North Walsham,
Holt and King's Lynn, and now opened full branches in Yarmouth,
Halesworth and Lynn, which itself had an agency in Wisbech. The
Yarmouth branch was a separate but interlocked partnership, the
others under the head office. All told, with developments like these,
the banking capital and business of the kingdom must have grown
enormously. But during the subsequent recession and depression,
especially after 1813, the number of country banks fell away; by 1842
it was down to just over three hundred. A slackening of industrial
borrowing and a swing to paying off loans was felt very strongly by
banks in the manufacturing districts. This turn of events, however,
was due to the inflation caused by government overspending and the
consequent suspension of payment on its notes by the Bank of
England in 1797, rather than to inherent weakness in the banking
system as a whole, which stood generally on a firm foundation of trade
bills.[255]

From 1826 onwards, joint-stock banks, i.e. ones formed by much
enlarged partnerships, increasingly replaced and supplanted those run
by families and small partnerships. These new banks had much the
same functions as the old, but many more shareholders and much
larger capitals. After 1844, in order to circumvent government
restrictions on the issue of bank-notes, the new banks brought cheques
into much greater use. This was facilitated by their membership of
the London clearing house from 1854. From 1858 private country

banks also cleared cheques in London. In this period, the great steam transport boom ushered in a new upsurge of prosperity and a great swelling of the number and value of inland bills of exchange. Limited liability having been allowed to joint-stock banks in 1858, they readily adopted it. Meanwhile, the great financial crisis of 1857 gave the first impulse to the amalgamation, merging and absorption of the many unitary banks into a small number of nationwide concerns. At much the same time a second and overlapping circle of bankers undertook the similar and parallel task of providing the imperial and international joint-stock banks that served the new worldwide metropolitan market through the Bill on London, which in our colonies was essentially the old inland bill of exchange in a new form.[256]

The Bill on London remained the great financial instrument. Even though its use between British banks was reduced by their amalgamation, the Bill on London was still of the first importance to inland trade, especially at times of industrial expansion, and had become the linchpin of world trade. In the meantime, the London discount market had undergone modification. Ever since 1487 at the latest, sworn brokers had been acting on commission between would-be deliverers and takers of bills of exchange. Much later, as the Bank of England would only discount bills with two good London names on them and most country bills had only one when they came up to Town, bill-brokers made a trade of supplying a second. Then, from 1825, London banks took to lodging part of their cash reserves with bill-brokers, at call, and the brokers in turn to use this call money to deal in bills on their own accounts, only needing to go into the Bank to discount bills when no call money was available. The bill-brokers, now really bill-dealers, thus acted as a buffer between the commercial banks and the Bank of England, and their new business expanded rapidly during the railway boom, still more with the development of imperial and international banks. But banking still stood on the discounting of bills of exchange, largely inland ones, and on the handling of that special form of inland bill called the cheque, which long remained the most distinctive and easily recognised feature of the English system.[257]

Some Continental countries, meanwhile, had eventually developed metropolitan markets not unlike those in England, and had begun to use inland bills of exchange. Thus, from about 1850, small, sight, inland bills solved the difficulty occasioned by a shortage of currency in the Rhineland. Continental banks, including the new joint-stock

ones, discounted bills of exchange, but private investment banks still
overshadowed the others, stamping their mark on banking in general,
and inland bills, especially in the form of cheques, never took the same
hold as they had done in England.[258]

The inland bill of exchange is the red thread that runs through all
our banking history, and this thread was spun in the third quarter
of the sixteenth century. If I send A. Smith a written order to my
bankers to pay him Fifty pounds only, I am only doing what William
Leonard did in 1580, when he sent William Morris a written order
to his factor to pay him Fifty pounds only.

Nowhere was this red thread less conspicuous or more important
than in the first half of the early modern period, from about 1560
to 1660. The inland bill of exchange, formal or informal, came in as
the coping stone of the whole edifice of credit. Without it, residual
debts would have had to have been met by the conveyance of coins
at high freight rates and insurance premiums. The inland bill settled
balances left outstanding even when all debts and bills obligatory had
been made over, and went on to replace the bill obligatory in its most
common and essential function. Metropolitan markets gave rise both
to inland bills and to the English banking system, and all three
advanced hand in hand.

6

The 'price revolution'

Our argument already suffices to put the final nail in the coffin of the deceased crude quantity-of-money explanation of the second phase of the so-called 'Price Revolution' in England, according to which it was caused by the influx of precious metals from America and elsewhere.

The first phase of this supposed revolution in England was caused by successive debasements of the coinage in 1543, 1545, 1546, 1548 and 1551. The Crown effectually purloined precious metal from its subjects' coins, leaving them with a base and inflated currency and making nearly all prices, some of which would have risen anyway, higher than otherwise they would have been. Social, economic and political chaos ensued; but this inflation was self-destructive, for the end of it was, the king was paid back in his own coin, and then true coinage had to be restored. The final recoinage in 1560–61[259] failed some expectations, in that, though it marked the complete end of inflation, it could not prevent non-inflationary price rises. It is these rises after 1561 that were formerly most usually explained by an influx of precious metals;[260] and it was on this sand that was built the folly of assuming a consequent fall in real wages, which was then imagined to have been the cause of a supposed general swelling of profits and of the fancied rise of what had gratuitously been dubbed 'capitalism'.[261] How dangerous these particular notions, and monetary monomania itself, have been to free societies, can be gauged by the glee with which they were taken up by such people as J. M. Keynes and M. Dobb.[262] Lest those unfamiliar with the early modern period be further deceived, let us point out that the indices of wage rates and other prices used in support of these notions have been proved worthless for the purpose.[263] We know English people generally, including wage workers, enjoyed more and better food, drink, clothing, furnishing, and housing than ever before, and also indulged in such minor luxuries as tobacco, sweetmeats and dried fruit. This rise in real wages came about in consequence of improvements and innovations in agricultural, extractive, processing and manufacturing industry and in commercial and financial practice.[264]

Some precious metals came into England,[265] and some were even mined here,[266] but some also went out, especially to the Baltic region and the Orient.[267] As had been amply demonstrated, there was an increase in the amount of precious metal coined during the reigns of Elizabeth and the early Stuarts; but some coins were melted down and others wasted away by one means or another, so we have no method of ascertaining the cumulative total of coinage in circulation at any single time.[268] It is unlikely to have risen much per head, and then only gradually.

Nor can we learn what proportion of the available precious metal went into coins and what into non-monetary artefacts. We have good reason to suppose that, off and on, more gold and silver than ever before went into such things as clocks, watches, chains, rings, seals, sheaves, vessels, jewellery and gold-and-silver thread. Gold went into rings, jewellery and plate and into gilt, double gilt and part-gilt crucifixes, saltcellars, cups, tankards, goblets, lids and covers. Silver was used for silver plate, spoons and other cutlery, drinking bowls, cans, cups, goblets, beakers, dishes, pots, basins, ewers, saltcellars, whistles, bells, candlesticks, fan-handles, buttons, hooks, hat-pins, and so on; and also for garnishings for the feet, tops, covers, lids, lips and tips for treen and pottery cups, pots, bowls and such like. Silver spoons, often in dozens and half-dozens, became commonplace. It was a poor child indeed not born, or at least weaned, with a silver spoon in its mouth. Half the Liverpool, perhaps half the Yorkshire, a third of the Lichfield and district, a fifth of the Ipswich, a sixth of the Devon, and a twelfth of the Frampton Cotterell and district, testators in the hundred years or so up to 1660 left silver or gold plate, spoons or other articles behind them when they died, as did a quarter of those in Southwell peculiar from 1512 to 1567 and a fifth of those in Chesterfield and district in the period 1521–1603.[269] Not only wealthy landowners and widows,[270] merchants, industrialists, and professional and business men generally,[271] but also clerks, yeomen, husbandmen, farmers, innkeepers, craftsmen, tradesmen, mariners, and even sailors, shoemakers and maidservants[272] accumulated precious wares like the ones described whenever they had more money than they had any other immediate use for. About 1620 it was estimated that £80,000 of silver a year was going into thread, spangles, purls, oaes, and such, while the plate being made in London alone was absorbing £50,000 or £60,000 a year more. At this time trade was depressed and prices low, so hardly any silver was being coined.[273] Conversely, to meet financial exigencies, plate and such like were often melted down for coining. One has only to glimpse what happened to all the monastic plate and recall how both sides in the Civil War coined whatever plate they could lay their hands on. In short, when more coin was needed, bullion and plate went to be coined, and when less, coins were melted down and fashioned into other things.[274] Thus the influx of precious metals did not lead inevitably to an increase in the coinage. People only had coined what they themselves demanded, and it was their demand that decided the total value and volume of coins in circulation. If the size of the coinage helped to determine prices, yet demand determined the size of the coinage.

Of the alternative explanations of the price rises, the one now most fashionable is that they were caused by a rise in population. Such explanations have even been offered when least needed, for the period of the Great Debasement:

Yet the inflation (*sic*) had deeper roots than the debased currency and was derived, in large measure, from the growth of population at a faster pace than any possible means to feed or employ them. Hence, too many people were chasing too few goods and too few jobs and, as usually happens in these circumstances, prices rose and wages fell.

Professor Jordan is no less emphatic:

The principal causes, we now know, were the inability of a somewhat archaic and a tenaciously conservative agrarian economy to adapt itself quickly to the needs of a steadily increasing population, a sharply higher proportion of which was by 1553, urban in character.

But he only 'knows' this because he made a similar and likewise unsupported assertion in his previous volume.[275] Here we enter the realms of pure fantasy, without a shred of either economic theory or historical evidence.

In economic theory no place has ever been found for the proposition that a rise in population can cause a rise in prices, or a fall in one a fall in the other. Economic thinkers from Giovanni Botero in 1589 onwards, including such famous men as Beccaria, Cantillon, Petty, Smith and McCulloch, have studied the economics of population with great care and reflection, and have noted the tendency of population to increase as much as human fecundity will allow, limited only by the demand for labour, the availability of the means of subsistence and the possibility of increasing them, while recognising that human beings, unlike the lower animals, are not the mere slaves of instinct and appetite, and try to prevent the population outrunning its means. Any rise in population was a response to an increase in these means, often perceived through an increase in the demand for the labour with which to earn what it took to buy them. From Botero onwards, too, it was understood that when the means appeared insufficient, the population was checked, for the most part, by the simple expedients of foregoing or postponing marriage. By and large, people only married when they could afford to.[276] Marshall followed along these lines, repeating that the opposing forces of desire and means were complicated in the human race 'by the influences of forethought and self-control, of prudence and sense of duty', and adding that the average age of marriage was lowest amongst unskilled labourers, low amongst artisans, and highest amongst the middle classes, corresponding to their respective ages of maximum income. Von Mises, like Beccaria before him, pointed out that an increase in population was not necessarily accompanied by a proportionate increase in wealth. Schumpeter, after re-affirming that 'short-time variations in marriage rates are obviously the reflex of business fluctuations and do not cause them', goes on to observe an often overlooked feature of population growth, that the monthly increase in the number seeking gainful employment is always small compared with that of those already gainfully employed, and that even a yearly increase is insufficient to disturb the markets. These are all matters of great interest, but what is of most immediate importance to us is that one may run through the whole gamut of economists without finding one who postulates a causal relationship between a rise in population and a general rise in prices.[277]

Assume the arrival of a first-born child. It has to be provided for out of the family's income, which may have fallen due to the mother's loss of earnings. What is spent on or about the baby will have to be saved on other things. The pattern of demand will change, but not total demand. The demand for foods, especially meat and dairy produce, may rise, but not demand in general, so the general level of prices will not thereby be changed. As the family grows and the elder children start to earn their own livings, the household's income and demand will rise, but only to the extent by which it increases its supply, so the balance of supply and demand will not be upset. Since prices depend on the balance of supply and demand, prices in general will not have been raised. It follows that no increase in population can cause a general rise in prices. Besides, it is difficult to imagine an increase in the birth rate of more than one per cent. a year or that such an increase in the rate would cause a price revolution either in a township of one hundred souls or in a nation of one million or more. Those who argue a rise in population will cause a rise in prices in general, have not grasped that it is the balance of supply and demand, not mere demand, still less mere need or want, that regulates prices. They have also overlooked how slowly populations rise and how small the increment is relative to the cumulative total.

This is not to say a rise in population has no economic effect. An increase in the birth rate will bring about a lowering of the average age and increase the proportion of young, vigorous, ambitious, adventurous and ingenious people, well able to increase the quantity of goods produced. But this will tend to lower rather than to raise prices.

Now let us turn to the historical evidence. No one doubts an increase in the population occurred during the period 1540–1640; but no one knows exactly when this increase occurred or how great it was. Since the population was never counted, every writer on the subject is free to form his own opinion on these matters, and we consequently find as many estimates as writers and wide variations between the estimates, which are obviously accurate only to the nearest million or so.[278] The sets of estimates that appear both most worthy of confidence and relevant to our purpose are those produced by Rickman and by Professor Wrigley and Dr Schofield. They have relied mainly on parish registers. Rickman had them read and tabulated by local parsons, Messrs Wrigley and Schofield were helped by amateurs. Which of the two methods was more accurate and by how much is difficult to discover. Rickman estimated the population of England and Wales in 1570 at 4,123,708, in 1600 at 4,811,718, in 1630 at 5,600,517; Messrs Wrigley and Schofield arrive at figures for England alone (but less Monmouthshire) of 2,774,000 in 1541 and 5,092,000 in 1641. These estimates for 1541 and 1641 have been made by means of 'back projections' in quinquennial stages starting in 1871. The ages of death were largely estimated from life tables, but London parishes were excluded from the aggregations because of their high and rapid turnover of population, and a series of ratios of London births and deaths was constructed from the Bills of Mortality. Unfortunately, emigration and immigration were not taken into account as fully as they might have been. A fair comment on this work was made by the late Professor Flinn:

However well founded and skilfully devised the techniques may be, the multiplicity of assumptions and sheer number of cumulative modifications to raw data diminish the accuracy of the end-products. And the further back in time the reconstruction goes the more this must be true. Every five-year reconstruction of population by the back projection method necessarily involves, since it is an estimate, some error; but the error in that reconstruction becomes the base for the next quinquennium going backwards. For the early seventeenth century, when the back projection has already passed through between fifty and sixty stages, the frailties are compounded by the diminution in the number of aggregations available and the increasing role of corrections ... Some modest scepticism ... is scarcely avoidable.

Nevertheless, as Flinn says, Messrs Wrigley and Schofield have produced a good basic framework, and 'Theirs will be the orthodoxy for the foreseeable future, and many of their findings will inevitably be quoted, regardless of criticism, by non-specialist writers as gospel.'[279]

We have no need to take this work as holy writ, least of all for the period that concerns us. Particularly worrying are the London parishes, for it is common knowledge that London, with Westminster, Southwark and the suburbs and liberties, maintained and increased its population mainly by recruitment from the country. Dr Rowse has shown by the registers back to 1558 that rural or semi-rural towns like Halifax, Ormskirk, Askham and Shap usually had a surplus of births over deaths, while large towns like Durham, Exeter, and, above all, London, usually had a surplus of deaths over births, leading to the conclusion that the rural surplus went to great towns and was largely cancelled out there, thus partially accounting for the surplus of births over deaths in its native towns. Thus a surplus of births over deaths in rural townships fails to prove an increase in the population at large. Nevertheless, from all the studies made, it seems the population started to rise, or rise more rapidly, about 1560 or 1570, when sound coinage, prosperity and rising prices coincided. But we still remain in ignorance as to whether the rise in population preceded, succeeded or coincided with the resumption of price rises. And even if this ignorance were dispelled, we would still know nothing about the causal relationship between these events. Indeed, Messrs Wrigley and Schofield wisely concede the possibility that population movements reflected changes in real wages.[280]

Even were the impossible to happen and we came into possession of precise statistics of population movements, we would not be much further forward, because we lack, and cannot hope for, accurate and detailed price statistics. Prices can be compared only over short periods of time, for the obvious reason that over long periods, a dozen years or so, the goods against which money is exchanged have themselves altered, often out of all recognition. A kersey bought in 1580 is unlikely to have been the same in quality and dimensions as one bought in 1560. Cereals were grown in many different varieties and sold in various qualities and measurements, not all of which are usually recorded with precision at the time of sale and purchase. We are thus in perpetual danger of comparing like with unlike, and whenever we do, the nominal price has little meaning for us. Moreover, the terms of a transaction are of crucial importance in determining price. Unless we know what reduction was made for quantity, what credit terms were agreed upon, when delivery was to be made and at whose expense, we are not much further forward. Then expectations must be taken into account, especially in relation to farm goods and produce, and not least wool. 'The wheat quotations from month to month depended entirely on the home harvest. A bad harvest, or the prospect of one, would double the price of corn in a few weeks; and the promise of a good yield would lower it as rapidly.' The climate being so changeable, no one could be certain whether the harvest was to be good or bad until it was gathered in and samples of threshed grain had been examined. Until then men were guided only by prognostications based on natural occurrences.[281] And by the time one harvest was known, speculation had started about the next. So such markets were akin to futures ones, with dealers going long or short according to whether they expected higher or lower prices. Therefore it will not serve to compare prices from year to year or between fixed dates in two or more years. The comparison has to be between like market situations in one year and another. Moreover, wholesale trade was conducted on credit, so we need to know when payment was due and by how many instalments, for the nominal price took account of these details. In fine, to attain accuracy, one must know the unknowable.

Turning to such indications of price movements as we have, we find a composite index of a 'shopping basket' of certain goods in the mainly larger towns of southern England from 1264 to 1954, with 1451–75 as one hundred. Throughout the period 1550–70 and beyond, disregarding seasonal and annual fluctuations, prices rose in something like an exponential curve. But when one looks at the five-year averages, a plateau of relatively stable prices appears in the years 1551–81.[282] A better understanding of these thirty years comes from an index of wheat price fluctuations from a thirty-one year moving average, for what immediately concerned young people was not the level of prices as compared with 1451–75, or even the quinquennial average, but whether the current cost of living was low enough in three or more successive years to allow them to save up and get married with confidence. Prices were well or appreciably below average in sixteen harvest years: 1552, 1553, 1557, 1558, 1561, 1563, 1564, 1566, 1567, 1568, 1569, 1570, 1571, 1572, 1578 and 1579. In eight years they were at or near average: 1554, 1559, 1574, 1575, 1576, 1577, 1580 and 1581. In seven they were well above average: 1551, 1555, 1556, 1560, 1562, 1565 and 1573.[283] It thus seems early marriage was encouraged most in the years 1566–72. Thus what little we know about prices fits in roughly with what little we know about population, which we inferred was increasing, or rising more rapidly, from about 1560 or 1570. So it appears that a rise in population coincided with a period of low prices. From this it would be reasonable to assume that so far from an increase in population causing a rise in prices, low prices caused the population to increase.

For an explanation of the price rises after 1560, we had better look at that offered by economists, and particularly by J. A. Schumpeter. In a nutshell, he argues that credit was created to finance enterprises with enhanced productivity, allowing enterprising men to command the resources they needed, so withdrawing them from production for immediate consumption and committing them to the creation of new and better productive facilities that came into operation only after some delay, during and after which prices generally were forced first up and then down. A protracted period of overlapping innovations thus gave rise to a Kondratieff long wave, first to a long rise and then a long fall in prices.

What is often called 'capitalist economy' is always changing. It is ceaselessly being revolutionised from within by new enterprises, new commodities, new methods of production, new commercial ventures and new sources of supply. Profits come from supplying new things or supplying old things in new and better ways. New goods and methods drive out the old-fashioned ones, transforming the whole scene. There has been a whole series of such long waves, each consisting of an industrial revolution and the absorption of its effects: 'the "Industrial Revolution" dear to the hearts of textbook writers', the wave of steam transport, then another based on electricity and the internal combustion engine, and now, in our day, one rooted in electronics.[284] Schumpeter gives a sketch of such a long wave in early modern England, and all we have learned since confirms, modifies and fills out his narrative, which he summarised in these words:

> Agriculture was the leading branch of production and taking the period from about 1500 to about 1780 as a whole, the most important field of extra-commercial entrepreneurial activity. The latter statement sounds strange, no doubt, and the reader will be still more reluctant to follow if he be invited to look upon what happened in post-medieval agriculture as analogous to such a process as, for instance, the rise of the electrical industry in the course of our third Kondratieff. Yet it is necessary for us to be familiar with this view.

He goes on to recount what was known in his day about the innovations in agriculture, textiles, the extractive and processing industries and commercial and colonial enterprise, from which he concludes, 'All the durable achievements of English industry and commerce can be accounted for without reference to the plethora of precious metals.'[285]

We can now see more clearly than Schumpeter how the great innovations in agriculture released surplus labour for other occupations; how they raised the joint productivity of labour, capital and enterprise; how they profited innovators and improvers, landowners, servants, merchants, seedsmen, drovers, dealers, and carriers; how they helped to quicken and transform domestic trade; how, in short, a succession of innovations in agriculture, manufactures, mining, processing, transport, trade and finance, all overlapped and interacted to create the great prosperity that set in motion a more rapid rise in population through a heightened demand for labour, especially in jobs needing new skills and commanding high wages. It was this whole process of development that caused prices after 1560 to be higher than otherwise they would have been.[286]

The innovations and improvements were financed, directly or indirectly, by the extension of credit in one form or another. A crucial role was played by the setting over of debts, leaving merely the balance to be settled by means of actual money. This had all the freedom associated with the use of money combined with the technical simplicity of barter. Once setting over became customary, it stimulated itself. By means of credit, transactions between two men could be treated as simultaneous for purposes of settlement even if they actually took place at different times. Money was still the medium of exchange, but its use in this capacity was independent of its physical existence. Use was made of money that was not present, money that worked even in its absence, merely by being able to be present if needed. Claims to money were transferred instead of actual money. 'Since it was the general custom to make payments in this way, anybody would accept a bill that still had some time to run even when he wanted cash immediately, for he could be fairly sure that the people he had to pay would, in their turn, accept a similar bill.' Thus the demand for actual, physical money was much lower than otherwise it would have been.[287]

Producers and traders got and gave credit by book entries and bills obligatory and of exchange. Production and trade grew enormously, without any commensurate increase in the coinage, because credit instruments were used to increase out of all proportion the velocity of circulation of the existing coinage. In 1603 the coinage available amounted at most to £3,500,000, in 1640 to at most £10,000,000. Leafing through the bill transactions we have run across, and bearing in mind the huge credit structure revealed in Restoration times, it is hard not to believe the volume of credit was always much greater than that of the coinage.[288]

To gain some notion of by how much the volume of credit exceeded that of actual money, we turn to probate inventories. These are tantalising documents that appear to record and value all goods and chattels, but often omit some or lump them together under general or miscellaneous heads. Nor was there uniformity of style and content between various bishoprics and different times, so some inventories are highly detailed and others aggregate under a few main heads. Nowhere is diversity of form more conspicuous than in the listing of money and debts. Some inventories itemise money by itself, others together with debts or plate or both, and many list and value the deceased's purse and apparel without making it clear if the money they contained was included. Many or most inventories listing purse and apparel make no specific mention of coins, perhaps because there were none. But every man needed at least a little money about him.

In some instances, no doubt, the absence of money in inventories is due to it having been spent or given away in the man's last hours, or to it having been stolen or concealed before or after his death. However it is to be explained, two thirds of the Ipswich, Liverpool, and Frampton Cotterell and district, over half the Devon, half the Lichfield and district, and perhaps a quarter of the Yorkshire inventories in the hundred years or so up to 1660, failed to mention coins or money at all, as did half the Southwell peculiar court ones from 1512 to 1567, half the Chesterfield and district ones from 1521 to 1603, and nine tenths of the Oxford consistory and archdeaconry ones from 1550 to 1590.[289] We are invited to believe that all these people died penniless; that a widow who had kept a tavern and left good book debts of £16 10s for wine sold and for money lent from her purse, died without either any purse or any money; that a Liverpool gentleman dying in 1588 with plate worth £8 9s 8d, with £592 2s 4d owing to him, and a total of goods and chattels valued at £703 0s 4d, had not two halfpennies to rub together; and that a gentleman who was lord farmer of the manor of Dunston near Chesterfield and had goods and chattels worth well over £500 in 1593, left neither money, nor any apparel, not as much as a nightcap. Explanations are occasionally found, when appraisers make such comments as, 'by her confession', 'there is monie more confessed', 'in mony as John Busschope confessethe', with the implication that some was suspected stolen or concealed. One set of appraisers reported ignorance of what money had been left, listing £40 'and some more which wee knowe not certainly'. In 1577 some Chesterfield appraisers noted 'some other goodes detayned by persons as yet to us unknowne'. Appraisers for a Winterbourne gentleman could find no money, but abruptly ended their inventory with the laconic note, 'The rest is stolen.'[290] Incidentally, such thefts were probably to defeat the dead man's will, for no tax was involved and probate fees were modest. The fact remains that the absence of money from an inventory does not prove the deceased had none.

Debts, too, were appraised in a variety of ways, some being lumped together with money or plate. Often they were classified as sperate, desperate or bad, and often also as by specialty, by bond, by bill or by book, or as wages, rents, and so on. We know that most wholesale and many retail transactions were conducted by credit; but by no means all inventories mention credit. Some frankly excluded debts, for a list of them could be drawn up separately from, and in addition to, the inventory, and was not always preserved once all the debts had been received.[291] Besides, much depended on the manner of a man's going and whether he had had the chance of calling in his debts. Moreover, unless debts were listed in the will, it was often difficult for appraisers to discover them all. Furthermore, the matter was not always urgent, for outstanding debts could be collected after probate, and many were not due immediately. Above all, appraisers and executors had to consider their own positions. They were concerned not to charge themselves with debts they might not be able to collect. Hence their eagerness to classify them as doubtful, desperate or bad. This attitude is explained in the inventory for Matthew Wilson of London and Eshton Hall in Yorkshire. To a list of his hopeful debts it adds, 'butt the executores will not charge themselves with any parts thereof untill they shall bee received'. Desperate debts are listed, 'butt the same are all desparate and not to bee received, butt if they or any of them bee, the executores will be accomptable and charge themselves therewith'. This was one safe approach. Another was to list the debts 'according to the will', which left a way of escape.[292] Bonds and bills obligatory found could hardly be ignored, but barring accidents, the law courts could be relied on to ensure payment. For a variety of reasons, then, we cannot always take at face value inventories that list no debts, or be absolutely sure those that listed them did so exhaustively.

In comparing volumes of money and credit, then, we do best to play safe and use only those inventories that we believe listed all money and debts.

Out of 260 Liverpool inventories[293] from 1571 to 1681, only fifty-six record debts by specialty, i.e. by bond or bill obligatory. We suppose a quarter of the heads of families had debts owing them by specialty, including what one inventory, that of Thomas Johnson, clothworker, 1622, says was from Michael Shaw 'by a note under his own hand'. This inventory, being that of a humble craftsman with goods and chattels not worth much above £100, is instructive, not only in showing the extent of his credit operations, the debts owing him by bill and book being £38 odd, but also what small sums many of the bills were for. Five were for less than £1, one for 9s, one for 9s 1d, the highest for £9. Disregarding a legacy due to his wife, Johnson was owed twenty-three debts, about half by bill and half by book. The bill debts were not generally larger than the book ones; on the contrary, the bill average was £1 16s 11d, the book one £2 2s 9d.

It was just that bills were safer and Johnson probably converted debts from book to bill from time to time as he saw fit. To say, 'In quiet times, the ledger is the real instrument of exchange' exaggerates slightly, for even in quiet times disquieting debtors may be encountered. But most bills were likely given and taken merely for convenience, much as one uses a credit or charge card nowadays. Small bills were far from unusual. In 1597 Thomas Boulton, a merchant, and a hatter by trade, left bills for such sums as 18*s* and 28*s*. John Bolton, husbandman, held two specialties in 1627, one for £1 and the other for 4*s*. Most of the Liverpool bills were for small sums. They were given and taken in the normal course of business by ordinary people like maltsters, hatters, joiners, carpenters, shoemakers and blacksmiths.

What we witness in Liverpool and throughout England, is the bill as currency. Inland bill drawing was universal even amongst the smallest traders and manufacturers in the early eighteenth century, not that giving and taking bills was a new practice, but because long-dated inland bills of exchange had now mostly replaced bills obligatory. Ordinary small provincial traders now generally took and made full payment by inland bills whose tenor did not exceed the one customary in the trade engaged in. Nine tenths of Manchester business was done this way. Even after the rise of country banks with note issues, inland bills remained by far the greater part of the medium of circulation in Lancashire, Worcestershire and probably most industrial and commercial regions. Bank-notes came into use more rapidly in Somerset and, generally, in more purely agricultural districts. But, then, bank-notes were only a special kind of bill obligatory.[294]

Going back to the Liverpool inventories, out of the fifty-six that list specialties, many fail to show how much money, if any, was left behind. Disregarding widows and others who seem to be mere money-lenders or usurers, only seventeen inventories allow us to determine the ratio of money to specialties. Three farmers or cultivators give a ratio of 1:19; a mercer and two ironmongers of 1:16; and ten tradesmen and manufacturers of 1:4. Chronological differences seem to have been slight. What mattered most was the nature of the trade. Nine inventories tell us about the ratio of book debts to specialties. This, too, differed greatly between trades. Merchants, mercers and tailors, for example, tended to have about eight times as much owing by book as by specialty; but much depended on the trade cycle.

However, one firm conclusion may be drawn from these inventories: in this period the ratio of coin to credit was about 1 : 30.

We turn now to what falls somewhat short of a cross-section of 351 trusted inventories from various parts of the kingdom in the period 1538–1660.[295] They are only a small fraction of the thousands read, but in order to make up even this small number we have had to make do with 106 that refer simply to 'purse and apparel', twenty-one to 'purse, apparel and money' and one each to 'girdle and money in purse', 'money and books', 'clothes, saddle and money', 'purse, apparel, saddle, bridle and boots', 'purse, sword and apparel', 'purse, apparel, girdle and money', 'girdle, purse and money', 'purse, clothes and books', and 'purse, box and money in purse', and, finally, one where the money amounted not exactly but at most to £40. Occasionally foreign coins were amongst those appraised. It follows from the inclusion of items other than money that our figures tend to exaggerate the amount of money held, and if our assumption that all the purses contained money be unfounded, then this exaggeration will be so much the greater. We have omitted debts arising from rents, wages and legacies and all those that appear to derive from loans at usury or interest or from deposits with bankers. Debts owed by the testators are ignored altogether. We recognise that other students making similar surveys would achieve different numerical results, but remain confident that they would confirm our argument, which is all that concerns us.

We find that in the period 1538–1660 the ratio of money (coins) to debts by bond, bill obligatory and book was on average 1 : 9; among merchants, shipowners, merchant tailors and others of similar rank, 1 : 26; among farmers and cultivators, 1 : 6; among graziers, drapers, ironmongers, haberdashers, mercers, grocers and high-class shop-keepers, 1 : 7; among textile manufacturers, clothiers, bonelacemen, silkweavers, threadtwisters, yarnmasters, market spinners, maltsters, brewers, millers, tanners, whittawers, saddlers, fellmongers, wheelwrights and upholsterers, 1 : 5; among labourers, manual workers in textile trades, cutting butchers, bakers, small retailers, blacksmiths, locksmiths, curriers, tailors, shoemakers, cooks, sailors, mariners, glovers, domestic servants, servants in husbandry, petty chapmen, innholders and innkeepers, 1 : 3; among the lower landed gentry, 1 : 2. Ratios vary greatly between these groups, reflecting, in part, the varying degree of use made of inland bills of exchange, which do not come into the reckoning. In considering the general ratio of 1 : 9, we must remember that London inventories are but little represented here; they mostly perished in the Great Fire. The same is true of the inventories relating to the greater part of the higher ranks of landowners, merchants and others, for their wills were mostly proved in the Prerogative Court of Canterbury, whose records went the same way. Bearing in mind that the bigger of the London merchants between them dealt in all the commodities of the realm and the wider world, their almost complete omission is of the first importance. Were they included, we guess the general ratio would change to about 1:12; If we were then to add the moneylenders, usurers and bankers, who were an integral part of the financial structure, the ratio might be 1:15. The volume of inland bills of exchange is unknown, except that it must have been great and increasing. Their inclusion would probably change the general ratio to something like 1:20. Then we must not forget the mass of humble people, roughly the lower ranks of servants and self-employed, who engaged in hardly any credit transactions beyond deferred payment, pawning, personal loans, and the use of tokens. Yet, though they had little debt owing them, they had very little money either. Petty transactions were usually settled in leather, lead, or, later, brass and copper tokens, credit instruments even the most modest trader could make at will or buy from his borough or city government. In the mid-seventeenth century some ten or twelve million tokens were circulating, but few were for so much as a penny, so their total value could scarcely have exceeded £10,000. Nevertheless, their inclusion would raise the credit ratio.[296]

If we now re-arrange our data chronologically, we find the ratio of money to credit by bond, bill obligatory and book, in the period 1538–61, was 1:1; in the period 1563–89, 1:4·5; in 1590–1620, 1:12; in 1621–39, 1:11; in 1640–60, 1:6. Thus the price rises after the great recoinage coincided with a great upsurge of credit, even without taking inland bills of exchange into account.

In fine, the price rises in England were not caused by the influx of precious metals, but by the same forces that caused the prosperity, the upsurge of credit and the rise of banking and of the inland bill of exchange.

References

1 M. ROSTOVTZEFF, *Economic and Social History of the Hellenistic World* (3 vols., Oxford, 1941), I, 406; II, 1276 sqq.; *Social and Economic History of the Roman Empire* (2 vols., Oxford, 1947), I, 180–3; T. FRANK, *Economic History of Rome* (Baltimore, 1927), pp. 288–9; *Economic Survey of Ancient Rome* (6 vols., Baltimore, 1933–40), II, 445 sqq., III, 200, 310–13; iv, 224–5; M. M. AUSTIN and P. VIDAL-NAQUET, *Economic and Social History of Ancient Greece* (London, 1977), pp. 149, 292, 360, 370–1; A. P. USHER, 'Origins of Banking: primitive banks of deposit 1200–1600', *Economic History Review*, IV, 1934, pp. 401–2; *Early History of Deposit Banking in Mediterranean Europe* vol. I (Cambridge, Mass.), 1943, p. 4.

2 *Ibid.*, 4,237, 242, 246 sqq., 255; 'Origins', 399, 400, 404, 408; MATT. xxi.12; xxv.26–7; JN ii.14, 15; M. POSTAN and E. E. RICH (eds), *Cambridge Economic History of Europe* vol. II (Cambridge, 1952), pp. 108–9, 266–7, 286; R. S. LOPEZ and I. W. RAYMOND, *Medieval Trade in the Mediterranean World* (New York, 1955), pp. 16, 147–9, 418–19; R. DE ROOVER, *Business, Banking and Economic Thought in late medieval and early modern Europe* ed. J. Kirshner (Chicago and London, 1974), pp. 200–3, 213 sqq.; *Money, Banking and Credit in Medieval Bruges* (Cambridge, Mass., 1948), pp. 171–3, 185–6, 199, 202 sqq., 231–4, 247 sqq., 272, 275–6, 278–9, 281, 283, 293–5, 297 sqq., 303, 305–6, 308 sqq., 318 sqq., 331, 339–41, 346–8; *Gresham on Foreign Exchange* (Cambridge, Mass. and London, 1949), pp. 231 sqq.; M. W. HALL, 'Early Bankers in Genoese Notarial Archives', *Economic History Review*, VI, 1936, pp. 73 sqq.; T. W. BLOMQUIST, 'Dawn of Banking in an Italian Commune: 13th-century Lucca' in *Dawn of Modern Banking* (Center for Medieval and Renaissance Studies, University of California, New Haven and London, 1979), pp. 53 sqq.; 'Early History of European Banking: merchants, bankers and lombards of thirteenth-century Lucca in the county of Champagne', *Journal of European Economic History*, XIV, 1985, pp. 522–3, 526 sqq., 533–4, 536; R. A. GOLDTHWAITE, 'Local Banking in Renaissance Florence', *ibid.*, pp. 6 sqq.

3 ROSTOVTZEFF, *Hellenistic World*, I, 404–5; II, 1278–80, 1282–5; FRANK, *Ancient Rome*, IV, 224–5.

4 USHER, 'Origins', 403–5; *Deposit Banking*, 270–1, 278–9, 287, 295,

301–2, 304, 313, 318, 332, 334, 356 sqq., 369 sqq., 387, 391, 407, 422, 436, 442–5, 464–7, 473 sqq., 486 sqq., 501 sqq.; A. SMITH, *Wealth of Nations*, ed. E. Cannan (2 vols., London, 1961), I, 502 sqq.; J. G. VAN DILLEN (ed.), *History of the Principal Public Banks* (London, 1964), pp. 2 sqq., 39 sqq., 79 sqq., 161 sqq.; C. TE LINTUM, *De Merchant Adventurers in de Neder-landen* (The Hague, 1905), pp. 93, 112, 114, 205, 251; DE ROOVER, *Bruges*, 210, 280, 341, 351–2; *Business*, 215, 217–19, 223 sqq.

5 *Ibid.*, 39 sqq., 195, 204 sqq., 222–3, 230–1, 239 sqq.; *Bruges*, 11–13, 16, 17, 29 sqq., 48 sqq., 55 sqq., 72, 84, 86–9, 91, 314, 341, 349; *Rise and Decline of the Medici Bank 1397–1494* (Cambridge, Mass., 1968), pp. 2, 3, 8, 13, 16, 35–6, 39, 42–3, 47, 53, 55, 59, 70–1, 76–8, 80, 88, 95, 100–2, 109–11, 123–5, 132, 141, 143–4, 149 sqq., 195–6, 199, 201, 205, 210–11, 213, 224–5, 228, 239, 324, 326–9, 331 sqq., 338, 348, 353, 357 sqq., 370; *Gresham*, 104; M. PRESTWICH, 'Italian Merchants in late 13th and early 14th century England' in *Dawn of Modern Banking*, 77–80, 82–4, 86–8, 92, 95–6; BLOMQUIST, 'Dawn of Banking', *ibid.*, 53 sqq.; 'Early History', 523–6, 530–1, 535–6; R.S. LOPEZ, 'Dawn of Medieval Banking', *loc. cit.*, 12 sqq., 21; *The Commercial Revolution of the Middle Ages 950–1350* (Englewood Cliffs, N.J., 1970), pp. 56 sqq.; 'Trade of Medieval Europe' in *Cambridge Economic History of Europe*, II, 289 sqq.; E. RUSSELL, 'Societies of the Bardi and Peruzzi and their dealings with Edward III, 1327–45' in G. UNWIN (ed.), *Finance and Trade under Edward III* (Manchester, 1918), pp. 110–11, 115–16, 121–2, 126–7, 129–30, 144; UNWIN, 'Estate of Merchants, 1336–65', *ibid.*, 180, 200; USHER, 'Origins', 403, 406–7; R. EHRENBERG, *Capital and Finance in the Age of the Renaissance* (London, 1928), pp. 64 sqq.; W. E. RHODES, 'Italian Bankers in England and their loans to Edward I and Edward II' in T. F. TOUT and J. TAIT, *Historical Essays by Members of Owens College, Manchester* (London, 1902), pp. 138 sqq., 152–5; A. V. JUDGES, 'Philip Burlamachi: financier of the 30 Years War', *Economica*, VI, 1926, pp. 285 sqq.; 'Origins of English Banking', *History*, XVI, 1931, p. 141; E. B. FRYDE, 'Deposits of Hugh Despenser the younger with Italian Bankers', *Economic History Review*, 2nd ser., III, 1951, pp. 344 sqq.; R. J. WHITWELL, 'Italian Bankers and the English Crown', *Transactions of the Royal Historical Society*, XVII, 1893, pp. 175 sqq.; R. W. KAEUPER, *Bankers to the Crown: the Riccardi of Lucca and Edward I* (Princeton, N.J., 1973), pp. viii, 6, 8, 11, 12, 17, 20–1, 25–6, 34–5, 37, 41, 45 sqq., 76, 82–3, 86, 88, 91–2, 173 sqq., 209 sqq., 216, 219, 237, 239, 253; L. STONE, *An Elizabethan: Horatio Palavicino* (Oxford, 1956), pp. 3 sqq., 41 sqq., 71–2, 75–7, 85, 140–1, 184–5, 188 sqq.; R. ASHTON, *The Crown and the Money Market 1603–40* (Oxford, 1960), pp. 18 sqq.; H. VAN DER WEE, *Growth of Antwerp and the European Economy 14th–16th centuries* (3 vols., The Hague, 1963), II, 359; R. D. RICHARDS, *Early History of Banking in England* (London, 1929), pp. 3–6, 8, 9; 'Pioneers of Banking in England', *Economic History*, I, 1929, pp. 485 sqq.; E. T. POWELL, *Evolution of the Money Market 1385–1915* (London, 1915 and 1966), pp. 18, 86; also I. ORIGO, *Merchant of Prato: Francesco di Marco Datini* (London, 1957).

6 My 'Early Modern English Markets' in B. L. ANDERSON and A. J. H. LATHAM (eds), *The Market in History* (London, 1986), pp. 121, 144; L. VON MISES, *Human Action* (Chicago, 1966), pp. 257–8, 327; *Theory and History* (London, 1958), pp. 29, 30.

7 N. S. B. GRAS, *History of Agriculture in Europe and America* (London, n.d.), pp. 133–5, 137; *Evolution of the English Corn Market* (Cambridge, Mass., 1915), pp. 77, 95 sqq., 111 sqq., 188, 245, 256–8, 437; R. B. WESTERFIELD, *Middlemen in English Business 1660–1760* (Transactions of the Connecticut Academy of Arts and Sciences, XIX, New Haven, 1915), pp. 135–7, 145, 149, 152, 189–90, 205–6, 208, facing p. 328; A. P. USHER, *History of the Grain Trade in France 1400–1710* (Cambridge, Mass., 1913), frontis., pp. 3 sqq., 21, 37 sqq., 299, 362; R. MUNDAY, 'Legal History of the Factor', *Anglo-American Law Review*, VI, 1977, pp. 223, 230–2, 243; D. G. BARNES, *History of the English Corn Laws from 1660 to 1846* (London, 1930), p. 299; W. CAMDEN, *Britannia* ed. Gibson (London, 1695), col. 367; A. H. JOHN, 'English Agricultural Improvement and Grain Exports 1660–1765', in D. C. COLEMAN and A. H. JOHN (eds), *Trade, Government and Economy in Pre-Industrial England* (London, 1976), pp. 49, 56; D. DAVIS, *History of Shopping* (London and Toronto, 1966), pp. 60–3, 68–70, 74, 93–5, 100 sqq., 146 sqq., 181 sqq.; T. S. WILLAN, *Inland Trade* (Manchester, 1976), pp. 59 sqq., 77, 79 sqq.; W. B. STEPHENS, *Seventeenth Century Exeter: a study of industrial and commercial development, 1625– 1688* (Exeter, 1958), pp. 80–1; P. R. EDWARDS, 'Horse Trade in the Midlands in the 17th century', *Agricultural History Review*, XXVII, 1979, p. 92; R. REYCE, *Breviary of Suffolk*, (1618) ed. F. Hervey (London, 1902), pp. 32, 41; D. WOODWARD (ed.), *Farming and Memorandum Books of Henry Best of Elmswell 1642* (London, 1984), pp. 105–6, 118; E. LEIGH, *England Described* (London, 1659), pp. 181, 184; *Journals of the House of Commons*, XIII, 570, 720; my *Textile Manufactures in Early Modern England* (Manchester, 1985), pp. 149–50, 216–18; F. J. FISHER, 'Development of the London Food Market 1540–1640' in E. M. CARUS-WILSON, *Essays in Economic History* (London, 1954), pp. 149–50; cf. F. BRAUDEL, *Civilization and Capitalism: 15th–18th century* (3 vols., London, 1982–4), II, 26 sqq., 400 sqq.; III, 89 sqq., 280 sqq.

8 W. H. B. COURT, *Rise of the Midland Industries 1600–1838* (London, 1953), pp. 135 sqq.; T. S. WILLAN, *English Coasting Trade* (Manchester, 1938), pp. 97–8; M. G. DAVIES, *Enforcement of English Apprenticeship: a study in applied mercantilism 1563–1642* (Cambridge, Mass., 1956), pp. 136–7; M. B. ROWLANDS, *Masters and Men in the West Midland Metal Trades before the Industrial Revolution* (Manchester, 1975), pp. 11, 12, 75; P. RIDEN (ed.), *George Sitwell's Letterbook 1662–66* (Derbyshire Record Society, X, 1985), pp. vii, xii, xix, xliv; Cheshire R. O., Cholmondeley Coll., box K, Vouchers to Account 1698–1700, no 39.

9 J. U. NEF, *Rise of the British Coal Industry* (2 vols., London, 1932), I, facing page 19, pp. 81–2, 110–11, 444–5; WILLAN, *Coasting Trade*, 60 sqq., 210–11; P. MILLICAN, *History of Horstead and Stallinghall* (Norwich, 1937), p. 118; N. J. WILLIAMS, 'Maritime Trade of the East Anglian Ports 1550–1590', typescript thesis D. Phil., Oxford University,

1952, pp. 162sqq.; R. SMITH, *Sea-Coal for London: history of the coal factors in the London market* (London, 1961), pp. 45–7.

10 J. YOUINGS, *Dissolution of the Monasteries* (London, 1971), pp. 126sqq.; S. J. MADGE, *Domesday of Crown Lands* (London, 1938), pp. 59, 210, 216, 220–1, 224; J. THIRSK, 'Sales of Royalist Land during the Interregnum', *Economic History Review*, 2nd ser., V, 1952, pp. 191–4, 196–7, 204; D. C. COLEMAN, 'London Scriveners and the Estate Market in the later 17th century', *ibid.*, IV, 1951, pp. 222sqq.

11 A. D. DYER, 'Market Towns of Southern England 1500–1700', *Southern History*, I, 1979, pp. 123sqq.; W. HARRISON, 'Description of England' in R. HOLINSHED, W. HARRISON and J. HOOKER, *Chronicles* (3 vols., London, 1587), I, 203; WILLAN, *Inland Trade*, 77; J. MORTON, *Natural History of Northamptonshire* (London, 1712), p. 22; J. H. HAMER, 'Trading at Saint White Down Fair, 1637–49', *Somerset Archaeology and Natural History* (Proceedings of the Somerset Archaeological and Natural History Society), CXII, 1968, pp. 61sqq.; C. M. GARRARD, 'Taunton Fair in the Seventeenth Century', *ibid.*, CXXVIII, 1984, pp. 66–7; EDWARDS, 'Horse Trade', 92sqq.; J. A. CHARTRES, 'Marketing of Agricultural Produce' in H. P. R. FINBERG and J. THIRSK, *Agrarian History of England and Wales* (8 vols., Cambridge, 1967– in progress), V, part 2, pp. 409sqq.; C. W. CHALKLIN, *Seventeenth-century Kent: a social and economic history* (London, 1965), pp. 162–4; W. SMITH, *Particular Description of England, 1588*, ed. H. B. Wheatley and E. W. Ashbee (London, 1879), pp. 65–8; Wiltshire R.O., Accession 88, Charlton Estate Papers, Remembrance Book; Bodleian Lib., Aubrey MSS, vol. 2, fos 149–51.

12 H. FISHWICK, *Survey of the Manor of Rochdale 1626* (Chetham Society, new ser., LXXI, 1913), p. ix; D. H. WILLSON (ed.), *Parliamentary Diary of Robert Bowyer 1606–1607* (Minneapolis, 1931), p. 34; D. DEFOE, *Tour through England and Wales* (2 vols., London, 1928), I, 210; T. C. MENDENHALL, *Shrewsbury Drapers and the Welsh Wool Trade in the XVI and XVII Centuries* (London, 1953), p. 223; R. GOUGH, *History of Myddle* (Sunninghill, Ascot, 1979), pp. 3, 4, 81; T. CAVE and R. A. WILSON, *Parliamentary Survey of the Lands and Possessions of the Dean and Chapter of Worcester* (Worcestershire Historical Society, 1924), p. 131; T. G. BARNES, *Somerset 1625–1640: a county's government during the 'personal rule'* (London, n.d.), p. 4; M. POSTLETHWAYT, *Universal Dictionary of Trade and Commerce, translated from the French of M. Savary, with large editions and improvements* (2 vols., London, 1757), I, 768; II, 350, 848–9; C. BROWN, *Annals of Newark-on-Trent* (London, 1879), p. 88; R. BLOME, *Britannia* (London, 1673), p. 207; R. DAVIES, *Life of Marmaduke Rawdon of York* (Camden Society, LXXXV, 1863), p. 128; J. THOMSON, *History of Leicester* (Leicester, 1849), p. 304; J. CHARLESWORTH, *Wakefield Manor Book 1709* (Yorkshire Archaeological Society Record Series, CI, 1939), p. 52; W. BEAUMONT, 'Some Instructions given by William Booth esquire to his stewards John Carrington and William Rowcrofte upon the purchase of Warrington by Sir George Booth bart. and William Booth his son, A.D. 1628', in *Miscellanies relating to Lancashire and Cheshire vol. III* (Chetham Society, LVII, 1862), p. 4; STEPHENS, *Exeter*, 143; R. POCOCKE, *Travels* *through England of Dr Richard Pococke, successively bishop of Meath and Ossory, during 1750, 1751, and later years* (2 vols., Camden Society, new ser., XLII, XLIV, 1888–9), I, 166; II, 58; K. J. BONSER, *Drovers* (London, 1970), pp. 126, 128–30, 133, 135, 137–9, 143, 183; D. WOODWARD, *op. cit.*, 117–20; J. DE L. MANN, *Documents Illustrating the Wiltshire Textile Trades in the Eighteenth Century* (Wiltshire Record Society, XIX, 1963), p. 24; M. W. BARLEY, *Lincolnshire and the Fens* (London, 1952), p. 81; CHARTRES, 'Marketing', 420 sqq.; Leicester Museum MS 35/29/378; Denbighshire R.O. (Clwyd R.O.), Denbigh Borough Records, A. 120; Bodleian Lib., Aubrey MSS, vol. 2 fo 148; British Lib. (B.L.), Harleian MSS 3696 fo. 25; 4716 fo. 8v.; Worcestershire R.O. (Herefordshire and Worcestershire R.O.), 705: 128 (BA 1188), parcel I, particular of Bromsgrove c. 1660; Public Record Office (P.R.O.), Exchequer, Treasury of Receipt, Books 148, p. 27; 157 fo. 8 (p. 17); Land Revenue, Miscellaneous Books 185 fo. 59; 255 fo. 78; 285 fo. 163; Augmentation Office, Parliamentary Surveys, Bedfordshire 19 fo. 1; Cheshire 19 fo. 1; Nottinghamshire 19 fos 1, 2; 27 fo. 2.

13 *Ibid.*, Leicestershire 7 fo. 3; Monmouthshire 7 fo. 2; 9 fo. 2; Land Revenue, Misc. Books 186 f. 9v.; 255 fos 77–8; Duchy of Lancaster, Misc. Book 117 fo. 188; Gloucestershire R.O., D.36/N.19; Northamptonshire R.O., Fitzwilliam (Milton) Coll., Miscellaneous Vol. 433, pp. 14, 15; T. S. WILLAN, *River Navigation in England 1600–1750* (London, 1964), pp. 23, 26, 38, 42, 50–1, 66, 71–2, 74, 91, 111, 114 sqq., 122, 126–8, 130; W. M. and F. MARCHAM, *Court Rolls of the Bishop of London's Manor of Hornsey 1603–1701* (London, 1929), p. xxii; J. STRADLING, *Storie of the Lower Borowes of Merthyrmawr*, ed. H. J. Randall and W. Rees (South Wales and Monmouthshire Record Society, I, n.d.), end map; J. BRADNEY, *History of Monmouthshire* (4 vols., London, 1904–34), II, part 1, p. 21; *Journals of the House of Lords*, VI, 47.

14 Northamptonshire R.O., Misc. Ledger 138, pp. 89, 90; Leicestershire R.O., DE.23/2/45; P.R.O., Exch., Land Revenue, Misc. Book 220 fo. 284; Augmentation Office, Parliamentary Surveys, Cornwall 29 fo. 4; Oxfordshire 12 fo. 32; B.L., Lansdowne MS 758 fo. 2 (pp. 1, 2); H. STOCKS, *Records of the Borough of Leicester 1603–88* (Cambridge, 1923), pp. 142–4, 183.

15 *Ibid.*, 142–4, 183, 427; *Journals of the House of Lords*, VI, 47; W. MARSHALL, *Rural Economy of Glocestershire* (2 vols., Gloucester, 1789), I, 109–10; P. J. BOWDEN, *Wool Trade in Tudor and Stuart England* (London, 1962), pp. 94–5; S.H.A.H. (ed.), *Letter-Books of John Hervey First Earl of Bristol 1651–1750* (3 vols., Wells, 1894), I, 71; T. ROBINSON, *Essay towards a Natural History of Westmorland and Cumberland* (London, 1709), p. 48.

16 My *Agricultural Revolution* (London, 1967), pp. 111–12, 133, 153–4, 165, 180, 244; WILLAN, *Inland Trade*, 2 sqq.; J. CROFTS, *Packhorse, Waggon and Post* (London, 1967), pp. 1 sqq., 9, 10, 45–6; W. T. JACKMAN, *Development of Transportation in Modern England* (London, 1962), pp. 32–3; FISHER, 'London Food Market', 150; DEFOE, *Tour*, I, 99; II, 117–18, 121–2, 127–8, 130–1; C. FIENNES, *Journeys* ed. C. Morris (London, 1947), pp. 192, 194, 245, 251, 264–5, 271; J. STOW, *Survey of London*, ed. H. B. Wheatley (London, 1956), p. 168; E. G. R. TAYLOR,

'Leland's England' in H.C.DARBY, *Historical Geography of England before 1800* (Cambridge, 1948), pp. 337 sqq.; J. N. L. BAKER, 'England in the 17th century', *ibid.*, 426–9; J. AUBREY, *Natural History of Wiltshire*, ed. J. Britton (London, 1847), p. 115; MORTON, *op. cit.*, 18; R. H. COX, *Green Roads of England* (London, 1927), facing pp. 18, 36, 142, 174; C. SKEEL, 'Cattle Trade between England and Wales from the Fifteenth to the Nineteenth Centuries', *Transactions of the Royal Historical Society*, 4th ser., IX, 1926, pp. 145–8; FITZHERBERT, *Boke of Surveyinge and Improvementes* (London, 1535), fo. 53v.; B. AUSTEN, *English Provincial Posts 1633–1840: a study based on Kent examples* (London and Chichester, 1978), pp. 24, 27–8; NEF, *Coal Industry*, I, 380–4; J. COX, *Records of the Borough of Northampton*, vol. II (Northampton, 1898), pp. 197, 201–2; F. M. STENTON, 'Road Systems of Medieval England', *Economic History Review*, VII, 1936, p. 20; MENDENHALL, *op. cit.*, 34; M. E. JAMES (ed.), *Estate Accounts of the Earl of Northumberland 1562–1637* (Surtees Society, CLXIII, 1955), p. liv; D. HEY, *Packmen, Carriers and Packhorse Roads: trade and communication in north Derbyshire and south Yorkshire* (Leicester, 1980), pp. 86 sqq.; J. TAYLOR, *New Discovery by Sea*, reprinted in *Miscellanea Antiqua Anglicana*, vol. III (London, 1873), pp. 25–6; W. MARSHALL, *Rural Economy of the West of England* (2 vols., London, 1796), I, 30–1; II, 227; B.L., Lansdowne MS 691 fo. 20(21); Cheshire R.O., Quarter Sessions Records, Quarter Session Book 1695–1708, 9 Apr. 7 Wm 3; P.R.O., State Papers Domestic (S.P.D.), Charles, vol. 182 no 67; vol. 379 no 61; vol. 380 no 83.

17 FIENNES, *op. cit.*, 120, 147, 155, 177, 184, 226, 250; Historical Manuscripts Commission (H.M.C.), *13th Report*, Appendix, part II (London, 1893), p. 291; J. LELAND, *Itinerary*, ed. L. T. Smith (5 vols., London, 1906–10), I, 170, 299; II, 58; IV, 192; V, 110, 144; J. OGILBY, *Britannia* (London, 1675), p. 130; B. G. CHARLES (ed.), *Calendar of the Records of the Borough of Haverfordwest 1539–1660* (Cardiff, 1967), p. 185; DEFOE, *Tour*, II, 119–20; T. PROCTER, *A Profitable Worke to this whole Kingdome* (London, 1610); TAYLOR, 'Leland's England', 341–2; GOUGH, *op. cit.*, 21; Statute 1 Mary statute 3 capita 5, 6; Lancashire R.O., Kenyon of Peel Correspondence 19/32; B. L., Harleian MS 4716 fo. 4; Bodleian Lib., Hearne's Diaries, 158 p. 14.

18 J. PARKES, *Travel in England in the Seventeenth Century* (Oxford, 1925), pp. 7, 22–3; N. BACON, *Annalls of Ipswiche*, ed. W. H. Richardson (Ipswich, 1884), p. 331; J. F. LARKIN and P. L. HUGHES (eds), *Stuart Royal Proclamations* (2 vols., Oxford, 1973–83), I, 396, 551–2; II, 487–9; R. STEELE, *Bibliography of the Royal Proclamations of the Tudor and Stuart Sovereigns* (2 vols., Oxford, 1910), I, 205; A. H. A. HAMILTON, *Quarter Sessions from Queen Elizabeth to Queen Anne* (London, 1878), pp. 270–1; my *Agricultural Revolution*, 36, 179–80; ANON., *Reasons Humbly Offered to the Honorable House of Commons, Why Wagoners ought not to be obliged to a certain Weight* (sine loco nec data); *Case of Richard Fielden, in relation to the Petition of the Waggoners* (s.l.n.d.); *Case of John Littlebales, against the pretended Petition of the Waggoners travelling the Northern Roads of England* (s.l.n.d.); P.R.O., S.P.D., James 14/55; Charles 170/28; CROFTS, *op. cit.*, 19.

19 *Ibid.*, 7, 9–11, 19; W. MARSHALL, *Rural Economy of Yorkshire* (2 vols., London, 1788), II, 273; N. BACON, *op. cit.*, 311, 331, 447; NEF, *Coal Industry*, I, 101–2, 381–4; MORTON, *op. cit.*, 71; R. PLOT, *Natural History of Oxfordshire* (Oxford, 1677), p. 257; FIENNES, *op. cit.*, 8; R. H. TAWNEY and E. POWER, *Tudor Economic Documents* (3 vols., London, 1924), I, 193; STOCKS, *op. cit.*, 168, 240–1, 462; J. HARLAND (ed.), *House and Farm Accounts of the Shuttleworths of Gawthorpe Hall* (Chetham Society, XXXV, XLI, XLIII, XLVI, 1856–8), pp. 49, 50, 103, 194; STOW, *op. cit.*, 77; E. LODGE (ed.), *Illustrations of British History* (3 vols., London, 1838), III, 20, 29; F. P. VERNEY (ed.), *Memoirs of the Verney Family during the Civil War* (3 vols., London, 1892), I, 259; D. WOODWARD, *op. cit.*, 121; J. W. BURGON, *Life and Times of Sir Thomas Gresham* (2 vols., London, [1839], I, 241–2, 486–7; Leicestershire R.O., DE. 10 Beaumanor Coll., Court Roll of Beaumanor 30 Mar. 1 Chas; B.L., Additional MS 34162 fo. 63; Harleian MS 7186 fos 17, 18.

20 CROFTS, *op. cit.*, 17, 19; JACKMAN, *op. cit.*, 33–6, 52–3, 58 sqq., 65; K. H. BURLEY, 'Economic Development of Essex in the later 17th and early 18th centuries', ts. thesis, Ph.D., London University, 1957, pp. 195, 197–8; J. A. CHARTRES, 'Road Carrying in England in the 17th century: myth and reality', *Economic History Review*, 2nd ser., XXX, 1977, p. 74; E. C. K. GONNER, *Common Land and Inclosure* (London, 1912), pp. 83–5, 300, end maps; HAMILTON, *op. cit.*, 271–2; DEFOE, *Tour*, II, 121 sqq.; R. A. PELHAM, 'Fourteenth-century England' in DARBY, *op. cit.*, 260; TAYLOR, 'Leland's England', *ibid.*, 342; J. N. L. BAKER, 'England in the 17th century', *ibid.*, 427–9; S. and B. WEBB, *Story of the King's Highway* (London, 1963), pp. 20–1, 115; LARKIN and HUGHES, *op. cit.*, I, 396; II, 487–9; W. MATHER, *Of Repairing and Mending the Highways* (London, 1696), pp. 11, 29; PROCTER, *op. cit.*; Statutes 2 and 3 Philip and Mary c. 8; 5 Elizabeth c. 13; 18 Eliz. c. 10; 27 Eliz. c. 19; 29 Eliz. c. 5; 39 Eliz. c. 19; 14 Charles 2 c. 6; 22 Chas 2 c. 12; 3 William and Mary c. 12; 8 and 9 Wm 3 c. 6; *Journals of the House of Commons*, XIX, 227, 381; WILLAN, *Insland Trade*, 3; W. ALBERT, *Turnpike Road System in England 1663–1840* (Cambridge, 1972), pp. 14 sqq.; E. PAWSON, *Transport and Economy: the turnpike roads of eighteenth century Britain* (London and New York, 1977), pp. 71, 76 sqq.

21 B.L., Lansdowne MS 691 fos 16, 17 (17, 18) (13, 15); Manchester R.O., M91/M1/26.

22 *Ibid.*; HEY, *op. cit.*, 211; G. L. TURNBULL, *Traffic and Transport: an economic history of Pickfords* (London, 1979), p. 6; 'Provincial Road Carrying in England in the 18th century', *Journal of Transport History*, IV, 1977, pp. 20 sqq.; J. TAYLOR, *Carriers Cosmographie* (London, 1637); CHALKLIN, *op. cit.*, 165, 186; CROFTS, *op. cit.*, 40, 43, 47, 49, 51; BURLEY, *op. cit.* 217–18; D. DAVIS, *op. cit.*, 144–5, 226, 228, 231; T. S. WILLAN, *Elizabethan Manchester* (Chetham Society, 3rd ser., XXVII, 1980), p. 126; *Inland Trade*, 5 sqq., 11–14, 21; D. GARDINER (ed.), *Oxinden Letters 1607–42* (London, 1933), pp. 83, 105; STEPHENS, *op. cit.*, 133; A. D. DYER, *City of Worcester in the Sixteenth Century* (Leicester, 1973), p. 105; H.M.C., *14th Report*, App. pt VIII (London, 1895), p. 141;

CHARTRES, 'Road Carrying', 74 sqq.; M. BATESON (ed.), *Records of the Borough of Leicester* (3 vols., Cambridge, 1899–1905), III, 115; D. DAWE, *Skilbecks: drysalters 1650–1950* (London, 1950), p. 9; E. POWELL (ed.), 'Pryce (Newton Hall) Correspondence etc.', *Collections Historical and Archaeological relating to Montgomeryshire*, XXXI, 1900, p. 83; STOCKS, *op. cit.*, 222; VERNEY, *op. cit.*, I, 233, 235; E. LODGE, *op. cit.*, III, 15, 26; LELAND, *op. cit.*, I, 10; GOUGH, *op. cit.*, 83, 160–1; J. S. PURVIS, *Select XVI Century Causes in Tithe from the York Diocesan Registry* (Yorkshire Archaeological Society Record Series, CXIV, 1949 [1947]), p. 86; HARLAND, *op. cit.*, 67, 221; C. R. HUDLESTON (ed.), *Naworth Estate and Household Accounts 1648–60* (Surtees Society, CLXVIII, 1958 [1953]), pp. 30, 36–7, 42, 50–1, 81–2, 120, 148–9, 195–6, 232; D. R. HAINS-WORTH (ed.), *Correspondence of Sir John Lowther of Whitehaven 1693–8: a provincial community in wartime* (London, 1983), pp. 123, 125–6, 146, 152, 321, 377, 393; N. J. WILLIAMS, *Tradesmen in Early Stuart Wiltshire* (Wiltshire Record Society, XV, 1960 [1959]), pp. 19, 35, 37; JOHN MILTON, 'On the University Carrier'; STEELE, *op. cit.*, I, 144; Northamptonshire R.O., Fitzwilliam (Milton) Coll., Misc. 225 fo. 15v.; Hampshire R.O., Winchester City Records, Chamberlain's Accounts Michaelmas 21 Jas-Michaelmas 22 Jas; B.L., Additional MSS 34258 fo. 7; 36908 fo. 45; Harleian MSS 570 fo. 15; 4716 fo. 8; Bodleian Lib., Aubrey MSS vol. 2 fo. 89; Hearne's Diaries, 159 p. [181]; P.R.O., Exchequer, Land Revenue, Particulars of Grants, Leases etc. vol. 15 fo. 166 (161).

23 CROFTS, *op. cit.*, 40; HUDLESTON, *op. cit.*, 42; WILLAN, *Inland Trade*, 76, 82–3; Lancashire R.O., Petre of Dunkenhalgh Coll., account book starting 1630, at 1635; Northamptonshire R.O., Fitzwilliam (Milton) Coll., Miscellaneous Vol. 20, housekeeping account 1638.

24 D. WOODWARD, *op. cit.*, 108; H. C. JOHNSON (ed.), *Minutes of Proceedings in Sessions 1563 and 1574 to 1592* (Wiltshire Record Society, IV, 1949), pp. 1 sqq.; E. S. GODFREY, *Development of English Glassmaking 1560–1640* (Oxford, 1975), p. 182; W. SMITH and W. WEBB, *Vale Royall of England* (London, 1656), p. 18; J. SMYTH, *Names and Surnames of all the Able and Sufficient Men in the Body fit for His Majesty's Service in the Wars, within the County of Gloucester ... in the month of August 1608* (London, 1902), pp. 109, 138–9; H.M.C., *Report on Manuscripts in Various Collections* (8 vols., London, 1901–14), I, 166, 173.

25 W. NOTESTEIN, F. H. RELF and H. SIMPSON (eds), *Commons Debates 1621* (7 vols., New Haven, 1935), VII, 45.

26 TAYLOR, *Carriers Cosmographie*; STEPHENS, *op. cit.*, 133; J. SMYTH, *Description of the Hundred of Berkeley* Berkeley MSS, III ed. J. Maclean (Gloucester, 1885), p. 30; J. D. MARSHALL, 'Kendal in the late 17th and 18th centuries', *Transactions of the Cumberland and Westmorland Antiquarian and Archaeological Society*, new series, LXXV, 1975, p. 196; J. RAINE (ed.), *Wills and Inventories from the Registry of the Archdeacon of Richmond* (Surtees Society, XXXVI, 1853), p. 107; BURLEY, 'Economic Development of Essex', p. 310.

27 SMITH and WEBB, *op. cit.*, 18; B.L., Sloane MS 3815 fo. 79 (p. 173).

28   CROFTS, *op. cit.*, 29 sqq., 47; N. BACON, *op. cit.*, 331, 453–4, 476–8; TURNBULL, *Traffic and Transport*, 6, 9; 'Provincial Road Carrying', 21; A. H. A. HAMILTON, *op. cit.*, 259–60; H.M.C., *14th Report*, pt VIII (London, 1895), p. 141; G. A. THORNTON, *History of Clare, Suffolk* (Cambridge, 1930), p. 207; J. W. HORROCKS (ed.), *Assembly Books of Southampton* (4 vols., Southampton, 1917–25), I, 70, 94, 101; III, 35, 49, 60; W. ALBERT, 'Justices' Rates for Land Carriage 1748–1827', *Transport History*, I, 1968, pp. 105–6; Hampshire R.O., Winchester City Records, Chamberlain's Accounts for 21–22 Jas.

29   WILLAN, *River Navigation*, frontis., 32, 68, 84 sqq., 119 *et passim*, and *Inland Trade*, 14 sqq. are drawn on hevily here; also T. GERARD, *Particular Description of the County of Somerset (1633)*, ed. E. H. Bates (Somerset Record Society, XV, 1900), p. 209; TAYLOR, *Carriers Cosmographie*, ad fin.; W. P. W. PHILLIMORE and G. S. FRY, *Abstracts of Gloucestershire Inquisitiones Post Mortem in the Reign of King Charles the First* (3 pts [vols.], Index Lib., British Record Society, 1893–9), II, 51; Statute 3 Jas c. 20; W. T. MacCAFFREY, *Exeter, 1540–1640* (Cambridge, Mass. and London, 1975), pp. 19, 23, 68, 126 sqq., 180; STEPHENS, *op. cit.*, 133; T. G. BARNES, *op. cit.*, 8; COURT, *op. cit.*, 10; C. C. OWEN, 'Early History of the Upper Trent Navigation', *Transport History*, I, 1968, pp. 233 sqq.; MENDENHALL, *op. cit.*, 36; BURLEY, 'Economic Development of Essex', 190–1; B. F. DUCKHAM, *Yorkshire Ouse: the history of a river navigation* (Newton Abbot, 1967), pp. 37 sqq., 43 sqq., 59 sqq.; *Inland Waterways of East Yorkshire 1700–1900* (East Yorkshire Local History Society, XXIX, 1973), pp. 7, 46–8; 'The Fitzwilliams and the Navigation of the Yorkshire Derwent', *Northern History*, II, 1967, pp. 45 sqq.; MORTON, *op. cit.*, 5, 16, 484; I. S. BECKWITH, 'River Trade of Gainsborough 1500–1850', *Lincolnshire History and Archaeology*, no 2, 1967, pp. 3, 4; Liverpool R.O., Norris Papers (920 NOR), 1/37, 133; P.R.O., S.P.D., Chas 313/17; 321/38; 331/30; Privy Council Register, 1637–8, pp. 48–9, 74 (fos 22v.–3,35v.); Exch., Land Revenue, Misc. Book 201 fo. 176; Northamptonshire R.O., Fitzwilliam (Milton) Coll., Misc. 225 fo. 6v.; Westmorland Coll., box 5, found loose, Woodston Court Roll 16 Sept. 25 Eliz.; Misc. Ledger 145, p. 541; John Rylands Lib., English MS 216 fo. 17; Bodleian Lib., Aubrey MSS vol. 3 fo. 84v. (p. 83); Deene House, Brudenell MS O.xxii.4 fo. 123v.; B.L., Harleian MS 702 fo. 1. For mud-dredgers, see BURLEY, *op. cit.*, 99; B.L., Lansdowne MS 691 fo. 19(20); Norfolk R.O., Norwich City Records, Mayor's Court Book 20 fo. 394v.

30   WILLAN, *Inland Trade*, 1, 2, 21–2; *River Navigation*, 119 sqq.; B.L., Lansdowne MS 691 fo. 20(21); P.R.O., S.P.D., Chas 321/38; 331/30.

31   NEF, *Coal Industry*, I, map facing page 19; MORTON, *op. cit.*, 16.

32   H.M.C., *MSS in Various Colls*, VIII, 96.

33   P.R.O., Exch., Treasury of Receipt, Book 157 fo. 8 (p. 17); B.L., Additional MS 14850 fo. 151; Gloucestershire R.O., D.326/E.1 fo. 89v.

34   WILLAN, *Coasting Trade*, *passim*; *Inland Trade*, 7 sqq., 20; D. WOODWARD, *op. cit.*, 105; L. A. HARPER, *English Navigation Laws: a 17th-century experiment in social engineering* (New York, 1939), pp. 335–6, 339, 390–2; NEF, *Coal Industry*, I, 79 sqq.; Statute 13 Anne c. 20 par. 19;

P.R.O., S.P.D., Chas 182/67; Norfolk R.O., Archdeaconry Court of Norwich, inventory 1674–5/24.

35 STEPHENS, *op. cit.*, 143; POCOCKE, *op. cit.*, II, 20; CHALKLIN, *op. cit.*, 160; D. DAVIS, *op. cit.*, 92–5, 100 sqq., 145 sqq., 171 sqq., 191 sqq., 216 sqq.; WILLAN, *Elizabethan Manchester*, 74–5; *Inland Trade*, 60 sqq., 79 sqq., 89 sqq.; Norfolk R.O., inventories: Consistory Court of Norwich, 1631/18; Archdeaconry Court of Norwich, 1706–7/30; Peculiar Court of the Dean and Chapter, 1727–37/21; Bodleian Lib., MS Top. Devon b.9; Suffolk R.O. (Ipswich) Archdeaconry of Suffolk inv. 1 (390/16); 3/144; Leicestershire R.O., Archdeaconry of Leicester inv. Ric. Byllyng 1561 St Mary's, Leicester; Middlesex R.O., Archdeaconry Court of Middlesex (Middlesex Division) invs: John Hoptkins 1673, William Williams 1676, John Meades 1678 – all of St Clement Danes; P.R.O., Privy Council Register 1637–8, p. 179 (fo. 87).

36 ANDERTON, 'Delaval Papers', 151–2; AUSTEN, *op. cit.*, 56.

37 H. ROBINSON, *British Post Office: a history* (Princeton, N.J., 1948), pp. 5, 12; CROFTS, *op. cit.*, 39, 40, 46, 49, 51 sqq., 62; D. GARDINER, *op. cit.*, 105; A. H. A. HAMILTON, *op. cit.*, 116; HARLAND, *op. cit.*, 221; VERNEY, *op. cit.*, I, 233, 235; P.R.O., S.P.D., Chas 379/61; 380/80, 83; 459/81; Kent R.O., Consistory Ct of Canterbury, Register of Accounts and Inventories 5 fo. 67 v.; Archdeaconry Ct of Canterbury, Inventory Register 7 fos 252, 259, 295 v.; R. E. G. and E. F. KIRK, *Returns of Aliens dwelling in the City and Suburbs of London from the reign of Henry VIII to that of James I*, Pubs of Huguenot Society of London, X, in 4 pts, 1900–1908, pt III, 163; J. N. MILTON, 'On the University Carrier – another of the same'; TAYLOR, *Carriers Cosmographie*; E. A. PARRY, *Letters from Dorothy Osborne to Sir Wm Temple 1652–54*, London, n.d., pp. 46, 53–5, 82, 85, 93, 191, 199, 200, 220; HUDLESTON, *op. cit.*, 32, 44 sqq., 95 sqq., 127–8, 161–2, 202–3.

38 *Ibid.*, 18, 32, 44, 46, 95 sqq., 127–8, 160–2, 202–3; CROFTS, *op. cit.*, 58 sqq., 65 sqq., 75–8, 84–7, 90–2, 94 sqq.; H. ROBINSON, *op. cit.*, 7, 17, 31–2, 65–6; MacCAFFREY, *op. cit.*, 241; STOCKS, *op. cit.*, 39; E. LODGE, *op. cit.*, III, 159–61; NEF, *Coal Industry*, I, 145; Statute 2 and 3 Edward 6 c. 3; AUSTEN, *op. cit.*, 2 sqq., 35–7, 41 sqq., 104–5; H.M.C., *Calendar of the Manuscripts of the Marquess of Salisbury at Hatfield House*, several pts, London, 1883– in progress, XIX, 324; Colchester Town Hall, Borough Assembly Book 1576–99, at 31 May 33 Eliz.; *Calendar of Treasury Papers 1697–1701/2*, Rolls ser., London, 1871, pp. 307–8; P.R.O., S.P.D. Jas 146/93; Chas 378/45; 379/37,61; 380/80–3; 383/42.

39 *Ibid.*, 378/45; 380/80–3; 383/42; Norfolk R.O., City Records, Assembly Book 5 fo. 32(42) v.; TURNBULL, *Traffic and Transport*, 12; cf. *Reasons Humbly Offered to the Honorable House of Commons, Why the Wagoners ought not to be obliged to any Certain Weight.*

40 My *Textile Manufactures*, 214 sqq.

41 *Ibid.*, 142 sqq.

42 P. KALM, *Kalm's Account of his Visit to England* (London, 1892), p. 205; my *Agrarian Problems in the Sixteenth Century and After* (London, 1969), pp. 96 sqq., 105, 109, 112–13, 115, 117 sqq., 130, 164 sqq., 176, 180,

182, 184–6, 188–91; my *Agricultural Revolution*, 45–6, 60, 65, 68, 71, 87, 89, 92, 115, 148, 195, 213–14, 216 sqq.

43 *Ibid.*, 116; D. WOODWARD, *op. cit.*, 48, 53, 57, 104–5; MORTON, *op. cit.*, 479; AUBREY, *Natural History of Wiltshire*, 36; Bodleian Lib., Aubrey MSS 1 fo. 62(59); 2 fo. 84; Hearne's Diaries 158, pp. 33, 82; R. PLOT, *Natural History of Staffordshire* (Oxford, 1686), p. 348; *Natural History of Oxfordshire*, 152–3; E. LISLE, *Observations in Husbandry* (London, 1757), pp. 83, 147–50, 165–7, 169; W. BLITH, *English Improver Improved* (London, 1652), p. 128; J. LAURENCE, *New System of Agriculture* (London, 1726), p. 96; W. MARSHALL, *Review (and Complete Abstract) of the Reports to the Board of Agriculture from the Midland Department of England* (London, 1815), p. 139; *Rural Economy of the Midland Counties* 2 vols., London, 1790), II, 214; W. FOLKINGHAM, *Feudigraphia: the synopsis or epitome of surveying* (London, 1610), p. 42; J. BILLINGSLEY, *General View of the Agriculture of the County of Somerset* (London, 1798), p. 279; GRAS, *English Corn Market*, 403 sqq.; H. GILL and E. L. GUILFORD, *Rector's Book of Clayworth 1672–1701* (Nottingham, 1910), p. 42; H. C. BRENTNALL, 'Document from Great Cheverell', *Wiltshire Archaeological Magazine*, LIII, 1950, p. 437; R. V. LENNARD, 'English Agriculture under Charles II: the evidence of the Royal Society's "Enquiries"', *Economic History Review*, IV, 1943–4, reprinted in W. E. MINCHINTON (ed.), *Essays in Agrarian History* (2 vols., Newton Abbot, 1968), I, 177; R. CAREW, *Survey of Cornwall (1602)* (London, 1769), fo. 20; J. RAY, *Historia Plantarum* (3 vols., London, 1686–1704), I, 891–2 (recte) 891–4 (erron.); II, 1243; Bristol University Lib., Shrewton MS 37; H.M.C., *Portland MSS*, II, 276; Lancashire R.O., Petre of Dunkenhalgh Coll., 1: account book starting 1616, at 7 Feb. 1616; Derby of Knowsley MSS 1542/2; Somerset R.O., DD/SH, Natural History of Somerset, sect. 116; Berkshire R.O., D/EP2 E2/2.

44 Suffolk R.O. (Bury St Edmunds) Episcopal Consistory Court for Bury St Edmunds (with Archdeaconry of Sudbury) inv. 1702/5; MORTON, *op. cit.*, 483; my *Agricultural Revolution*, 284–5.

45 *Ibid.*, 319; T. FULLER, *History of the Worthies of England* ed. P. A. Nuttall (3 vols., London, 1840), I, 193; A. CAMPLING, *History of the Family of Drury* (London, n.d.), p. 72; B. WINCHESTER, *Tudor Family Portrait* (London, 1955), p. 173; K. J. ALLISON, 'Wool Supply and the Worsted Cloth Industry in Norfolk in the 16th and 17th centuries', ts. thesis, Ph.D., Leeds University, 1955, p. 326; M. E. FINCH, *Wealth of Five Northamptonshire Families 1540–1640*, Northants. Record Society, XIX, 1956, p. 45; B.L., Additional MS 25079 fo. 55.

46 FULLER, *op. cit.*, III, 395; Northamptonshire R.O., Fitzwilliam (Milton) Coll., Misc. 904; my *Agricultural Revolution*, 79, 91, 215, 301, 318, 320.

47 *Ibid.*, 49, 50, 113, 238, 317–18; WESTERFIELD, *op. cit.*, 202; J. COX, *op. cit.*, 186; LAURENCE, *op. cit.*, 129; DEFOE, *Tour*, II, 86–7; G. R. BATHO (ed.), *Household Papers of Henry Percy Ninth Earl of Northumberland*, Royal Historical Society, Camden ser., CXIII, 1962, pp. 59, 64; POCOCKE, *op. cit.*, I, 166; H.M.C., *Portland MSS*, II, 290; J. THIRSK, *English Peasant Farming: the agrarian history of Lincolnshire from*

Tudor to recent times (London, 1957), p. 176; Bodleian Lib., Hearne's Diaries 158, p. 131; P.R.O., Exchequer, Land Revenue, Miscellaneous Book 221 fo. 219; Worcestershire R.O., 705: 85 (BA 950) parcel 9 no 183 inv. Francis Hull 1656 Worcester; POSTLETHWAYT, *op. cit.*, I, 230.

48 *Ibid.*, I, 768; II, 763, 848–9; D. LUPTON, *London and the Countrey Carbonadoed and Quartred into severall Characters* (London, 1632), pp. 35–7; EDWARDS, 'Horse Trade', 92 sqq.; THIRSK, *op. cit.*, 176; FITZ-HERBERT, *Boke of Husbandrie* (London, 1523) fo. 44v.; J. A. GILES, *History of the Town and Parish of Bampton* (London, 1848), p. 75; STOW, *op. cit.*, 505; HUDLESTON, *op. cit.*, 44; WESTERFIELD, *op. cit.*, 202; Liverpool R.O., 920 MD 172, at 16 Dec. 1681; Lancashire R.O., Towneley of Towneley Coll., K. 35.

49 *Cal. of Wynne (of Gwydir) Papers*, 155, 281, 312, 352; E. C. LODGE (ed.), *Account Book of the Kentish Estate 1616–1704* (British Academy, London, 1927), pp. 488–9; my *Agricultural Revolution*, 111–12, 116, 119, 124, 126, 130, 131, 133, 135, 138, 146, 149, 158, 164, 171, 178–9, 206, 221, 316–17, 319–20; HAMER, 'Trading at St White Down', 65; SMITH and WEBB, *op. cit.*, 17; E. MELLING, *Kentish Sources III: aspects of agriculture and industry* (Maidstone, 1961), 36, 50; W. PITT, *General View of the Agriculture of Northamptonshire* (London, 1809), pp. 270–1; A. M. MIMARDIERE, 'Warwickshire Gentry, 1660–1730', ts. thesis, M.A., Birmingham University, 1963, p. 152; FULLER, *op. cit.*, III, 508; BLOME, *op. cit.*, 232; GOUGH, *op. cit.*, 61; POSTLETHWAYT, *op. cit.*, I, 768; II, 350; J. M. COWPER, 'Tudor Prices in Kent, chiefly in 1577', *Transactions of the Royal Historical Society*, I, 1875, pp. 170 sqq.; B.L., Harleian MSS 127 fos 17, 18 (28, 29), 22–4 (37–8); 570 fo. 15; Essex R.O., D/DP.F.234.

50 POSTLETHWAYT, *op. cit.*, I, 768; II, 350; G. ELAND (ed.), *Shardeloes Papers of the 17th and 18th centuries* (London, 1947), pp. 60–1; NOTESTEIN *et al.*, *op. cit.*, III, 214; EVANS and BECKETT, 'Cumberland, Westmorland und Furness', 13; T. C. SMOUT, *Scottish Trade on the Eve of Union 1660–1707* (Edinburgh and London, 1963), p. 213; D. WOOD-WARD, 'Comparative Study of the Irish and Scottish Livestock Trade in the Seventeenth Century' in L. M. CULLEN and T. C. SMOUT (eds), *Comparative Aspects of Scottish and Irish Economic and Social History 1600–1900* (Edinburgh, sine data), pp. 150, 152–3, 158; E. HUGHES, *North Country Life in the Eighteenth Century, vol. II: Cumberland and Westmorland 1700–1830* (London, 1965), p. 12; G. CULLEY, *Observations on Livestock* (London, 1786), p. 51; Northamptonshire R.O., Fitzwilliam (Milton) Coll., Misc. 792–3, 921; Leicestershire R.O., Archdeaconry inv. 1710/20; Lincolnshire R.O., Monson Deposit, Newton Papers, 7/13/232; Norfolk R.O., Consistory Court of Norwich invs: Misc. 1628–68/3; 1668/27; 1669/53; 1673/44, 51; 1674–5/92, 148; my *Agricultural Revolution*, 138, 238, 295, 298, 303, 307, 346.

51 *Ibid.*, 346; NOTESTEIN *et al.*, *op. cit.*, II, 307, 356–7, 382; III, 213–14; IV, 363; V, 157; A. K. LONGFIELD, *Anglo-Irish Trade in the Sixteenth Century* (London, 1929), pp. 107–8; L. M. CULLEN, *Anglo-Irish Trade 1660–1800* (Manchester, 1968), pp. 30–3; *Economic History of Ireland since 1660* (London, 1972), pp. 7, 8, 10 sqq.; Statutes 18 and 19 Chas 2 c. 11;

19 and 20 Chas 2 c. 12; Liverpool R.O., 920 MD 172, at 6 July 1681; P.R.O., S.P.D., Jas 130/81; 138/68; EVANS and BECKETT, 'Cumberland, Westmorland and Furness', 13, 15; E. HUGHES, *op. cit.*, 12; WOODWARD, 'Comparative Study', 149–50.

52 DEFOE, *Tour*, I, 210.

53 J. H. BETTEY, 'Marketing of Agricultural Produce in Dorset in the 17th century', *Dorset Natural History and Archaeological Soc.'s Proceedings*, IX(XCIX), 1977, p. 3; A. EVERITT, 'Marketing of Agricultural Produce' in FINBERG and THIRSK, *op. cit.*, IV, 551; my *Agricultural Revolution*, 43, 51–2, 55, 59, 69, 96, 113, 116, 119, 122, 131, 133, 135–6, 138, 146, 164, 173, 178–9, 220, 311, 313–15; W. ELLIS, *Compleat System of Experienced Improvements made on Sheep, Grass-lamb and House-lamb* (London, 1749), pp. 41, 294; *Cal. of Wynne (of Gwydir) Papers*, 155, 281, 312, 352; WESTERFIELD, *op. cit.*, 189; LISLE, *op. cit.*, 309; W. K. BOYD, 'Chancery Proceedings *tempore* Elizabeth, A.D. 1560–A.D. 1570', *Collections for the History of Staffordshire*, new ser., X, pt 1, 1907, pp. 93–4; B. H. CUNNINGTON (ed.), *Records of the County of Wiltshire: extracts from quarter sessions rolls* (Devizes, 1932), pp. 109–10; B.L., Harleian MS 127 fos 17, 18, 22–3, 25, 36v. (28–9, 37–8, 80v.); Bristol University Lib., Shrewton MS 37; POSTLETHWAYT, *op. cit.*, I, 768; Bodleian Lib., Aubrey MS 2 fo. 148.

54 STEPHENS, *op. cit.*, 143; LISLE, *op. cit.*, 26; DEFOE, *Tour*, I, 99, 100; MARSHALL, *Yorkshire*, II, 273; B.L., Sloane MS 3815 fo. 79 (p. 173); my *Agricultural Revolution*, 67, 89, 132, 196, 203, 207, 243, 248, 250.

55 *Ibid.*, 55, 62, 67, 256.

56 *Ibid.*, 170; A. P. WADSWORTH and J. DE L. MANN, *Cotton Trade and Industrial Lancashire 1600–1780* (Manchester, 1931), p. 356; D. WOODWARD, *op. cit.*, 105; *Acts of the Privy Council*, new ser., ed. J. R. Dasent (32 vols., London, 1890–1907), XIV, 69, 70; XV, 66; XXV, 159; XXVI, 227–8, 479–80; FIENNES, *op. cit.*, 188, 193; T. CHURCHYARD, *Worthines of Wales (1587)* (London, 1776), p. 49; S. SEYER, *Memoirs of Bristol* (2 vols., Bristol, 1821), I, 253; *Victoria History of the Counties of England (V.C.H.): Derbyshire*, II, 180; WILLAN, *Coasting Trade*, 80; *Inland Trade*, 20; GRAS, *Corn Market*, 298–300, 315, 322–3; HUDLESTON, *op. cit.*, 38–9, 81, 89, 90, 198; MORTON, *op. cit.*, 16; STOCKS, *op. cit.*, 396; P. KYNDER, 'Historie of Darbyshire' (1663), *Reliquary*, XXII, 1881–2, p. 20; J. WEBB, *Memorials of the Civil War between Charles I and the Parliament of England, as it affected Herefordshire and the adjacent counties* (2 vols., London, 1879), I, 2.

57 *Ibid.*; R. P[OWELL], *Depopulation Arraigned* (London, 1636), App.; S. R. GARDINER (ed.), *Reports of Cases in the Courts of Star Chamber and High Commission* (Camden Society, new ser., XXXIX, 1886), p. 83; J. NORTH, *Lives of the Rt Hon. Francis North, Baron Guilford; the Hon. Sir Dudley North; and the Hon. and Rev. Dr John North*, ed. A. Jessop (3 vols., London, 1890), I, 180; TAYLOR, *New Discovery by Sea*, 25–6; J. BANKES and E. KERRIDGE (eds), *Early Records of the Bankes Family at Winstanley* (Chetham Society, 3rd ser., XXI, 1973), pp. 6, 56, 62, 68–9, 75–6, 81; KALM, *op. cit.*, 205; FULLER, *op. cit.*, I, 366–7; WILLAN,

River Navigation, 137; BLOME, *op. cit.*, 231, 242; D. M. WOODWARD, *Trade of Elizabethan Chester* (Hull, 1970), p. 69; D. WOODWARD, *op. cit.*, 174, 203; ROBERT HERRICK, *Hesperides*, A Hymne to the Lares; Lancashire R.O., Petre of Dunkenhalgh Coll., account book starting 1616, at 7 Feb. 1617; Bodleian Lib., Aubrey MS 2 fo. 63v.; Somerset R.O., DD/SH, Natural History of Somerset, sect. 116; P.R.O., S.P. Ire., 80/35; 83/33; my *Agricultural Revolution*, 119, 146, 336–7.

58 *Ibid.*, 117 sqq.; H.M.C., *MSS in Various Colls*, I, 79, 80; W. B. WILLCOX, *Gloucestershire: a study in local government* (New Haven, 1940), p. 135; J. RUTHERFORD (ed.), *Miscellaneous Papers of Capt. Thomas Stockwell 1590–1611* (2 vols., Southampton Record Society, 1932–33), II, 44; WESTERFIELD, *op. cit.*, 147; CUNNINGTON, *op. cit.*, 25, 105, 124; Somerset R.O., DD/SH, Natural History of Somerset, sect. 116; Basset Down House, Neville Maskelyne's Account Book fos 41–2; P.R.O., S.P.D., Jas 142/14.

59 My *Agricultural Revolution*, 86–7, 119–20, 122, 124–5, 128, 131, 133, 215; Bodleian Lib., Herrick Papers, MS English History c. 475 fo. 118; Aubrey MS 2 fos 100, 148, 151; Berks, R. O., Archdeaconry Court of Berks., Original Wills etc. 87/53; 113/123; 219/109; Manchester R.O., M91/M1/26; B.L., Harleian MS 4716 fo. 8; Kent R.O., Archdeaconry Court of Canterbury, Inventory Register 5 fo. 196; H.M.C., *Portland MSS*, II, 278, 299; WILLAN, *Coasting Trade*, 139; *Inland Trade*, 34; CHALKLIN, *op. cit.*, 176, 271–2; BLOME, *op. cit.*, 52, 95, 207, 209, 213, 215, 251; STEPHENS, *op. cit.*, 143; DEFOE, *Tour*, I, 53, 55, 253; WESTERFIELD, *op. cit.*, 205; FULLER, *op. cit.*, I, 263; D. WOODWARD, *op. cit.*, 110; E. A. LEWIS (ed.), *Welsh Port Books (1550–1603)* (Hon. Cymmrodorion Society, Cymmrodorion Record Series, XII, 1927), pp. 7, 30 sqq., 42–3, 216, 220; J. T. CLIFFE, *Yorkshire Gentry from the Reformation to the Civil War* (London, 1969), p. 2; CUNNINGTON, *op. cit.*, 26, 86, 107; R. W. BLENCOWE (ed.), 'Extracts from the Journal and Account Book of the Rev. Giles Moore', *Sussex Archaeological Collections*, I, 1848, p. 69; J. H. ANDREWS, 'Trade of the Port of Faversham 1650–1750' in M. ROAKE and J. WHYMAN (eds), *Essays in Kentish History* (London, 1973), p. 132; A. R. BAX, 'Notes and Extracts from the Account Book of Richard Bax, a Surrey yeoman', *Antiquary*, VI, 1882, p. 162; COWPER, 'Tudor Prices', 174; GERARD, *op. cit.*, 171–2; J. WAYLEN, *History Military and Municipal of the Town … of Marlborough* (London, 1844), pp. 517–18; E. H. BATES (ed.), *Quarter Sessions Records for the County of Somerset*, vol. I, James I, 1607–1625 (Somerset Record Society, XXIII, 1907), pp. 2, 3; E. H. B. HARBIN (ed.), *Quarter Sessions Records for the County of Somerset*, vol. II, Charles I, 1625–1639 (Somerset Record Society, XXIV, 1908), pp. 19–20.

60 W. MARSHALL, *Review (and Complete Abstract) of the Reports to the Board of Agriculture from the Southern and Peninsular Departments of England* (London, 1817), pp. 238, 250; T. DAVIS, *General View of the Agriculture of the County of Wiltshire* (London, 1794), p. 123; J. AUBREY, *Wiltshire: the topographical collections of John Aubrey, F.R.S., A.D. 1659–70* ed. J. E. Jackson (Devizes, 1862), p. 216; *Natural History of Wiltshire*, 37, 114–15; POCOCKE, *op. cit.*, II, 265; J. SPRATT, 'Agrarian

Conditions in Norfolk and Suffolk, 1600–50', ts. thesis M.A., London University, 1935, p. 210; P.R.O., Court of Requests, Proceedings, bundle 26 file 63; D. DEFOE, *Plan of the English Commerce* (London, 1738), p. 283; my *Agricultural Revolution*, 119, 126.

61 *Ibid.*, 51, 69, 79, 113, 119, 144, 146, 149, 154, 158, 164–5, 169–71, 173, 177–80, 221, 238, 317–20.

62 *Ibid.*, 49, 59, 69–72, 74, 86–7, 89–91, 109 sqq., 116, 119–20, 122, 124 sqq., 131, 133, 135–8, 146, 198–9, 212, 215, 236–8, 260, 273, 295–6, 298–300, 302–4, 306–7, 320 sqq.

63 *Ibid.*, 55–6, 59, 76, 79, 81, 83, 85–6, 88, 114–15, 119, 121–2, 125, 139, 152–3, 177, 196, 212–13, 215, 228, 231, 268, 274, 310, 332, 336–7; BECKWITH, 'Gainsborough', 5; P.R.O., Duchy of Lancaster, Misc. Books 108 fos 50v., 82v.–3; 115 fos 27, 55; Exch., Augmentation Office, Parliamentary Surveys, Wiltshire, 19; D. DEFOE, *Complete English Tradesman* (Edinburgh, 1839), p. 77; *Tour*, I, 55; BLOME, *op. cit.*, 78–9, 116, 209, 213–15, 225, 254; STOW, *op. cit.*, 168; LELAND, *op. cit.*, I, 259; WILLAN, *Inland Trade*, 29; STEPHENS, *op. cit.*, 125, 143; GERARD, *op. cit.*, 231; POSTLETHWAYT, *op. cit.*, II, 763, 765; WILLCOX, *op. cit.*, 4; FULLER, *op. cit.*, I, 548; FOLKINGHAM, *op. cit.*, 42; R. C. TEMPLE (ed.), *Travels of Peter Mundy in Europe and Asia 1608–67: vol. IV, Travels in Europe 1639–47* Hakluyt Society, ser. II, vol. LV, 1925), pp. 20–1; H.M.C., *Portland MSS*, II, 266; J. KIRBY, *Suffolk Traveller* (London, 1764), p. 144; J. C. K. CORNWALL, 'Agrarian History of Sussex, 1560–1640', ts. thesis, M.A., London University, 1963, p. 235; Bodleian Lib., Aubrey MSS 2 fo. 103; Hearne's Diaries 159, p. 173.

64 My *Agricultural Revolution*, 206 sqq., 235–8, 242 sqq., 256, 259–60, 271–3, 275, 278–9, 282, 320 sqq., 328 sqq.

65 *Ibid.*, 157, 168–9, 215, 244–5, 249–50, 310. For demands set up by agric. rev. v. my paper in A. GUARDUCCI (ed.), *Agricoltura e Transformazione dell'Ambiente secoli XIII–XVIII* (Prato, n.d.), pp. 238 sqq.

66 MORTON, *op. cit.*, 16; FIENNES, *op. cit.*, 8; D. WOODWARD, *op. cit.*, 105, 121; WILLAN, *Coasting Trade*, 79; *V. C. H. Nottinghamshire*, II, 283; BARLEY, *op. cit.*, 81; P.R.O., S.P.D., Jas 113/22; Leicester Museum MS 4D.51/1, p. 159; J. HOUGHTON, *Husbandry and Trade Improv'd, being a Collection of many valuable materials* (4 vols., London, 1692 and var. edns), no XXXVII.

67 WADSWORTH and MANN, *op. cit.*, 5, 6; Statutes 23 Eliz. cc. 8, 9; 14 Chas c. 30; J.L., *Discourse concerning the great Benefit of Drayning and Imbanking and of Transportation by Water within the Country* (sine loco, 1641), pp. 3, 4; J. MOORE, *History or Narrative of the Great Level of the Fenns called the Bedford Level* (London, 1685), p. 62; my *Agricultural Revolution*, 79, 85, 119, 127, 130, 132, 137, 143, 145, 148, 152, 176, 194, 196–7, 204, 209 sqq., 236–7, 268, 298.

68 Bodleian Lib., Aubrey MSS 2 fo. 151.

69 MARSHALL, *West of England*, I, 38; T. RISDON, *Chorographical Description or Survey of the County of Devon* (London, 1723), pp. 5, 6; [J.] COKER, *Survey of Dorsetshire* (London, 1732), p. 5; R. REYCE, *Breviary of Suffolk (1618)* ed. F. Hervey (London, 1902), pp. 20, 37; *Acts of the Privy*

Council, XIV, 69, 70; XV, 39, 40; XXV, 109, 159; XXVIII, 372; XXX, 794–5; B. PEARCE, 'Elizabethan Food Policy and the Armed Forces', *Economic History Review*, XII, 1942, pp. 39 sqq.; CORNWALL, 'Agrarian History of Sussex', 224–6; B.L., Additional MS 34258 fo. 5v.

70 MARSHALL, *Midland Counties*, I, 229–30; my *Agricultural Revolution*, 112.

71 *Ibid.*, 221; MARSHALL, *Review of the Reports to the Board of Agriculture from the Northern Department of England* (London, 1808), p. 96; GRAS, *Corn Market*, 223, 297, 302–3, 305 sqq., 312–14, 321–2; WILLIAMS, 'Maritime Trade', 177–8; WILLAN, *Coasting Trade*, 79; D. WOODWARD, *op. cit.*, 105.

72 MARSHALL, *Midland Counties*, I, 370; *Yorkshire*, I, 409; CLIFFE, *op. cit.*, 2; DEFOE, *Tour*, II, 199; HOUGHTON, *op. cit.*, no XXXVII; my *Agricultural Revolution*, 131, 215.

73 *Ibid.*, 119; WESTERFIELD, *op. cit.*, 205; WILLAN, *Coasting Trade*, 83–4, 167, 172; DEFOE, *Tour*, I, 283; II, 42; *Acts of the Privy Council*, XXVI, 227–8, 479–80; W. E. MINCHINTON, 'Bristol – Metropolis of the West in the 18th century', *Transactions of the Royal Historical Society*, 5th ser., IV, 1954; T. DAVIS, *op. cit.*, 4, 120, 123; HARBIN, *op. cit.*, 145–6; R. C. GAUT, *History of Worcestershire Agriculture and Rural Evolution* (Worcester, 1939), p. 68; CAMDEN, *op. cit.*, cols 89, 104; TAYLOR, *New Discovery by Sea*, 25–6; R. BAXTER, 'Poor Husbandman's Advocate', *Bulletin of the John Rylands Lib.*, X, 1926, p. 186; P.R.O., S.P.D., Chas 210/18; Gloucestershire R.O., D.326/E.1 fo. 89v.; Bodleian Lib., Aubrey MSS 2 fo. 149; Hearne's Diaries 159, p. 225; D. WOODWARD, *op. cit.*, 174, 203; GRAS, *Corn Market*, 122, 298, 315.

74 *Ibid.*, 75; FISHER, 'London Food Market', 136; FULLER, *op. cit.*, I, 193–4; my *Agricultural Revolution*, 177–9.

75 GRAS, *Corn Market*, 47, 105 sqq., 121–2, 124, 186–9, 223, 300–1, 310 sqq., 319–20, 330 sqq., 342 sqq., 350 sqq., 357–60, 363; POCOCKE, *op. cit.*, II, 163; CHALKLIN, *op. cit.*, 175, 185–6; POSTLETHWAYT, *op. cit.*, II, 392; R. POWELL, *op. cit.*, App.; J. AUBREY, *Natural History and Antiquities of the County of Surrey* (5 vols., London, 1719), III, 346–7; WILLAN, *Coasting Trade*, 79 sqq., 148; *Inland Trade*, 27–8, 33–4, 36; FISHER, 'London Food Market', 136, 138–9, 144, 148; J. WEBB, *op. cit.*, 115; WESTERFIELD, *op. cit.*, 169–70, 172, 178–80, App., map I; DEFOE, *Tour*, I, 135, 142, 144, 157; II, 113; *Complete English Tradesman*, 77; W. MARSHALL, *Rural Economy of Norfolk* (2 vols., London, 1787), I, 195; *Southern Dept.*, 9; CORNWALL, 'Agrarian History of Sussex', 224, 243; FIENNES, *op. cit.*, 42; FULLER, *op. cit.*, I, 164; BLITH, *op. cit.*, 82–3; PLOT, *Oxfordshire*, 280; W. HEWETT, *History and Antiquities of the Hundred of Compton* (Reading, 1844), pp. 46–7; H. HALL, *Society in the Elizabethan Age* (London, 1887), p. 199; STEPHENS, *op. cit.*, 80–1; J. NORDEN, *Speculi Britanniae Pars: the Description of Hartfordshire* (London, 1598), p. 1; *V.C.H. Hertfordshire*, IV, 208–10; TAYLOR, *New Discovery by Sea*, 25–6; SPRATT, 'Agrarian Conditions in Norfolk and Suffolk', 166; J. H. ANDREWS, 'Thanet Seaports 1650–1750' in ROAKE and WHYMAN, *op. cit.*, 123–4; 'Trade of Faversham', 130; P. V. McGRATH,

'Marketing of Food, Fodder and Livestock in the London area in the 17th century', ts. thesis, M.A., London University, 1948, p. 120; Bodleian Lib., Aubrey MSS 2 fos 63v., 84; P.R.O., S.P.D., Eliz. 261/30; Chas 182/67; B.L., Additional, Roll 16280; MS 41305 fos 7, 8; Sloane MS 3815 fo. 79 (p. 173); Harleian MS 570 fo. 15v.; Kent R.O., Archdeaconry Court of Canterbury, inv. John Ashley 1678 Faversham; D. O. PAM, *Tudor Enfield: the maltmen and the Lea navigation*, Edmonton Hundred Historical Society, Occasional Papers, new ser., 18, s.l.n.d., pp. 3, 4.

76 WILLAN, *Coasting Trade*, 84–7, 118, 122, 124, 126, 132, 134–6, 185; *Inland Trade*, 28–9, 33–4, 137; WESTERFIELD, *op. cit.*, 204–6, 208; E. LEIGH, *England Described* (London, 1659), 42, 165, 181, 184; GERARD, *op. cit.*, 172; D. HENSTOCK, 'Cheese Manufacture and Marketing in Derbyshire and North Staffordshire 1670–1870', *Derbyshire Archaeological Journal*, LXXXIX, 1969, pp. 40–2; BECKWITH, 'Gainsborough', 5; J. A. CHARTRES, *Internal Trade in England 1500–1700* (London, 1977), p. 29; 'Marketing', 486–9; DEFOE, *Complete English Tradesman*, 19, 77; *Tour*, I, 53, 55, 270–1, 283; II, 42, 72, 131; T. DAVIS, *op. cit.*, 120; AUBREY, *Natural History of Wiltshire*, 105; *Acts of the Privy Council*, XXVIII, 372–3; W. MARSHALL, *Review of the Reports to the Board of Agriculture from the Western Department of England* (London, 1810), p. 158; *Glocestershire*, I, 313–14; II, 179–80; *Yorkshire*, 409; II, 195; POSTLETHWAYT, *op. cit.*, II, 765; BLOME, *op. cit.*, 52, 201, 207, 213, 215; McGRATH, 'Marketing', 220–1; E. POWELL, 'Pryce Correspondence', 83, 86; OGILBY, *op. cit.*, 108; C. B. FRY, *Hannington: the records of a Wiltshire parish* (Gloucester, 1935), p. 8; *Wiltshire Archaeological Magazine*, XXVIII, 1894–6, p. 254; PLOT, *Staffordshire*, 108; FULLER, *op. cit.*, III, 158; J. A. FAREY, *General View of the Agriculture and Minerals of Derbyshire* (3 vols., London, 1811–17), III, 61–3; FISHER, 'London Food Market', 137, 139, 144; REYCE, *op. cit.*, 41; STOCKS, *op. cit.*, 222; Bodleian Lib., Aubrey MSS 2 fos 99v., 148, 151; 3 fo. 84v. (p. 83); Berks. R.O., Archdeaconry Court of Berkshire, Original Wills etc., 87/53; 113/123; 138/35; 219/107; P.R.O., Privy Council Register 1640–5, pp. 20, 31, 123 (fos 3v., 9, 57); WILLIAMS, 'Maritime Trade', 188–90; Basset Down House, Neville Maskelyne's Account Book fo. 123; Leicestershire R.O., Archdeaconry inv. 1665/28; B.L., Additional MS 34653 fo. 33 (p. 65); Norfolk R.O., invs, Consistory Ct of Norwich 1663/33B; Archdeaconry Ct of Norfolk 1665/28; W. STERN, 'Cheese Shipped Coastwise to London towards the middle of the Eighteenth Century', *Guildhall Miscellany*, IV, 1973, pp. 208–9, 211–12, 221; D. HEY, 'Yorkshire and Lancashire' in Finberg and Thirsk, *op. cit.*, V, pt 1, p. 73; J. THIRSK, 'South-west Midlands', *ibid.*, 183; my *Agricultural Revolution*, 87, 114, 125, 131, 215, 280.

77 *Ibid.*, 72, 112, 119, 126, 176, 322; W. MARSHALL, *Rural Economy of the Southern Counties* (2 vols., London, 1798), I, 115; *Norfolk*, I, 195; *Southern Department*, 238, 250; COKER, *op. cit.*, 4; MIMARDIERE, 'Warwickshire Gentry', 151–2; BETTEY, 'Marketing', 3; J. BOYS, *General View of the Agriculture of the County of Kent* (London, 1796), p. 150; MORTON, *op. cit.*, 483; THIRSK, *English Peasant Farming*, 195; K. J. ALLISON, 'Flock Management in the 16th and 17th centuries', *Economic*

History Review, 2nd ser., XI, 1958, p. 109; 'Wool Supply', 354; LUPTON, *op. cit.*, 38; FISHER, 'London Food Market', 144–5; WINCHESTER, *op. cit.*, 173, 179; DEFOE, *Tour*, I, 125, 270–1; II, 230–1; WESTERFIELD, *op. cit.*, 190; CHALKLIN, *op. cit.*, 185; BAXTER, 'Poor Husbandman's Advocate', 186; BARLEY, *op. cit.*, 81; BURLEY, 'Economic Development of Essex', 64–5; T. DAVIS, *op. cit.*, 123; T. B. FRANKLIN, *British Grasslands* (London, 1953), p. 90; E. C. LODGE, *op. cit.*, 488–9; Statute 16 and 17 Chas 2 c. 11; Lincolnshire R.O., Massingberd-Mundy Deposit, VI/5/9; Bodleian Lib., Aubrey MSS 1 fo. 64 (61); Essex R.O., Petre MSS, A. 18; W. R. EMERSON, 'Economic Development of the Estates of the Petre Family in Essex in the 16th and 17th centuries', ts. thesis, D. Phil., Oxford Univesity, 1951, pp. 330–1; Northamptonshire R.O., Fitzwilliam (Milton) Coll., Correspondence 222/52, 54.

78 GRAS, *Corn Market*, 126; G. ATTWELL, *Faithfull Surveyour* (Cambridge, 1662), p. 102; M. CAMPBELL, *English Yeoman under Elizabeth and the early Stuarts* (New Haven, 1942), p. 90; my *Agricultural Revolution*, 179.

79 *Ibid.*, 79, 81, 85, 88, 215; H.M.C., *Portland MSS*, II, 275, 283, 297, 300; ANDREWS, 'Faversham', 130–1; BLOME, *op. cit.*, 116; FISHER, 'London Food Market', 149–50; WILLAN, *Inland Trade*, 29; *Coasting Trade*, 112–13, 118, 120, 126–7, 129–32; STOW, *op. cit.*, 168; D. G. BARNES, *op. cit.*, 299; JOHN, 'English Agricultural Improvements', 49, 56; ANON., 'Natural History of Dorking', *Gentleman's Magazine*, XXXIII, 1763, p. 220; POCOCKE, *op. cit.*, I, 164; II, 163; REYCE, *op. cit.*, 37; EDWARDS, 'Horse Trade', 92; DEFOE, *Tour*, I, 59, 113–14, 153; MARSHALL, *Yorkshire*, I, 409; CROFTS, *op. cit.*, 5, 6; WESTERFIELD, *op. cit.*, 203–4, App. map I; J. NORDEN, *Surveiors Dialogue* (London, 1618), p. 215; AUBREY, *Natural History of Surrey*, III, 346–7; GATU, *op. cit.*, 92; GRAS, *Corn Market*, 77, 113–14, 116; EVERITT, 'Marketing', 509; W. M. STERN, 'Fish Marketing in London in the first half of the Eighteenth Century' in COLEMAN and JOHN, *op. cit.*, 69, 70, 72; Lancashire R.O., Cavendish of Holker Coll.; 1/107; Aberystwyth, National Lib., Episcopal Consistory Court of St Asaph, Original Wills, Administrations and Inventories, Richard Hood 1695 Ledbury; Bodleian Lib., Aubrey MSS 3 fo. 147v. (p. 180).

80 Wiltshire R.O., ex-Salisbury Diocesan Registry invs, George Eames 1639 Calne; H.M.C., *MSS in Various Colls*, I, 79, 80; CUNNINGTON, *op. cit.*, 25.

81 *Ibid.*, 28, 86, 105, 107, 124; JOHNSON, *op. cit.*, 1sqq.; HEY, *op. cit.*, 178; *V.C.H. Hertfordshire*, IV, 208–10; *Leicestershire*, IV, 79; Leicester Museum MS BR. iv. 3.7; Leicester Town Hall, Quarter Sessions Rolls: '1609', at 21 April 10 Jas; '1626', at 26 Sept. 2 Chas; Colchester Town Hall, Orders etc. 1571–92 fo. 285; Cheshire R.O., Quarter Sessions Records, Quarter Sessions Books: 1618–40 Recognizances and Orders, fos 5, 15v., 30, 47, 69, 86, 98, 110, 120v., 126v., 133, 136, 145, 149v., 173v., 389v., 417, 443v., 499; 1683–94 fos 8, 39.

82 HARRISON, 'Description of England', in HOLINSHED *et al.*, *op. cit.*, I, 202; FISHER, 'London Food Market', 150; *V.C.H. Hertfordshire*, IV, 210.

83 CUNNINGTON, *op. cit.*, 26, 96; CHARTRES, 'Marketing', 471; P.R.O., Exch., King's Remembrancer, Special Commission 122; Depositions by Commission 42 Eliz. Trinity 9; Leicester Town Hall, Quarter Sessions Roll '1609'; W. J. HARDY (ed.), *Hertford County Records: notes and extracts from the sessions rolls 1581–1698*, vol. I (Hertford, 1905), p. 144; W. LE HARDY and G. L. RECKITT (eds), *County of Buckingham: Calendar to the Sessions Records*, vol. III (Aylesbury, 1939), p. 190; HARBIN, *op. cit.*, 152.

84 POCOCKE, *op. cit.*, II, 58; AUBREY, *Natural History of Wiltshire*, 114–15; *Natural History of Surrey*, III, 346–7; Bodleian Lib., Aubrey MSS 2 pp. 149–51; Somerset R.O., DD/SH, Natural History of Somerset, sect. 116; J. S. COCKBURn (ed.), *Western Circuit Assize Orders 1629–48* (Royal Historical Society, Camden 4th ser., XVII, 1976), p. 273; 'Natural History of Dorking', 220; M. BATESON (ed.), *Records of the Borough of Leicester* (3 vols., Cambridge, 1899–1905), III, 228; WESTERFIELD, *op. cit.*, 145; W. MARSHALL, *Minutes, Experiments, Observations and General Remarks on Agriculture in the Southern Counties* (2 vols., London, 1799), I, 34–5; HARRISON, 'Description of England', in HOLINSHED *et al.*, *op. cit.*, I, 202.

85 D. WOODWARD, *op. cit.*, 105.

86 MARSHALL, *Norfolk*, I, 195, 351; WESTERFIELD, *op. cit.*, 188–90, 199, facing p. 328; M. A. HAVINDEN (ed.), *Household and Farm Inventories in Oxfordshire, 1550–90* (H.M.C. Joint Publication X, Oxford Record Society XLIV, 1965), pp. 234–7; THIRSK, *English Peasant Farming*, 195; *V.C.H. Leicestershire*, IV, 92–3; J. S. PURVIS, 'Note on XVI Century Farming in Yorkshire', *Yorkshire Archaeological Journal*, XXXVI, 1944–7, pp. 449–50; CHARTRES, 'Marketing', 483–5; Bodleian Lib., Hearne's Diaries 158, p. 35; Northamptonshire R.O., Fitzwilliam (Milton) Coll., Correspondence 222/52; my *Agricultural Revolution*, 112, 176, 178–9.

87 GRAS, *Corn Market*, 186, 196 sqq.; CHARTRES, 'Marketing', 472 sqq.; CHALKLIN, *op. cit.*, 185; AUBREY, *Natural History of Surrey*, III, 346; CORNWALL, 'Agrarian History of Sussex', 224.

88 REYCE, *op. cit.*, 32.

89 H.M.C., *Portland MSS*, II, 282; WINCHESTER, *op. cit.*, 173; FRANKLIN, *op. cit.*, 90; BURLEY, 'Economic Development of Essex', 64–6; SKEEL, 'Cattle Trade', 145–8.

90 NORDEN, *Surveiors Dialogue*, 215; my *Agricultural Revolution*, 55–6.

91 *Ibid.*, 87, 120, 122, 125, 128, 131, 199, 215; *Acts of the Privy Council*, XXVIII, 372–3; WESTERFIELD, *op. cit.*, 206; REYCE, *op. cit.*, 41; FAREY, *op. cit.*, III, 61–3; BLOME, *op. cit.*, 201, 207; J. H. E. BENNETT (ed.), *Rolls of Freemen of the City of Chester* (Record Society for Lancashire and Cheshire, LI, LV, 1906–8), pp. 190, 210, 238; W. R. and R. K. SERJEANT, *Index of the Probate Records of the Court of the Archdeaconry of Suffolk, 1444–1700* (Index Lib., British Record Society, XC, XCI, 1979–80), pp. 402, 463, 530; McGRATH, 'Marketing', 220–1; PLOT, *Staffordshire*, 108; DEFOE, *Complete English Tradesman*, 19; HENSTOCK, 'Cheese Manufacture', 40; MARSHALL, *Glocestershire*, I, 313–14; II, 163;

Western Department, 158; HARRISON, 'Description of England' in HOLINSHED *et al.*, *op. cit.*, I, 203; Cheshire R.O., Cholmondeley Coll., box K, Vouchers to Account: 1696–7, 1698–1700; Liverpool R.O., Norris Papers (920 NOR), 1/58; Berks. R.O., Archdeaconry Court of Berkshire, Original Wills etc., 87/53; 113/123; 138/35; 219/109; Aubrey MSS 2 fos 103, 151; Norfolk R.O., Consistory Court of Norwich inv. 1663/33B; WAYLEN, *op. cit.*, 517–18.

92 MARSHALL, *Western Department*, 159; WILLAN, *Coasting Trade*, 85–7; STERN, 'Cheese', 208–9, 211, 213; DEFOE, *Tour*, II, 72; *Journal of the House of Commons*, XIX, 227, 381; Liverpool R.O., Norris Papers (920 NOR) 1/58; C. ARMOUR, 'Trade of Chester and the State of the Dee Navigation 1600–1800', ts. thesis, Ph.D., London University, 1956, p. 291.

93 GRAS, *Corn Market*, 77; FISHER, 'London Food Market', 136, 138.; and see, R. W. K. HINTON, *Port Books of Boston 1601–40* (Lincolnshire Record Society Publications, L, 1956), pp. xxxii–xxxiii; G. D. RAMSAY, 'Smugglers' Trade: a neglected aspect of English commercial development', *Transactions of the Royal Historical Society*, 5th ser., II, 1952, pp. 131 sqq., 157; N. J. WILLIAMS, 'Francis Shaxton and the Elizabethan Port Books', *English Historical Review*, LXVI, 1951, pp. 387 sqq.; 'Maritime Trade', 56–7.

94 MARSHALL, *Minutes … on Agriculture*, I, 34–5; *Southern Department*, 135; FULLER, *op. cit.*, I, 164; WESTERFIELD, *op. cit.*, 169–70; McGRATH, 'Marketing', 119–20; FISHER, 'London Food Market', 136, 148; B.L., Harleian MS 570 fo. 15v.; Bodleian Lib., Hearne's Diaries 158, p. 41; P.R.O., S.P.D., Chas 177/50.

95 GRAS, *Corn Market*, 108, 111–12, 243, 282, 287, 290–1, 295; my *Agricultural Revolution*, p. 332; and see, FISHER, 'London Food Market', 140; ANDREWS, 'Faversham', 129; JOHN, 'English Agricultural Improvements', 49.

96 GRAS, *Corn Market*, 75, 256; WILLIAMS, 'Maritime Trade', 150.

97 GRAS, *Corn Market*, 77, 111–13, 192, 196–7, 245, 437. Cf. C. W. J. GRANGER and C. M. ELLIOTT, 'Fresh Look at Wheat Prices and Markets in the Eighteenth Century', *Economic History Review*, 2nd ser., XX, 1967, pp. 257 sqq.

98 *Letters and Papers, foreign and domestic, of the reign of Henry VIII, preserved in the P.R.O., the British Museum and elsewhere in England* (23 vols., P.R.O., 1862–1932), IV, pt 2, no 3649; and see C. S. L. Davies, 'Provisions for Armies, 1509–50', *Economic History Review*, 2nd ser., XVII, 1964, p. 236.

99 H.M.C., *Portland MSS*, 11, 278; Statute 21 Jas c. 22; P.R.O. Privy Council Register 1640–5 pp. 20, 31, 48 (fos 3v., 9, 17v.); BLENCOWE, 'Extracts', 69; WESTERFIELD, *op. cit.*, 205; CHALKLIN, *op. cit.*, 176, 271–2; Kent R.O., Archdeaconry Court of Canterbury, Inventory Register 7 fo. 196; Bristol R.O., Consistory Court inv. 1662/31; MARSHALL, *Southern Counties*, I, 322; DEFOE, *Tour*, I, 53, 55, 253; *Complete English Tradesman*, 77; my *Agricultural Revolution*, 215; FISHER, 'London Food Market', 137; REYCE, *op. cit.*, 41; BLOME, *op. cit.*, 207; LEIGH, *op. cit.*, 181; C. H. FIRTH and R. S. RAIT (eds), *Acts and Ordinances of the Interregnum* (3 vols., London, 1911), II, 1044; CAMDEN, *op. cit.*, col. 367.

100 MARSHALL, *Southern Department*, 9.

101 PITT, *Northamptonshire*, 271; Shakespeare's Birthplace Lib., Stratford-on-Avon, Willoughby de Broke Coll., 1711, at 7 July.

102 R. SHARROCK, *History of the Propagation and Improvement of Vegetables by the Concurrence of Art and Nature* (Oxford, 1660), p. 21; BARLEY, *op. cit.*, 81; P.R.O., S. P. Ire, 80/35; 83/33; my *Agricultural Revolution*, 284.

103 *Ibid.*, 51, 131, 135, 179, 215; E. C. LODGE, *op. cit.*, 24; W. O. WILLIAMS, 'Anglesey Gentry in Tudor and Stuart Times', *Anglesey Antiquarian Society and Field Club Transactions*, 1948, p. 109; NEF, *Coal Industry*, I, 101; BLOME, *op. cit.*, 52; SMITH and WEBB, *op. cit.*, 17; BATHO, *op. cit.*, 59, 64; FISHER, 'London Food Market', 144; COWPER, 'Tudor Prices', 170 sqq.; B.L., Harleian MS 570 fo. 15.

104 WILLIAMS, 'Maritime Trade', 150.

105 PITT, *Northamptonshire*, 270–1; DEFOE, *Tour*, I, 153; my *Agricultural Revolution*, 176–9.

106 Sup. pp. 5 sqq.

107 Sup. pp. 6, 15, 17, 18, 29–31, 42–4; inf. Ch. 4 pass.

108 Historical Manuscripts Commission (H.M.C.), *Calendar of the Manuscripts of the Marquess of Salisbury* (several parts, 1883– in progress), part XIII, p. 560; M. G. DAVIES, 'Country Gentry and Payments to London, 1650–1714', *Economic History Review*, 2nd ser., XXIV, 1971, pp. 22 sqq.; N. LOWE, *Lancashire Textile Industry in the 16th century*, Chetham Society, 3rd ser., XX, 1972, pp. 41–2; T. D. HIBBERT, 'Letters relating to Lancashire and Cheshire *tempore* James I, Charles I and Charles II', Historic Society of Lancashire and Cheshire, *Proceedings and Papers*, session IV, 1852, p. 190; R. D. RICHARDS, 'Pre-Bank of England Banker – Edward Backwell', *Economic History*, I, 1929, p. 341; ANDERTON, 'Delaval Papers', p. 145; Cheshire R.O., Cholmondeley Coll., box K, Vouchers to Account 1696–7; 1698–1700 nos. 1–5, 7, 9, 10, 17–19, 21, 24–5, 27–8, 31–3, 35–6, 38–9; Lancashire R.O., Cavendish of Holker Coll. 1/107; Hopwood Coll. 39/13; Consistory Ct of Chester, Supra inv., John Gregory 1675 Rochdale; Essex R.O., Peculiar Ct of Bocking, inv. William Deeks 1740 Hadleigh; Suffolk R.O. (Bury St. Edmunds), Episcopal Commissary Ct of Bury (with the Archdeaconry Ct of Sudbury), invs. 1665/22; 1667/1; 1735–9/10; Suffolk R.O. (Ipswich), Blois Fam. Archives, HA. 30:787 Hy Blois's Acct Ledger, fo. 59; Norfolk R.O., Business Records, no. 79; Worcester and Hereford R.O. (Worcester), Consistory Ct of Worcester, inv. 1614/169; Gloucestershire R.O., Marcham Coll., F. 26; Devon R.O., Marwood Tucker Coll., E. 1; Kent R.O., Consistory Ct of Canterbury, Inv. Registers, 7 fos 5, 6, 456; 12 fos 247–8; 14 fo. 588; 20 fos 567–8; Leicestershire R.O., Archdeaconry Ct of Leicester, inv. Nicholas Alsop 1707 Leicester; Wiltshire R.O., Consistory Ct of Salisbury, inv. Jn Willmott 1698 Reading; P.R.O., Prerogative Ct of Canterbury, parchment invs post 1660, nos 3672, 3715, 8687, 8752, 9658; paper invs 1660–*circa* 1725, nos 444, 3127, 3279.

109 H.M.C., *Salisbury MSS*, part XIII, 212 (reference owed to the kindness of Dr C. E. Challis); BIDWELL, *op. cit.*, pp. 11, 12; D. GURNEY, *Record of the House of Gournay* (privately published, 1848), pp. 514, 520,

529–30, 545; J. H. THOMAS, '17th-century Merchant's Acct Book' in J.
WEBB, N. YATES and S. PEACOCK, *Hampshire Studies presented to D.
Dymond* (Portsmouth, 1981), pp. 144, 146, 155–6; W. BRERETON, *Travels
in Holland, the United Provinces, England, Scotland and Ireland 1634–5*
Chetham Society, I, 1844, p. 89; WADSWORTH and MANN, *op. cit.*, pp.
92–3, 95–6; Chester R.O., Town Clerks Recs., Protested Bills etc. 1639–65,
fo. 34; P.R.O., State Papers Domestic (S.P.D.), Charles, vol. 351 no 2; NEF,
Coal Industry, II, 120–1.

   110   T. S. ASHTON, 'Bill of Exchange and Private Banks in Lancashire
1790–1830' in T. S. ASHTON and R. S. SAYERS, *Papers in English
Monetary History* (Oxford, 1953), p. 38; T. WILSON, *Discourse upon Usury*,
ed. R. H. Tawney (London, 1925 and 1962), p. 24; P. J. BOWDEN, *Wool
Trade in Tudor and Stuart England* (London, 1962), p. 101; M. MOSSE,
Arraignment and Conviction of Usurie (London, 1595), p. 62; Leicestershire
R.O., DE 10, Beaumanor Coll., DG9/2049, Sir William Herrick's Account
Book 1599–1637 (1610–36), p. 133.

   111   B. W. DEMPSEY, *Interest and Usury* (London, 1948), pp. 141–4,
165–6, 181, 209; WILLSON, *op. cit.*, 151; F. C. LANE, *Venice and History*
(Baltimore, 1966), p. 67; B. NELSON, *Idea of Usury* (Chicago, 1969), pp.
14, 32, 79, 83; F. BACON, *Essays*, 'Of Usury'; WILSON, *op. cit.*, 276–8;
E. COKE, *Institutes of the Lawes of England*, (4 parts, London, 1628–44
and various editions), part 3, p. 151; MOSSE, *op. cit.*, 2, 16, 17, 22 sqq.,
53, 57; J. BLAXTON, *English Usurer, or usury condemned* (London, 1634),
pp. 1, 2, 6–8, 11, 60–1; G. FENTON, *Treatise of Usurie* (London, 1611),
pp. 19, 26–7, 71–2.

   112   *Ibid.*, 19, 20, 24, 118–19, 127; DEMPSEY, *op. cit.*, 134, 166,
171 sqq., 189–90; WILSON, *op. cit.*, 250; BLAXTON, *op. cit.*, 3, 7, 8; J. T.
NOONAN, *Scholastic Analysis of Usury* (Cambridge, Mass., 1957), pp. 105,
107, 109, 114 sqq., 129–30, 267; DE ROOVER, *Gresham*, 100–1, 128, 141,
143 sqq., 157–8; *Business*, 27 sqq., 211; *Bruges*, 66–7; USHER, 'Origins',
415.

   113   NELSON, *op. cit.*, 33; LANE, *Venice*, 67; LOPEZ, 'Dawn', 3;
USHER, *Deposit Banking*, 78; MOSSE, *op. cit.*, 27.

   114   *Ibid.*, 62; WILSON, *op. cit.*, 24; D. NORTH, *Discourses upon Trade*
(London, 1691), p. 20.

   115   P.R.O., Ct of Requests, Proceedings, 29/38.

   116   MOSSE, *op. cit.*, 157; Statutes 3 Hy 7 cc. 5, 6; 11 Hy 7 c. 8; 37 Hy
8 c. 9; 5 and 6 Ed. 6 c. 20; 13 Eliz. c. 8; 21 Jas c. 17; 12 Chas 2, c. 13; 13 Anne
c. 15 (commonly called 12 Anne stat. 2 c. 16); FIRTH and RAIT, *op. cit.*,
II, 548 sqq.; BOWDEN, *op. cit.*, 101; R. ASHTON, *op. cit.*, 10, 37; F.
BACON, *Essays*, 'Of Usury'; WILLSON, *op. cit.*, 151; FENTON, *op. cit.*,
2, 62, 127–8; BLAXTON, *op. cit.*, 57, 60–1; COKE, *Inst.*, III, 151–2;
NOONAN, *op. cit.*, 365–6; S. D'EWES, *Compleat Journal of the House
of Lords and House of Commons throughout the whole reign of Queen
Elizabeth* (London, 1693), pp. 171–4; P.R.O., S.P.D., Supplementary vol.
87, fo. 79 (4); British Library (B.L.), Lansdowne MSS, 89 no 87 fos 169–70;
90 no 1 fos 2, 3; no 21 fos 42–3; no 34 fo. 67; 91 no 16 fos 45–6; no 26 fos
63–4; no 70 fos 143–4; 92 no 35 fos 64–5; no 93 fos 163–4; 93 nos 2 fos 4, 5;

J. F. BERGIER, 'Taux de l'Intérêt et Crédit à Court Terme à Genève dans la seconde moitié du XVIe siècle' in *Studi in Onore di Amintore Fanfani*, vol. IV (Milan, 1962), pp. 93, 95−8, 101−2, 104−5, 115, 119; A. BIELER, *La Pensée Economique et Sociale de Calvin* (Geneva, 1959), pp. 455, 457−9, 464, 473−6. Cf. M. M. KNAPPEN, *Tudor Puritanism* (Chicago and London, 1970), pp. 417−20. For prices, see F. P. BRAUDEL and F. SPOONER, 'Prices in Europe from 1450 to 1750' in E. E. RICH and C. H. WILSON (eds), *Cambridge Economic History of Europe* vol. IV, (Cambridge, 1967), pp. 474−477, 479, 483.

117   DE ROOVER, *Gresham*, 239; *Bruges*, 53−4; *Business*, 210−11; *L'Evolution de la Lettre de Change XIVe−SVIIe siècles* (Paris, 1953), pp. 121, 124−7; USHER, 'Origins', 415; A. E. FEAVEARYEAR, *Pound Sterling* (Oxford, 1931), pp. 52, 67, 102−3, 227; G. L. APPERSON, *Gleanings after Time* (London, 1907), p. 163; M. BELOFF, 'Humphrey Shalcrosse and the Great Civil War', *English Historical Review*, LIV, 1939, p. 688; HARLAND, *op. cit.*, 225−6; P.R.O., S.P.D., Chas, 162/72; B.L., Egerton MS 2983 fos 31v.−2; Harleian MS 4606, reversed; Leicestershire R.O., Archdeaconry inv. 1708/59.

118   *Ibid.*, 1636/217; B.L., Harleian MS fo. 10(9) (p. 8); DE ROOVER, *Gresham*, 101; *L'Evolution*, 121; HARRISON, 'Description of England', 189; G. WITHER cited in BLAXTON, *op. cit.*, 79, which I failed to find in Wither's major works; G. P. JONES, 'Some Sources of Loans and Credit in Cumbria before the Rise of Banks', *Transactions of the Cumberland and Westmorland Antiquarian and Archaeological Society*, new ser., LXXV, 1975, p. 289.

119   BIDWELL, *op. cit.*, 81 sqq.; HARRISON, *loc. cit.*, NOONAN, *op. cit.*, 367; MOSSE, *op. cit.*, 2.

120   WILSON, *op. cit.*, 322−5; COKE, *Inst.*, IV, 332; F. G. EMMISON, *Elizabethan Life: Morals and Church Courts* (Chelmsford, 1973), p. 73; TAWNEY and POWER, *op. cit.*, II, 137.

121   *Ibid.*, 163 sqq.; *Acts of the Privy Council (A.P.C.)*, XXXI, 379; N. J. WILLIAMS, *Tradesmen*, pp. 52, 63, 73, 78, 99; P.R.O., S.P.D., Eliz., 99/26; 127/76; Chancery, Proceedings, ser. I, Jas, bundle G17 no 15; Exchequer, King's Remembrancer, Memoranda Rolls, Recorda, 5 Jas, Hilary, rotulet 175; Michaelmas, rots 223−4; 6 Jas, Hil., rot. 87; Mich., rots 357−8, 499; 7 Jas, Easter, rots 70, 188; Trinity, rots 100−2, 203; Michaelmas, rots 206−9; Cheshire R.O., Quarter Sessions Records, no 19, Miscellaneous List of Informations etc. 1585−7 (27−9 Eliz.), nos 5, 7, 8, 10−13, 22, 28−30, 32−5, 39; 3 Co. Inst., 151−2; F. MOORE, *Cases Collect & Report*, (London, 1663, and various editions), pp. 397−8; E. ANDERSON, *Les Reports du treserudite Edmund Anderson* (2 pts, London, 1664−5, and var. edns), I, 48; II, 15, 16; J. GOLDESBOROUGH, *Reports of that learned and judicious clerk John Goldesborough* (London, 1653, and var. edns), p. 128.

122   J. RITCHIE, *Reports of Cases decided by Francis Bacon in the High Ct of Chancery (1617−21)* (London, 1932), pp. 143−4; G. STONE and D. MESTON, *Law relating to Money-lenders* (London, 1927), pp. 134−7, 145 sqq., 180−1; D. E. C. YALE (ed.), *Lord Nottingham's Chancery Cases* (Selden Society, 2 vols., 1957−61), II, 694−5; Statutes 3 and 4 Wm 4 c. 98; 63 and 64 Victoria c. 51.

123 M. M. POSTAN, 'Private Financial Instruments in Medieval England', *Vierteljahrschrift fuer Sozial-und-Wirtschaftsgeschichte* XXIII, 1930, pp. 27–9, 32–4, 36–7; D. WOODWARD, *op. cit.*, 181; J. CLAPHAM, *Bank of England: a History* (2 vols., Cambridge, 1944), I, 291; BOWDEN, *op. cit.*, 101 sqq.; W. SHEPPARD, *Touch-stone of Common Assurances* (London, 1648), pp. 353, 367; WILSON, *op. cit.*, 206; P.R.O., Ct of Requests, Proceedings, 308/6; Chancery, Proceedings, ser. II, 221/13; Duchy of Lancaster, Pleadings, bundle 48 no S.31; Exchequer, King's Remembrancer, Depositions by Commission, 23 Chas, Mich. 3; B.L., Harleian MS 70 fo. 27 (26). Hertfordshire R.O., Cashiobury and Gape Coll., 8442; J. VANES (ed.), *Ledger of Jn Smythe 1538–50*, H.M.C., Jt Pub. XIX, Bristol Rec. Soc. XXVIII, 1974, p. 237; J. M. HOLDEN, *History of Negotiable Instruments in English Law* (London, 1955), p. 61.

124 *Ibid.*; G. MALYNES, *Consuetudo vel Lex Mercatoria* (London, 1622), p. 103; POSTAN, 'Private Financial Instruments', 42 sqq., 58–61; P.R.O., Chancery, Judicial Proc. (Common Law Side), Rolls Chapel ser., bundle 8 no 39; Ct of Requests, Proc., 179/13; Norfolk R.O., Consistory Ct of Norwich, inv. 1628/156; P. J. BOWDEN, *op. cit.*, 105–6; DE ROOVER, *Gresham*, 121; *L'Evolution*, 110; T. F. T. PLUCKNETT, *Concise History of the Common Law* (London, 1956), pp. 666, 668–9.

125 DE ROOVER, *Business*, 210; *Gresham*, 101, 141; WILSON, *op. cit.*, 294; Statutes as cited in n. 116.

126 PLUCKNETT, *op. cit.*, 666; EHRENBERG, *op. cit.*, 330; MALYNES, *op. cit.*, 96 sqq., 103; POSTAN, 'Private Financial Instrs', 36–7, 54–5; E. LATTES, *La Libertà della Banche a Venezia del secolo XIII al XVII* (Milan, 1869), pp. 118, 121–2; DE ROOVER, *Gresham*, 110–11, 119, 121; *Bruges*, 340, 344; Statute 3 and 4 Anne c. 8; HOLDEN, *Negotiable Instruments*, 9, 11; G. J. PICCOPE (ed.), *Lancashire and Cheshire Wills and Invs from Ecclesiastical Ct, Chester* Chetham Society, XXXIII, 1857, pp. 111, 126–9; cf. J. H. MUNRO, 'Bullionism and the Bill of Exchange in England, 1272–1663' in *Dawn of Modern Banking*, 195; VAN DER WEE, *Growth of the Antwerp Market*, II, 343–5, 350–1.

127 G. D. RAMSAY, *Queen's Merchants and the Revolt of the Netherlands (End of the Antwerp Mart, pt II)* (Manchester, 1986), p. 63; HOLDEN, *Negotiable Instruments*, 17, 20, 22, 46, 63–4, 66 sqq., 73–4, 78–9; DE ROOVER, *Gresham*, 118–19, 121, 141, 239; *L'Evolution*, 87, 110; RICHARDS, *Early History*, 7, 15, 40; PLUCKNETT, *op. cit.*, 666, 669.

128 BOWDEN, 105–6; E. BULSTRODE, *Reports of Divers Resolutions and Judgements* (3 pts, London, 1657–9 and var. edns), III, 148–9.

129 My *Textile Manufactures*, 216–17; MELLING, *op. cit.*, III, 112–13; Devon R.O., Huntsham MSS, PZ 1, at 18, 25 Aug. 1621, 11 Feb. 1622, 16 Aug., 18 and 29 Oct. 1623, 8 May 1624; Somerset R.O., Somerset County Documents, Miscellaneous 3/12 c. 112.

130 H.M.C., *Salisbury MSS*, XIII, 560.

131 P.R.O., S.P.D., Supplementary vol. 80 fos 240, 243, 245; D. WOODWARD, *op. cit.*, 181.

132 E.g., R. SMITH, *op. cit.*, 45–7, 70; RIDEN, *op. cit.*, 59, 189–90; BOWDEN, *op. cit.*, 101 sqq.; W. WEST, *First Part of Simboleography*

(London, 1615), sections 105 (recte) 205 (erron.), 107 sqq.; H.M.C., *MSS of the Duke of Buccleuch and Queensberry at Montagu House* (3 vols. in 4, London, 1899–1926), III: Montagu Papers, 2nd ser., p. 12; M. CASH (ed.), *Devon Inventories of the 16th and 17th centuries*, Devon and Cornwall Record Society, XI, 1966, pp. 169–72; *Wills and Inventories from the Registry at Durham*, pt II, Surtees Society, XXXVIII, 1860, pp. 241–2; P.R.O., Chancery, Proceedings, ser. I, Eliz., C. 23/10; ser. II, 221/13; 223/95; Judicial Proceedings, (Common Law Side), Rolls Chapel ser., 8/10, 33, 36, 39, 66, 84–5, 91, 107, 113, 134, 167, 180; Ct of Requests, Proceedings, 29/22; 66/38; 169/34; 179/13, 23; 182/62; 186/67; 189/52; 198/16; 219/3; 265/28; 308/6; Duchy of Lancaster, Pleadings, 140/S. 28; 147/O. 2; 148/S. 31; Corporation of City of London R.O., Mayor's Ct, Depositions, 9 July 1644 Harvey *versus* Bovey; Ct of Orphans, Invs, box 11, Oliver Chadwell citizen and goldsmith 4 Apr. 23 Chas 2; Bodleian Library, Consistory and Archdeaconry Cts of Oxford, Original Wills etc., 299/7/32; Nottinghamshire R.O., Manorial Ct of Mansfield, probate records, portfolio 23 no 2b; Norfolk R.O., Consistory Ct invs 1593/289, 299; B.L., Harleian MS 70 fos 6 (5) v. (p. 1) sqq.

133   *Ibid.*, fos 18 (17) (p. 24), 27 (26); also 10, 11 (9, 10) (pp. 8, 10).

134   Devon R.O., Exeter City Library MS 1 (Q009.91/N539) fos 2 sqq.

135   *Ibid.*, fo. 41.

136   *Ibid.*, MS 36 Acct Book of Jn Hayne 1631–43, fo. 10v. (p. 8); also fo. 56v. (55); and see VANES, *op. cit.*, 237.

137   P.R.O., S.P.D., Supplementary vol. 80 fo. 238; Suffolk R.O. (Ipswich), Blois Fam. Archives, Hy Blois's Acct Led., fo. 59.

138   HOLDEN, *Negotiable Instruments*, 35–6.

139   Somerset R.O., Soms. County Documents, Misc., 3/12 c. 112; Manchester R.O., M91/M1/26; MUNDAY, 'Legal History', 231.

140   *Ibid.*, 232; Norfolk R.O., Consistory Court of Norwich inv. 1618/121; Devizes Museum, Wm Gaby His Booke, reversed, p. 45; Suffolk R.O. (Ipswich), Blois Fam. Archives, Hy Blois's Acct Led., fos 29v., 110; BIDWELL, *op. cit.*, 11, 12; GURNEY, *op. cit.*, 529–30; J. DE L. MANN, 'Clothiers and Weavers in Wiltshire during the 18th century' in L. S. PRESSNELL (ed.), *Studies in the Industrial Revolution presented to T. S. Ashton* (London, 1960), pp. 81–3.

141   E. F. GAY, 'Temples of Stowe and their Debts: Sir Thomas Temple and Sir Peter Temple, 1603–53', *Huntington Library Quarterly*, II, 1938–9, pp. 425–6, 428.

142   *Ibid.*, 425–6; DAVIES, 'Country Gentry', 16; my *Textile Manufactures*, 216–7.

143   E.g., H. M. JEWELL, *English Local Administration in the Middle Ages* (Newton Abbot and New York, 1972), pp. 101, 118 sqq.

144   RICHARDS, *Early History*, 10; STONE, *Palavicino*, 2 sqq., 140–1, 184–5; T. G. WYATT, 'Part Played by Aliens in the Social and Economic Life of England during the reign of Hy VIII', typescript M.A. thesis, London University, 1951, pp. 182–3, 194–5, 198; EHRENBERG, *op. cit.*, 194, 196, 200–1, 226; POSTLETHWAYT, *op. cit.*, I, 197; DE ROOVER, *Business*, 230; *Bruges*, 350; *L'Evolution*, 111, 139–40; *Gresham*, 17, 103–4, 124–5, 169–70, 228.

145 GAY, 'Temples of Stowe', 425–6; P.R.O., Ct of Requests, Proceedings, 123/56; 171/25; Chester R.O., Town Clerks Records, Protested Bills etc. 1639–65, fo. 34; Suffolk R.O. (Ipswich), Blois Fam. Archives, Hy Blois's Acct Led., fos 58v., 62–3, 89; Gloucestershire R.O., Marcham Coll., F. 26.

146 Somerset R.O., Soms. Co. Docs, Misc., 3/12 c. 112; Manchester R.O., M91/M1/26.

147 L. S. PRESSNELL, *Country Banking in the Industrial Revolution* (Oxford, 1956), pp. 4, 5, 12, 36 sqq., 45 sqq., 77 sqq.; J. DE L. MANN, *Wiltshire Textile Trades*, pp. xxii, xxiv; *Cloth Industry in the West of England from 1640 to 1880* (Oxford, 1971), pp. 65–6; 'Clothiers and Weavers', 81; HIBBERT, 'Letters', 190; WADSWORTH and MANN, *op. cit.*, 92–3, 95–6; WILLAN, *Inland Trade*, pp. 107–9, 112–13, 119–20; RIDEN, *op. cit.*, 77, 81, 94–5, 101, 125, 187, 189, 243; Devon R.O., Marwood Tucker Coll., E. 1; Lancashire R.O., Cavendish of Holker Coll., 1/46 fos 1, 2, pp. 5, 6; Norfolk R.O., Yarmouth Library MS L. 13, Pengelly Letters, 21 May 1667; P.R.O., S.P.D., Supplementary vol. 87 fos 283 sqq.; Manchester R.O., M91/M1/26; Corporation of London R.O., Mayor's Ct, Depositions, 21 Sept. 1644, Hill *versus* Webley; cf. CULLEN, *Anglo-Irish Trade*, 170, 173.

148 J. H. THOMAS, '17th-century Merchant's Acct Book', 155–6; Manchester R.O., M91/M1/26.

149 H.M.C., *Salisbury MSS*, XIII, 212 (ref. owed to kindness of Dr C. E. Challis). 'Letters' = 'letter' in modern parlance.

150 J. H. HESSELS (ed.), *Ecclesiae Londino-Batavae Archivum*, 3 vols, Cambridge, 1887–97, III, 736.

151 *Wills and Invs from Registry at Durham*, II, 237, 239, 242.

152 ANDERTON, 'Delaval Papers', 140, 159.

153 P.R.O., S.P.D., Supplementary vol. 42 fo. 157.

154 House of Lords R.O., House of Lords Papers 27 Jan. 1596–7 to 1 June 1607, fo. 140.

155 Suffolk R.O. (Ipswich), Blois Family Archives, Hy Blois's Acct Led., loose papers ad init., and fos 29v., 51v.

156 Manchester R.O., M91/M1/26.

157 Lancashire R.O., Cavendish of Holker Coll., 1/107; Devizes Museum, Wm Gaby His Booke, reversed, pp. 34–5.

158 B.L., Harleian MS 70 fos 9, 18 (8, 17) (pp. 6, 24).

159 Devon R.O., Exeter City Lib. MSS 1, (Q009.91) (N.539), Acct Book of Jn Newcombe, fos 12v., 13, 23v.–4, 28.

160 P.R.O., S.P.D., Supplementary vol. 80 fos 233–5.

161 Suffolk R.O. (Ipswich), Blois Fam. Archives, Hy Blois's Acct Led., fo. 52; Manchester R.O., M91/M1/26; Liverpool R.O., 920 MD 172, Sir Willoughby Aston's Diary, at 17 Sept. 1681; Devon R.O., Huntsham MSS, PZ1, 23 July, 13 Oct. 1621; Bodleian Lib., Herrick Papers, MSS English History c. 475 fo. 22; P.R.O., Exchequer, Land Revenue, Particulars of Grants, Leases, etc. vol. 15, fo. 166 (161); *Cal. of Wynn (Gwydir) Papers*, 352; HAINSWORTH, *Correspondence*, 123, 125–6, 146, 152, 290, 321, 377, 393, 582; M. E. JAMES, *op. cit.*, p. liv; H.M.C., *Salisbury MSS*, II, 533 (ref. owed to kindness of Dr C. E. Challis); L. STONE, *Crisis of the*

Aristocracy 1558–1641 (Oxford, 1965), p. 511; C. CLAY, *Public Finance and Private Wealth: the career of Sir Stephen Fox 1627–1716* (Oxford, 1978), p. 160.

162   Gloucestershire R.O., Marcham Coll., F.26; DAVIES, 'Country Gentry', 26.

163   STONE, *Crisis*, 511.

164   Bodleian Lib., Herrick Papers, MSS Engl. Hist. c.475, fos 12, 29, 45, 98; P.R.O., S.P. Ire. 83/33; cf. L. VON MISES, *Theory of Money and Credit* (Indianapolis, 1981), p. 318.

165   *Cal. Wynn (Gwydir) Papers*, 155, 352.

166   Friends House, London, case 110 (32), shelf 2, box 8, Jas Dix's MSS, no B.4.B.

167   HOLDEN, *Negotiable Instruments*, 43; DAVIES, 'Country Gentry', 17 sqq.; J. MARIUS, *Advice concerning Bils of Exchange*, in MALYNES, *Consuetudo*, 1655 edn, p. 9, 1656 edn, p. 3; ROWLANDS, *op. cit.*, 75; RIDEN, *op. cit.*, 125, 129; Cheshire R.O., Cholmondeley Coll., box K, Vouchers to Account 1696–7; 1698–1700, pass.; F. T. MELTON, *Sir Robert Clayton and the Origins of English Deposit Banking, 1658–1685* (Cambridge, 1986), pp. 79, 84, 87–9, 102, 111–12, 217, 220–1; J. THIRSK and J. P. COOPER, *17th Century Economic Documents* (Oxford, 1972), p. 687.

168   STONE, *Crisis*, 512–13; BRERETON, *op. cit.*, 89; G. S. THOMSON, *Life in a Noble Household 1641–1700* (London, 1937), p. 365; HUDLESTON, *op. cit.*, 145, 191–2; ANDERTON, 'Delaval Papers', 138, 140, 145; M. E. JAMES, *op. cit.*, pp. liv–lv; BIDWELL, *op. cit.*, 11, 12; J. P. COOPER, *Wentworth Papers 1597–1628*, Royal Historical Society, Camden 4th ser., XII, 1973, pp. 174, 227; GURNEY, *op. cit.*, 529–30, 545; H.M.C., *12th Report* (London, 1890), Appendices, pt I, p. 71; pt IV, p. 96; *Calendar (Report) of (on) the MSS of the Marquis (Marquess) of Bath* (5 vols., London, 1904–80), IV, 168; J. V. BECKETT, *Coal and Tobacco: the Lowthers and the economic development of West Cumberland 1660–1760* (Cambridge, 1981), pp. 115–16; *Cal. of Wynn Papers*, 155, 352; Bodleian Lib., MSS English History c.475 fos 8, 12; Leicestershire R.O., Beaumanor Coll., DG9/2049, pp. 91, 128; Manchester R.O., M91/M1/26; Northamptonshire R.O., Finch-Hatton Coll., nos 4197–8; Lancashire R.O., Cavendish of Holker Coll., 1/107; Devon R.O., Exeter City Library MS 1 (56/14), transcript of Courtenay Pole's Acct Book 1650–8; HAINSWORTH, *Correspondence*, 29, 30, 32, 36, 52, 79, 87, 89, 101, 118, 125–6, 135, 159, 163, 173, 177, 213, 227–8, 283, 286, 314–15, 318, 403, 412, 414, 453–4, 466–7, 470, 472, 482, 486, 491–2, 496, 498, 520, 532, 536, 544–5, 586, 603.

169   T. NORTH, 'Letters of Alderman Robert Heyricke of Leicester 1590–1617', *Transactions of the Leicestershire Architectural and Archaeological Society*, V, 1882, pp. 110 sqq.; Bodleian Lib., Herrick Papers, MSS English History c.475 fos 6, 12, 25–6, 98; c.479 fos 24 sqq., 35, 54, 94; Leicestershire R.O., Beaumanor Coll., DG9/2049, pp. 88–9, 91–3, 98–9, 104, 106, 108–9, 111, 114, 117–8, 121, 123–4, 128 sqq., 135, 138–9, 141–4, 154, 156, 158–9, 161–4, 177, 179, 182.

170   BIDWELL, *op. cit.*, 11, 12; GURNEY, *op. cit.*, 529–30; Manchester R.O., M91/M1/26.

171 P.R.O., S.P.D., Supplementary vol.63 fos 163–5.

172 THOMSON, *op. cit.*, 365.

173 P.R.O., S.P.D., Supplementary vol.42 fo.157.

174 BECKETT, *op. cit.*, 115–17; WADSWORTH and MANN, *op. cit.*, 92–3; *DAVIES*, *'Country Gentry'*, 25, 34; *CLAY*, *op. cit.*, 157; T. NORTH, 'Letters', 117; HAINSWORTH, *Correspondence*, 228; Bodleian Library, MS Top. Kent a.I fo.26v.; P.R.O., Privy Council Register, 1638, p. 210 (f.103v.); S.P.D., Chas 351/2; 352/3, 82; 458/42; 459/21; W. R. WARD, *English Land Tax in the Eighteenth Century*, London, 1953, pp. 47–8.

175 H.M.C., *Salisbury MSS*, II, 533 (reference owed to the kindness of Dr C. E. Challis); P.R.O., S.P. Ireland, 76/11; 80/55, 56; 83/33, 55; 88/6.

176 HESSELS, *op. cit.*, III, 736, 1098–9.

177 H.M.C., *Salisbury MSS*, XIII, 212; C. E. Challis, *Tudor Coinage* (Manchester, 1978), p. 33.

178 P.R.O., Chancery, Proceedings, ser. I, Eliz., G3 no 31.

179 ANDERTON, 'Delaval Papers', 138.

180 P.R.O., S.P.D., Supplementary vol.63 fos 163–6.

181 Suffolk R.O. (Ipswich), Blois Fam. Archives, Hy Blois's Acct Led., fo.59. (For 'The George', see RICHARDS, *Early History*, 64.)

182 Devon R.O., Huntsham MSS, PZ1.

183 Devon R.O., Exeter City Library MS 36 Acct Book of Jn Hayne 1631–43 fo.10v. (p. 8).

184 COOPER, *op. cit.*, 174, 227; H.M.C., *12th Report*, Apps, I, 71, 89; IV, 96; *Marquess of Bath's MSS*, IV, 168; Devon R.O., Huntsham Coll., PZ1; Norfolk R.O., Business Records, no 79.

185 H.M.C. *Salisbury MSS*, II, 532–3; P.R.O., S.P. Ireland, 76/11; 80/55, 56; 83/33, 55; 88/6.

186 STONE, *Crisis*, 512.

187 THOMSON, *op. cit.*, 365; BECKETT, *op. cit.*, 115; DAVIES, 'Country Gentry', 34.

188 Bodleian Library, MS Top. Kent a.I fo.26v.

189 Chester R.O., Town Clerks Records, Protested Bills etc. 1639–65 fo.46.

190 RICHARDS, *Early History*, 237.

191 DAVIES, 'Country Gentry', 17.

192 GAY, 'Temples of Stowe', 425; DE ROOVER, *Gresham*, 127–8.

193 P.R.O., S.P.D., Supplementary vol.80 fo.236.

194 *Ibid.*, fo.237.

195 DAVIES, 'Country Gentry', 17; HOLDEN, *Negotiable Instruments*, 209–10, plates 5 a and b; CLAPHAM, *op. cit.*, I, 6; RICHARDS, *Early History*, 50, 52, 54; 'Backwell', 354; J. B. MARTIN, *'The Grasshopper' in Lombard Street* (London, 1892), p. 129; J. A. S. L. Leighton-Boyce, *Smiths the Bankers 1658–1958* (London, 1958), p. 18; USHER, *Deposit Banking*, 89, 90, 447; 'Origins', 418–9, 426–8; DE ROOVER, *Business*, 216, 231; *Medici*, 18, 19.

196 *Ibid.*, 127; *L'Evolution*, 99, 112–13, 140, 143; *Gresham*, 122; RICHARDS, *Early History*, 44–5; PLUCKNETT, *op. cit.*, 668; HOLDEN, *Negotiable Instruments*, 44–6, 268; MARIUS, *op. cit.*, 1655 edn, p. 45;

and in MALYNES, *Consuetudo*, 1656 edn, p. 12; POSTLETHWAYT, *op. cit.*, I, 197; Devon R.O., Brookings-Rowe Bequest 59/7/1/11 nos 1–29; P.R.O., S.P.D., Supplementary vol. 80 fos 236–9.

197   DAVIES, 'Country Gentry', 18.

198   *Ibid.*, 18–20, 33–5; *Wills and Invs from the Registry at Durham*, II, 242; RIDEN, *op. cit.*, 94–5; ROWLANDS, *op. cit.*, 75; Leicestershire R.O., Beaumanor Coll., DG9/2049, pp. 93, 188; Devon R.O., Exeter City Library MS 1, transcript of Courtenay Pole's Acct Book 1650–8, vol. I; Suffolk R.O. (Bury), Episcopal Commissary Ct of Bury, inv. 1704/32; P.R.O., S.P.D., Supplementary vol. 63 fo. 163.

199   Sup. p. 45.

200   MARIUS, *op. cit.*, 1655 edn, pp. 4, 5; J. SCARLETT, *Stile of Exchanges* (London, 1682), p. 15.

201   RICHARDS, *Early History*, 44–5; DE ROOVER, *Gresham*, 122; *Business*, 232; MARIUS, *op. cit.*, 1655 edn, p. 45, and in MALYNES, *Consuetudo*, 1656 edn, p. 12; Suffolk R.O. (Ipswich), Blois Fam. Archives, Hy Blois's Acct Led., fo. 112. Marselza = Marseilles.

202   *Ibid.*, fo. 57; ANDERTON, 'Delaval Papers', 145; RICHARDS, 'Backwell', 340; HAINSWORTH, *Correspondence*, 173; DAVIES, 'Country Gentry', 32–3; RIDEN, *op. cit.*, 77, 94, 101, 189, 243; Devon R.O., Exeter City Library MS 1, transcript Courtenay Pole's Acct Book; Brookings-Rowe Bequest, 59/7/4/11 nos 1–29; Lancashire R.O., Consistory Ct of Chester, Supra inv. Jn Gregory 1675 Rochdale; Manchester R.O., M91/M1/26; P.R.O., S.P.D., Chas 352/3, 82; 458/42; 459/21; Supplementary vol. 80 fos 236 sqq.; Bodleian Lib., Herrick Papers, MSS English History c. 475 fos 6, 18, 45, 86, 96; c. 476 fo. 60; Cheshire R.O., Cholmondeley Coll., box K, Vouchers to Account 1698–1700, nos 2, 8; Chester R.O., Town Clerks Records, Protested Bills etc. 1639–65, fo. 16.

203   *Ibid.*, passim; also W. J. Smith, *Herbert Correspondence: 16th and 17th century letters of the Herberts of Chirbury, Powis Castle and Dolgnog* (Cardiff and Dublin, 1963), p. 309; HAINSWORTH, *Commercial Papers*, 11, 15, 18, 56; CULLEN, *Economic History*, 16, 30–1, 42.

204   J[N] B[ROWN], *Marchants Avizo* (London, 1607), pp. 53–4; MARIUS, *op. cit.*, 1651 edn, pp. 10–12, 1655 edn, pp. 65–6; W. FORBES, *Methodical Treatise concerning Bills of Exchange* (Edinburgh, 1703), p. 61; HOLDEN, *Negotiable Instruments*, 45, 48, 53–5; SCARLETT, *op. cit.*, 60. DAVIES, 'Country Gentry', 18, 35; Statutes 3 and 4 Anne c. 8; 7 Anne c. 25 par. 3; 9 Wm 3 c. 17.

205   HAINSWORTH, *Commercial Papers*, 204; USHER, *Deposit Banking*, 21; 'Origins', 410, 416, 418–19, 426, 428; DE ROOVER, *Bruges*, 199, 264, 335; *Business*, 202, 216; VAN DILLEN, *op. cit.*, 40–1.

206   RICHARDS, *Early History*, 194; DAVIES, 'Country Gentry', 24–6; *Cal. of Wynn (Gwydir) Papers*, 155, 352; P.R.O., S.P. Ire., 80/55; 83/33, 55; 88/6; WESTERFIELD, *op. cit.*, 199; R. J. COLYER, *Welsh Cattle Drovers*, Cardiff, 1976, pp. 52 sqq.; cf. CHARTRES, 'Marketing', 480–2.

207   JAMES, *op. cit.*, p. liv.

208   HESSELS, *op. cit.*, III, 1098–9.

209 House of Lords R.O., House of Lords Papers 27 Jan. 1596–7 to 1 June 1607, fos 129, 135.

210 P.R.O., S.P.D., Supplementary vol. 63 fos 164, 165v., 174.

211 Suffolk R.O. (Ipswich), Blois Fam. Archives, Hy Blois's Acct Led., fos 57, 59.

212 *Ibid.*, fos 62, 89.

213 Devon R.O., Huntsham MSS, PZ1.

214 ANDERTON, 'Delaval Papers', 145.

215 DAVIES, 'Country Gentry', 19; Bradford R.O., Cunliffe-Lister MSS, bundle 11: Masham: 'Part of my Grandfather Sir Thomas Danby's Acct'.

216 P.R.O., Privy Council Register, 1638, p. 210 (fo. 103v.); S.P.D., Chas, 351/2; 352/3, 82; 458/42; 459/21.

217 *Ibid.*, 380/80.

218 *Ibid.*, 478/10; Supplementary vol. 80 fo. 237v.

219 Chester R.O., Town Clerks Records, Protested Bills etc. 1639–65, fo. 46; Somerset R.O., Soms. Co. Docs, 3/12 c. 112.

220 Lancashire R.O., Hopwood Coll., 39/13; Consistory Ct of Chester, Supra inv. Jn Gregory 1675 Rochdale; H.M.C., *8th Report* (3 vols. in 5 pts, London, 1881), I, 11.

221 Manchester R.O., M91/M1/26.

222 Corporation of London R.O., Ct of Orphans, invs, box 5, Sir Martin Noell knight, citizen and scrivener 1666; C. H. CAVE, *History of Banking in Bristol from 1750–1899* (Bristol, 1899), pp. 2–4; NEF, *Coal Industry*, II, 120; P.R.O., S.P.D., Interregnum, 69/98; RIDEN, op. cit., 81; DAVIES, 'Country Gentry', 23.

223 *Ibid.*, 26; P.R.O., S.P.D., Chas 351/2; 352/3, 82; 459/21; Bodleian Lib., Herrick Papers, MS English History c. 475 fos 6, 29.

224 DAVIES, 'Country Gentry', 33–4.

225 *Ibid.*, 34; HAINSWORTH, *Correspondence*, 30, 32, 118.

226 MARIUS, *op. cit.*, 1651 edn, pp. 48–9 recte (1st occurrence, 48–5 erron.), 1655 edn, pp. 4, 5, 8, 9, 26–7; in MALYNES, *Consuetudo*, 1656 edn, pp. 2, 3; MALYNES, *op. cit.*, 1622 edn, pp. 96, 104–5; also A. F. UPTON, *Sir Arthur Ingram circa 1565–1642* (Oxford, 1961), p. 178.

227 E.G., Devon R.O., Exeter City Library MS 36, Acct Book of Jn Hayne 1631–43, fo. 10v. (p. 8); P.R.O., Chancery, Proceedings, ser. I, Eliz., G3 no 31.

228 *Ibid.*, G3 no 31; ser. II, 258/82; (cf. 221/15); Ct of Requests, Proceedings, 29/22; 182/62; 189/52; 198/16; 219/3; Ct of Star Chamber, Proceedings, Eliz., C30/7; C54/3; S.P.D., Supplementary vol. 65 fos 55 sqq.; (cf. S.P.D., Chas 162/66); Leicestershire R.O., Beaumanor MSS, inv. Nicholas Herrick, citizen and goldsmith of London 38 Eliz.; Beaumanor Coll., DG9/2049, pp. 1, 3, X7, 13, 43, 61, 81, 88–9, 91–2, 94, 98, 108, 114, 116, 122, 124, 127–8, 131, 134, 138, 146, 156, 162, 164–5, 168; Bodleian Lib., Herrick Papers, MS Engl. Hist. c. 475 fos 86, 96; Gay, 'Temples of Stowe', 428; BACON, *Essays*, 'Of Riches'; WILSON, *op. cit.*, 98; FENTON, *op. cit.*, 23; DEMPSEY, *op. cit.*, 174–5; DE ROOVER, *Bruges*, 205; UNWIN, *op. cit.*, 27–8; A. HEAL, *London Goldsmiths 1200–1800* (Cambridge,

1935), pp. 62, 73, 75, 88; D. K. CLARK, 'Restoration Goldsmith-Banking House: The Vine on Lombard Street' in *Essays in Modern English History in Honor of W. C. Abbott* (Cambridge, Mass., 1941), p. 3; Lancashire R.O., Cavendish of Holker Coll., 1/46, p. 15; Corporation of London R.O., Ct of Orphans, invs. box 2, Chas Everard, esq., citizen and goldsmith 1665.

229   *Ibid.*, box 5, Sir Martin Noell, knight, citizen and scrivener 1666; WILSON, *op. cit.*, 99–101; GAY, 'Temples of Stowe', 427; RICHARDS, 'Pioneers', 496–7; *Early History*, 16, 18; PRESSNELL, *Country Banking*, 36sqq.; R. NORTH, *op. cit.*, 21; MELTON, *op. cit.*, 25–6, 28–30, 44, 46 sqq., 96; COLEMAN, 'Scriveners', 222–3, 227, 229; BELOFF, 'Humphrey Shalcrosse', 687sqq.; Statute 21 Jas c. 19 par. 2; B.L., Egerton MS 2983, fo. 31v.; HOLDEN, *Negotiable Instruments*, 206.

230   *Ibid.*; FENTON, *op. cit.*, 118–19; WILSON, *op. cit.*, 262; J. C(HILD), *Tract against Usury presented to the High Ct of Parliament* (London, 1621 and 1668), 1621 edn, p. 1, 1668 edn, p. 23; W. NOTESTEIN, F. H. RELF and H. SIMPSON (eds), *Commons Debates 1621* (7 vols., New Haven, 1935), II, 317–18; III, 66; V, 93–4; VI, 94; EVANS and BECKETT, 'Cumberland, Westmorland and Furness', 25; Norfolk R.O., Cons. Ct invs 1588/57, 168; 1593/289, 299; 1599/195B; 1611/310; 1618/121; 1621/81; 1625/9; 1626/167A and B; 1628/156; 1637–68/36; 1640/137; P.R.O., Prerogative Ct of Canterbury, invs 1718–82, bundle 27 no 60; B.L., Additional MS 15559 fos 1, 11v., 12; Leicestershire R.O., Archdeaconry inv. 1631/107; Worcester and Hereford R.O. (Worcester), Consistory Ct of Worcester, inv. Sarah Turbervile widow 1719 Worcester.

231   W. S. PRIDEAUX, *Memorials of the Goldsmiths' Company* (2 vols., sine loco nec data), I, 134, 136; RICHARDS, *Early History*, 36–7; DE ROOVER, *Gresham*, 99, 103, 237; *Business*, 230–2; *Bruges*, 350; POSTLETHWAYT, *op. cit.*, I, 197; MARIUS, *op. cit.*, 1655 edn, pp. 21–2; W. R. BISSCHOP, *Rise of the London Money Market 1640–1826* (London, 1910), p. 43; J. F. LARKIN, *Stuart Royal Proclamations*, vol. II, Royal Proclamations of King Chas I, 1625–1646 (Oxford, 1983), pp. 144sqq.; JUDGES, 'Origins', 142–3; Anon., *Is not the Hand of Joab in all this? or an Inquiry into the Grounds of a late Pamphlet intituled The Mystery of the New-fashioned Goldsmiths or Bankers* (London, 1676), p. 7.

232   VAN DER WEE, *Growth of the Antwerp Market*, II, 340–1; 345sqq., 360; 'Anvers et les innovations de la technique financière aux XVIe et XVIIe siècles', *Annales: économies, sociétés, civilisations*, XXII, 1967, pp. 1071sqq., 1081–2, 1085, 1088; 'Sporen van disconto te Antwerpen tijdens de XVIe eeuw', *Bijdragen tot de Geschiedenis der Nederlanden*, X, 1955, pp. 68–70; E. AERTS, 'Prof. R. De Roover and Medieval Banking History', *Revue de la Banque*, 1980, cahier 8/9, pp. 257–8, 268 (reference owed to the kindness of Prof. J. R. S. Revell); G. LUZZATTO, 'Les Banques Publiques de Venise' in VAN DILLEN, *op. cit.*, p. 49; DE ROOVER, *Business*, 185–6, 194, 219–21, 230–2; *Gresham*, 6, 100–3, 105, 110, 118sqq., 128, 237; *L'Evolution*, 86–7, 90, 98sqq., 112–13, 121, 124–5, 139, 143, 146; *Bruges*, 54, 70, 269, 276sqq., 350–1; *Medici*, 137–40; USHER, 'Origins', 421sqq.; *Deposit Banking*, 21–2, 72, 99, 100; EHRENBERG, *op. cit.*, 104, 116, 246–8, 310–12, 323–4, 330–1; HOLDEN, *Negotiable Instruments*,

References   131

44–5; J. B[ROWN], *op. cit.*, 53–4; RICHARDS, *Early History*, 44–5; PLUCKNETT, *op. cit.*, 66–7; *Modern Reports, or Select Cases adjudged in the Cts of King's Bench, Chancery, Common Pleas and Exchequer from the Restoration of Chas II to the 28th year of George II*, ed. T. Leach (12 vols., London, 1793–6 and var. edns), XII, 36; MARIUS, *op. cit.*, 1651 edn, pp. 54–5; 1655 edn, pp. 45, 54–5; in MALYNES, *Consuetudo*, 1656 edn, pp. 10, 14, 30, 39; MALYNES, *op. cit.*, 1622 edn, pp. 96–8, 394–5; DEMPSEY, *op. cit.*, 179–80; M. GRICE-HUTCHINSON, *Early Economic Thought in Spain 1177–1740* (London, 1978), p. 48; LATTES, *op. cit.*, 118, 121–2; J. STRIEDER, *Aus Antwerpener Notariats Archiven* (Stuttgart, Berlin and Leipzig, 1930), pp. 165–6; S. T. BINDOFF, 'Greatness of Antwerp' in G. R. ELTON (ed.), *New Cambridge Modern History* vol. I (Cambridge, 1958), pp. 63–5; cf. S.-E. Åström, *From Cloth to Iron: the Anglo-Baltic trade in the late seventeenth century.* (Societas Scientiarum Fennica, Commentationes Humanarum Litterarum, tomus XXXIII, no 1, Helsingfors [Helsinki], 1963), pp. 213 sqq.

233 DE ROOVER, *Gresham*, 127–8, 184, 195; C. WILLIAMS (ed.), *Thomas Platter's Travels in England, 1599* (London, 1937), p. 157; BISSCHOP, *op. cit.*, 43; RICHARDS, *Early History*, 36–7; JUDGES, 'Origins', 142–3.

234 J.R., *Mystery*, p. 3; H. YELVERTON, *Reports of Sir Hy Yelverton*, translated from the French (London, 1792 and var. edns), 137, 147; W. LEONARD, *Reports and Cases of Law* (2 vols., London, 1658), III, 63; R. BROWNLOW and J. GOULDESBOROUGH, *Reports of Diverse Choice Cases in Law* (London, 1651), p. 103.

235 MARTIN, *op. cit.*, 117; RICHARDS, *Early History*, 37; J.R., *op. cit.*, 3–6; PRIDEAUX, *op. cit.*, I, 134, 136; Anon., *Is not the Hand of Joab in all this?*, 7; R. NORTH, *op. cit.* 21; DE ROOVER, *Gresham*, 99, 100, 103, 105, 118–19, 127–8; *Business*, 185, 230, 232; FEAVEARYEAR, *op. cit.*, 102–3; S.H.A.H. (ed.), *Diary of John Hervey, First Earl of Bristol* (Wells, 1894), p. 183; *Letter-Books of John Harvey, First Earl of Bristol* (3 vols., Wells, 1894), III, 139, 145, 158.

236 PRIDEAUX, *op. cit.*, I, 39, 40, 51, 54, 73, 159; T. F. REDDAWAY, 'London Goldsmiths *circa* 1500', *Transactions of the Royal Historical Society*, 5th ser., XII, 1962, pp. 50–1, 62; T. F. REDDAWAY and L. E. M. WALKER, *Early History of the Goldsmiths' Company 1327–1509* (London, 1975), pp. 221–3, 244–5.

237 RICHARDS, *Early History*, 28–30, 82, 245; 'Backwell', 340–1; CLAY, *op. cit.*, 157, 159–60; WARD, *op. cit.*, 47–8.

238 Devon R.O., Exeter City Library MS 1, transcript of Courtenay Pole's Acct Book 1650–8.

239 LEIGHTON-BOYCE, *op. cit.*, 12, 13, 15, 67.

240 Leicestershire R.O., Beaumanor Coll., inv. Nicholas Herrick 38 Eliz.; DG9/2049, pp. 43, 132, 192; Bodleian Lib., Herrick Papers, MS English History c. 475 fos 22, 25, 45.

241 COKE, *Inst.*, I, 182; H. WINCH, *Reports* (London, 1657 and var. edns), p. 24; T. CARTHEW, *Reports of Cases adjudged in the Ct of King's Bench* (London, 1741 and var. edns), pp. 369–70; T. HETLEY, *Reports and*

Cases (London, 1657 and var. edns), p. 167; G. CROKE, *Reports* (3 pts, [Eliz., Jas., Chas.] London, 1661–7 and var. edns), II, 306; J. KEBLE, *Reports in the Ct of King's Bench* (2 pts, London, 1685 and var. edns), I, 592, 636; II, 105, 132–3; W. DALISON, *Les Reports de divers Special Cases* (London, 1689 and var. edns), p. 104; F. MOORE, *op. cit.*, 667; RICHARDS, *Early History*, 47–9; HOLDEN, *Negotiable Instruments*, 33–6, 78; PLUCKNETT, *op. cit.*, 246, 668–9; Statute 3 and 4 Anne c. 8; cf. J. H. BAKER, 'Law Merchant and the Common Law before 1700', *Cambridge Law Journal*, 1979, pp. 297, 315 sqq.

242   E. LUTWYCHE, *Un Livre des Entries* (2 vols., London, 1704), II, 1585.

243   HOLDEN, *Negotiable Instruments*, 22, 28, 44, 65, 268, 324–5; PLUCKNETT, *op. cit.*, 644; E. COKE, *Inst*, I, 182; *Reports* (13 pts, London, 1777 and var. edns), IV, fo. 92v.; CROKE, *op. cit.*, II, 6, 7; III, 301–2; P.R.O., Ct of Requests, Proceedings, 134/28.

244   D. E. C. YALE, 'View of the Admiralty Jurisdiction: Sir Matthew Hale and the Civilians' in D. JENKINS (ed.), *Legal History Studies* (Cardiff, 1972), pp. 90, 98–101, 104; L. S. SUTHERLAND, 'Law Merchant in England in the 17th and 18th centuries', *Transactions of the Royal Historical Society*, 4th ser., XVII, 1934, p. 155; HOLDEN, *Negotiable Instruments*, 28, 31–2, 34–5; W. PRYNNE, *Brief Animadversions on Amendments of and Additional Explanatory Records to, The Fourth Part of the Institutes of the Lawes of England* (London, 1669), pp. 75–6, 98–101, 123–5; Anon., *Reasons for Setling Admiralty Jurisdiction … offered to the Two Houses of Parliament* (sine loco, 1690), pp. 15–18 reproduces Privy Council Register for 18 & 22 Feb. 1632; R. G. MARSDEN (ed.), *Select Pleas in the Ct of Admiralty*, 2 vols., Selden Society, VI, XI, 1894–7, II, 73, 126; W. HOLDSWORTH, *History of English Law*, vol. I (1956), 555–6; vol. VIII (1937), 159–60; FIRTH and RAIT, *op. cit.*, I, 1120–1; II, 78, 510, 712–13, 902, 1131; P.R.O., S.P.D., Chas, vol. 208; 231/35, 48–51.

245   CROKE, *op. cit.*, II, 306; P. VENTRIS, *Reports*, 2 pts, London, 1726, II, 152–3; *Modern Reports*, V, 13, 14; XII, 36–7; HETLEY, *op. cit.*, 167; ROBERT, LORD RAYMOND, *Reports of Cases*, 3 vols, London, 1696 and var. edns, I, 574; D. IBBETSON, 'Assumpsit and Debt in the Early Sixteenth Century: the origins of the indebitatus count', *Cambridge Law Journal*, 1982, pp. 142, 150 sqq.; BAKER, 'Law Merchant', 296–7, 308–9, 313; HOLDS-WORTH, *op. cit.*, III (1935), 428, 443–4, 446, 451; VIII (1937), 6, 7, 159–60.

246   KEBLE, *op. cit.*, I, 592, 636.

247   *Ibid.*, II, 105–6; LUTWYCHE, *op. cit.*, II, 1585; B. SHOWER, *Reports of Cases in the King's Bench during the reigns of Chas II, Jas II and Wm III*, London, 1794 and var. edns, I, 4, 5.

248   PLUCKNETT, *op. cit.*, 669; Statutes 9 Wm 3 c. 17; 3 and 4 Anne c. 8; *Modern Reports*, VI, 29; C. H. S. FIFOOT, *Lord Mansfield*, Oxford, 1936, p. 90; Cheshire R.O., Cholmondeley Coll., box K, Vouchers to Account 1696–7; 1698–1700, nos 1–22, 24–5, 27–8, 31–3, 35–6, 38–9; HOLDEN, *Negotiable Instruments*, 63–4.

249   *Ibid.*, 73–4, 77–80, 91; RICHARDS, *Early History*, 48; Statutes 3 and 4 Anne c. 8; 7 Anne c. 25 para. 3; *Modern Reports*, 29, 30.

250 Supp. pp. 6, 31–2, 68.

251 HEAL, *op. cit.*, 51 sqq., 58, 62–3, 66, 68–9, 71 sqq., 77, 79–82, 85, 87–8, 100.

252 JUDGES, 'Origins', 139, 141, 145; RICHARDS, *Early History*, 23–4, 27 sqq., 37, 40–2, 82, 88–9, 245; 'Backwell', 341–2; J.R., *op. cit.*, 4, 7; D. K. CLARK, 'Ed. Backwell as Royal Agent', *Economic History Review*, IX, 1938, pp. 45 sqq.; 'Restoration Goldsmith-Banking House, 13, 17; PRESSNELL, *Country Banking*, 12 sqq., 36 sqq., 45 sqq.; BISSCHOP, *op. cit.*, 206–7; HOLDEN, *Negotiable Instruments*, 90, 209–10; MARTIN, *op. cit.*, 31, 117; BIDWELL, *op. cit.*, 23; CLAPHAM, *op. cit.*, I, 10; D. NORTH, *op. cit.*, 21; NEF, *Coal Industry*, II, 120–1; VON MISES, *Money and Credit*, 342–3; LEIGHTON-BOYCE, *op. cit.*, 13, 15, 17, 18, 67.

253 *Ibid.*, 7, 12, 13, 15, 17, 18, 67; J. K. HORSEFIELD, 'Beginnings of Paper Money in England', *Journal of European Economic History*, VI, 1977, pp. 117, 121, 125; '"Stop of the Exchequer" Revisted', *Economic History Review*, 2nd ser., XXXV, 1982, pp. 526–7; D. M. JOSLIN, 'London Private Bankers 1720–85', *ibid.*, 2nd ser., VII, 1954, pp. 167 sqq., and CARUS-WILSON, *op. cit.*, II, 340 sqq.; E. R. SAMUEL, 'Sir Francis Child's Jewellery Business', *Three Banks Review*, 1977, no 113, pp. 43 sqq.; MELTON, *op. cit.*, 53–6, 81 sqq., 91–4, 96–7, 126 sqq.; PRESSNELL, *Country Banking*, 4, 5, 75 sqq., 225 sqq., 401 sqq.; WARD, *op. cit.*, 47; S.H.A.H., *Diary*, 183; *Letter-Books*, III, 145; W. T. C. KING, *History of the London Discount Market* (London, 1936), pp. 17, 18.

254 *Ibid.*, 12, 13, 72–3, 81, 87, 101, 103 sqq., 158, 167; CLARK, 'Backwell', 46–7, 53; HORSEFIELD, '"Stop"', 511 sqq.; W. BAGEHOT, *Lombard Street* (London, 1873), p. 92; CLAPHAM, *op. cit.*, I, 2–5, 10, 103, 121 sqq., 130, 134, 137, 158–9, 162, 168–9, 204–5, 208–10, 215, 273–6, 284–7, 290–1, App. E; II, 2, 3, 15, 58–9, 61–2, 132–4, 144–5; R. S. SAYERS, *Bank of England 1891–1944* (2 vols., Cambridge, 1976), pp. 1, 33, 45–6, 105 sqq.; RICHARDS, *Early History*, 24–5, 59–61, 64–6, 136 (quot.), 140–1, 145–7, 149, 153, 171–2, 179, 181, 183, 191, 193; 'First Fifty Years of the Bank of England (1694–1744)' in VAN DILLEN, *op. cit.*, 201–2, 204, 208, 210–11, 215–16, 219 sqq., 243, 245–7, 250–1, 254 sqq., 265, 271–2; Statute 5 and 6 Wm and Mary c. 20; J. K. HORSEFIELD, 'Bank of England as Mentor', *Economic History Review*, 2nd ser., II, 1949, pp. 80 sqq.; B. L. ANDERSON and P. L. COTTRELL, *Money and Banking in England: the development of the banking system 1694–1914* (London, 1974), pp. 40 sqq., 60 sqq.

255 *Ibid.*, 206–8, 214 sqq.; BIDWELL, *op. cit.*, 16, 38, 58–9; LEIGHTON-BOYCE, *op. cit.*, 36–9; E. CANNAN, *Paper Pound of 1797–1821* (London, 1919), pp. ix, xi, xii, xvii, xxix sqq.; PRESSNELL, *Country Banking*, 7 sqq., 14 sqq., 36 sqq., 45 sqq., 77 sqq., 91–4, 105 sqq., 115 sqq., 126 sqq., 136 sqq., 270 sqq., 292 sqq., 322 sqq., 356 sqq., 434–6; KING, *op. cit.*, 6, 9, 10, 27–8, 175–6.

256 *Ibid.*, 32, 39, 112–13, 115, 175–6, 216, 264–5, 271 sqq.; R. S. SAYERS, *Central Banking after Bagehot* (Oxford, 1957), p. 14; *Bank of England*, 236 sqq., 244–5, 250, 654; CLAPHAM, *op. cit.*, II, 134, 149; BISSCHOP, *op. cit.*, 161, 193–4, 199, 200, 213, 237, 240–1; E. T. POWELL,

op. cit., 299 sqq., 312, 415–6; RICHARDS, *Early History*, 197–9; J. R. T.
HUGHES, *Fluctuations in Trade, Industry and Finance: a study of British
economic development 1850–60* (Oxford, 1960), pp. 233–4, 236–7, 258 sqq.;
B. C. HUNT, *Development of the Business Corporation in England 1800–67*
(Cambridge, Mass., 1936), pp. 50, 62–5; J. SYKES, *Amalgamation Move-
ment in English Banking, 1825–1924* (London, 1926), passim; E. J. T.
ACASTER, 'Joint Stock Innovation: Joplin, Gilbart and Geo. Pollard',
Three Banks Review, no CXXVI, 1980, pp. 40 sqq.; W. F. CRICK and J.
E. WADSWORTH, *Hundred Years of Joint Stock Banking* (London, 1930),
pp. 16 sqq., 29, 32–4, 36 sqq., 43 sqq., 450; S. E. THOMAS, *Rise and Growth
of Joint Stock Banking*, vol. I (London, 1934), pp. 543 sqq., 552, 555, 559–61,
571, 575, 590–1, 599 *et passim*; PRESSNELL, *Country Banking*, 11, 130,
443 sqq., 510; A. M. TAYLOR, *Gilletts: bankers at Banbury and Oxford*
(Oxford, 1964), pp. 225 sqq.; R. P. HIGONNET, 'Bank Deposits in the
United Kingdom 1870–1914', *Quarterly Journal of Economics*, LXXI, 1957,
pp. 329 sqq., 340–3, 348, 353; Anon., 'Commercial Bills', *Bank of England
Quarterly Bulletin*, I, 1961, pp. 27 sqq.; J. A. HENRY, *First Hundred Years
of Standard Bank*, ed. H. A. Siepmann (London, 1963), pp. 1, 5, 6, 46,
109 sqq., 117 sqq., 155–6, 162, 193 sqq., 323–4; A. S. J. BASTER, *International Banks* (London, 1935), pp. 3–6, 10 sqq., 22, 24, 37, 39, 40, 46 sqq.,
57 sqq., 73–4, 76–8, 83, 92–4, 99, 101–2, 114, 116, 119 sqq., 128–9, 137–8,
140–2, 144–6, 156 sqq., 174, 177–8, 181, 184–5, 189, 192, 199 sqq., 206–8,
223–4, 233, 245, 247–9; *Imperial Banks* (London, 1929), pp. 8 sqq., 20 sqq.,
44, 46, 49, 51, 57–9, 63 sqq., 77 sqq., 86–8, 104–6, 109, 112, 120–1, 126 sqq.,
131, 144 sqq., 161, 169, 181, 187, 196, 198, 207, 216 sqq., 249–50, 253, 255–6,
269; S. J. BUTLIN, *Australia and New Zealand Bank: the Bank of
Australasia and the Union Bank of Australia Ltd., 1829–1951* (London,
1961), pp. 1 sqq., 8, 10, 305–6, 325, 426; D. JOSLIN, *Central Banking in
Latin America* (London, 1963), pp. 16, 17, 26, 28 sqq., 60 sqq., 79 sqq.,
85 sqq., 109–10, 113 sqq., 152 sqq., 174 sqq., 236, 244, 253, 289–90; K. LE
CHEMINANT, *Colonial and Foreign Banking Systems* (London, 1931), pp.
71, 84 sqq., 111–14, 119 sqq., 126–8, 204–6; ANDERSON and COTTRELL,
op. cit., 241 sqq.

257   *Ibid.*, 205 sqq.; RICHARDS, *Early History*, 13–15; Statutes 3 Hy
7 c: 6; 13 Eliz. c. 8; 12 Chas 2, c. 13; 13 Anne c. 15; THOMAS, *op. cit.*, 569;
BISSCHOP, *op. cit.*, 244; KING, *op. cit.*, 8 sqq., 12, 13, 22, 39–42, 47–8,
50–1, 60 sqq., 67–8, 115, 117, 121–2, 136, 145, 183, 185, 187–9, 217–18,
271 sqq., 280–2; CLAPHAM, *op. cit.*, II, 135–7, 142–3; R. S. SAYERS,
Gilletts in the London Money Market 1867–1967 (Oxford, 1968), pp. 1, 3–5,
90, 134, 139–41, 156–7, 185, 188; *Central Banking*, 10.

258   R. TILLY, *Financial Institutions and Industrialisation in the
Rhineland 1815–1870*, Madison, Milwaukee and London, 1966, pp. 14, 15,
34, 36, 49, 51, 64–5, 67, 69, 71–4, 81–3, 87, 91–2, 94 sqq., 106 sqq., 111,
113; M. IKLE, *Switzerland: an international banking and finance center*,
Stroudsburg, Pa., 1972, pp. 5 sqq.; P. B. WHALE, *Joint Stock Banking in
Germany*, London, 1930, pp. 9, 16, 48, 51 sqq., 80; J. RIESSER, *Great
German Banks and their Concentration in connection with the economic
development of Germany*, Washington, D.C., 1911, pp. 46 sqq., 53, 62–3,

69, 71–2, 75, 85–6; R. E. CAMERON, *France and the Economic Development of Europe*, Princeton, N.J., 1961, pp. 111, 118–21, 148–51, 160, 177–9, 181, 183–4, 194 sqq., 214, 219 sqq., 228, 276–7.

259 CHALLIS, *op. cit.*, 83 sqq., 118 sqq., 312 sqq.; 'Circulating Medium and the Movement of Prices in Mid-Tudor England' in P. H. RAMSEY (ed.), *Price Revolution in Sixteenth Century England*, London, 1971, pp. 117 sqq.; J. D. GOULD, *Great Debasement*, Oxford, 1970, pp. 43 sqq.; DE ROOVER, *Gresham*, 51 sqq.; T. SMITH, *De Republica Anglorum*, London, 1583, p. 45.

260 E. J. HAMILTON, *American Treasure and the Price Revolution in Spain 1501–1650*, Cambridge, Mass., 1934; A. R. B. CHABERT, 'More about the Sixteenth Century Price Revolution' in P. BURKE (ed.), *Economy and Society in Early Modern Europe*, New York and London, 1972, pp. 47 sqq.

261 E. J. HAMILTON, 'American Treasure and the Rise of Capitalism (1500–1700)', *Economica*, new ser., IX, 1929, pp. 338 sqq.; 'Prices as a Factor in Business Growth', *Journal of Economic History*, XII, 1952, p. 334.

262 KEYNES, *Treatise on Money*, 2 vols., London, 1930, II, 152 sqq.; DOBB, *Development of Capitalism*, London, 1946, pp. 232–3, 237–8.

263 E. H. PHELPS-BROWN and S. V. HOPKINS, 'Seven Centuries of Building Wages' in CARUS-WILSON, *op. cit.*, II, 168 sqq.; 'Seven Centuries of the Prices of Consumables compared with Builders' Wage Rates', *ibid.*, 179 sqq.; my 'Movement of Rent 1540–1640', *ibid.*, 208 sqq.; J. U. NEF, 'Prices and Industrial Capitalism in France and England 1540–1640', ibid., [I], 1954, pp. 108 sqq.; D. FELIX, 'Profit Inflation and Industrial Growth', *Quarterly Journal of Economics*, LXX, 1956, pp. 441 sqq.

264 NEF, *Coal Industry*; GRAS, *op. cit.*; GODFREY, *op. cit.*; WILLAN, *Inland Trade; River Navigation*; R. DAVIS, *Rise of the British Shipping Industry*, London, 1962; my *Agricultural Revolution; Textile Manufactures*.

265 CHALLIS, *op. cit.*, 192 sqq.

266 *Ibid.*, 151–3.

267 *Ibid.*, 186, 188 sqq.; NOTESTEIN *et al.*, *op. cit.*, II, 29, 30; W. RALEIGH, *Observations touching Trade and Commerce with the Hollander, and other Nations, as it was presented to King James*, London, 1653, pp. 16, 17; J. K. FEDOROWICZ, *England's Baltic Trade in the early 17th century*, Cambridge, 1980, pp. 58–60; P.R.O., S.P.D., Eliz. 260/23; 263/63.

268 CHALLIS, *Tudor Coinage*, 246–7; J. D. GOULD, 'Royal Mint in the early 17th century', *Economic History Review*, 2nd ser., V, 1952, pp. 240, 248; 'Great Debasement and the Supply of Money', *Australian Economic History Review*, XIII, 1973, p. 187.

269 HARRISON, loc. cit., 188; G. MALYNES, *Maintenance of Free Trade*, London, 1662, p. 19; H. STEWART, *History of the Worshipful Company of Gold and Silver Wyre-drawers*, London, 1891, pp. 1, 3, 18–21, 24 sqq.; G. J. PICCOPE, *Lancashire and Cheshire Wills and Inventories from the Ecclesiastical Court, Chester*, Chetham Society, 3 pts, XXXIII, LI, LIV, 1857–61, pt I, 105 sqq., 126–9, 155–7, 169 sqq.; pt II, 39; pt III, 2 sqq., 58 sqq., 91 sqq., 128 sqq., 201 sqq.; J. EARWAKER, *Lancs. and Ches. Wills and Invs at Chester*, Chetham Soc., n.s., III, 1884, pp. 17 sqq., 57 sqq.;

Lancs. and Ches. Wills and Invs, 1572–1696, now preserved at Chester, Chetham Soc., n.s., XXVIII, 1893, pp. 15 sqq.; J. S. MOORE, *Goods and Chattels of our Forefathers: Frampton Cotterell and District Probate Invs 1539–1804,* London and Chichester, 1976, pp. 57–8, 61, 64, 70–2, 74–5, 79; D. G. VAISEY, *Probate Invs of Lichfield and District 1568–1680,* Colls for Hist. of Staffs., 4th ser., Staffs. Rec. Soc., V, 1969, pp. 41, 47, 49, 51, 59, 62–5, 70, 77, 84–5, 88 sqq., 95–7, 100, 105 sqq., 114 sqq.; P. C. D. BREARS, *Yorks, Probate Invs 1541–1689,* Yorks. Archaeol. Soc., Rec. Ser., CXXXIV, 1972, pp. 3–5, 9 sqq., 14 sqq., 19, 28–30, 36 sqq., 43, 50, 59, 65, 67–70, 72, 84, 89–92, 94, 103, 106 sqq.; J. M. BESTALL and D. V. FOWKES, *Chesterfield Wills and Invs 1521–1603,* Derbys. Rec. Soc., I, 1977, pp. 28, 30, 40, 47, 50, 56, 62, 74, 79, 80, 86, 91–2, 95, 107–8, 111–12, 117, 120–2, 124, 134, 138, 147, 150, 160, 164–5, 168, 177, 188–91, 195, 201 sqq., 206, 212, 221, 228, 250–1, 256, 272, 277–9, 289–90; P. A. KENNEDY, *Notts. Household Invs,* Thoroton Soc., Rec. Ser., XXII, 1963, pp. 8 sqq., 26 sqq., 53–5, 57–8, 60–3, 75 sqq., 83–4, 97–9, 110–11, 114–16, 118 sqq., 125–6, 128–9; M. REED, *Ipswich Probate Invs 1583–1631,* Sfk Rec. Soc., XXII, 1981, pp. 13–15, 29–31, 34, 51, 65–8, 70–3, 80–1, 91–2, 103–4, 112; CASH, *op. cit.,* 2, 4, 5, 7, 9, 14 sqq., 25–6, 31–4, 38–41, 43, 47–8, 50, 53–4, 67, 70–1, 76 sqq., 84–7, 91–2, 97–9, 103–5, 108–9, 111–12, 118–20; HAVINDEN, *op. cit.,* 62, 86–7, 102–3, 138, 192 sqq., 199, 200; Lancs. R.O., Cons. Ct Cestr., Liverpool invs.

270   *Ibid.*; HARRISON, loc. cit., 188; CHALLIS, *Tudor Coinage,* 155; STONE, *Crisis,* App. XXIII; BATHO, *op. cit.,* 108 sqq., 124, 126; *Wills and Invs from Registry at Durham,* IV, 268–9; Birmingham Ref. Lib., MS 437935; Northants. R.O., Westmorland Coll., box 6, pcl 5, nos. 1, 2; Young (Orlingbury) Coll., 668; Finch-Hatton Coll., 2659; PICCOPE, *op. cit.,* pt I, 105 sqq., 126–9, 155–7, 169 sqq.; pt II, 39; pt III, 2 sqq., 58, 91 sqq., 128 sqq., 201 sqq.; J. S. MOORE, *op. cit.,* 48, 57–8, 79; BREARS, *op. cit.,* 19, 28–30, 65; BESTALL and FOWKES, *op. cit.,* 164, 250; BANKES and KERRIDGE, *op. cit.,* 43–6; REED, *op. cit.,* 29, 30, 65–8, 80–1, 103–4; CASH, *op. cit.,* 7, 14–16, 25–6, 71, 80–1, 87, 108–9; KENNEDY, *op. cit.,* 30–1, 118–19; EARWAKER, *op. cit.,* III, 1884, pp. 17 sqq., 57 sqq.

271   *Ibid.,* XXVIII, 1893, pp. 15 sqq.; BREARS, *op. cit.,* 106 sqq.; BESTALL and FOWKES, *op. cit.,* 91, 124, 150; VAISEY, *op. cit.,* 90–2; REED, *op. cit.,* 70–3; CASH, *op. cit.,* 2, 4, 5, 38–40, 54, 67; H. ELLIS (ed.), *Original Letters Illustrative of English History,* 3rd ser., vol. I, London, 1846, p. 379; WILLAN, *Elizabethan Manchester,* 117; HARRISON, loc. cit., 188; *Wills and Invs illustrative of the History, Manners, Language, Statistics, etc. of the Northern Counties of England,* Surtees Soc., II, 1835, pp. 335 sqq., 347 sqq.; B.L., Additional MS 15559 fos 1 sqq.; Essex R.O., D/DWY.17; Leics. R.O., Archdeaconry inv. 1637/222.

272   *Ibid.,* 1632/60; D. WOODWARD, *op. cit.,* 231, 242, 248; Corp. of London R.O., Ct of Orphans, invs Nic. Russell cit. and weaver 1672, Jn Dixon cit. and feltmaker 1665, Barack Justian cit. and weaver 1670, Ralph Lawrence cit. and dyer 1670, Jn Causton cit. and weaver 1666; HARRISON, loc. cit., 188–9; G. BUELOW, 'Journey through England and Scotland made by Lupold von Wedel in the years 1584 and 1585', *Trans. Royal Historical*

Society, n.s., IX, 1895, p. 268; C. A. SNEYD (ed.), *Relation, or rather a true Account, of the Island of England*, Camden Soc., XXXVII, 1847, p. 29; CASH, *op. cit.*, 9, 17 sqq., 31–4, 43, 47–50, 53–4, 67, 70–1, 76 sqq., 84–6, 91–2, 98, 103–5, 112, 118–20; J. S. MOORE, *op. cit.*, 57–8, 61, 64, 70–2, 74–5; VAISEY, *op. cit.*, 41, 47, 49, 51, 62–5, 70, 77, 84–5, 95–7, 100, 105 sqq., 114; BREARS, *op. cit.*, 3–5, 9 sqq., 14 sqq., 37 sqq., 43, 50, 59, 67–70, 72, 84, 89–92, 94, 103; BESTALL and FOWKES, *op. cit.*, 28, 30, 40, 47, 50, 56, 62, 74, 79, 80, 92, 95, 107–8, 111–12, 117, 120–2, 134, 138, 147, 160, 165, 168, 177, 188–91, 195, 201 sqq., 206, 212, 221, 228, 250–1, 256, 272, 277–9, 289–90; HAVINDEN, *op. cit.*, 86–7, 102–3, 138, 192 sqq., 199, 200; REED, *op. cit.*, 30–1, 34, 51, 91–2, 112; KENNEDY, *op. cit.*, 8 sqq., 26 sqq., 53–5, 57–8, 60–3, 75 sqq., 83–4, 97–9, 110–11, 114–16, 120–2, 125–6.

273 MALYNES, *Free Trade*, 19; GOULD, 'Royal Mint', 240, 248; NOTESTEIN *et al.*, *op. cit.*, II, 29.

274 CHALLIS, *Tudor Coinage*, 157 sqq.; D. NORTH, *Discourses upon Trade*, London, 1691, PS., pp. ii, iii; R. DAVIES, *op. cit.*, 33.

275 J. HURSTFIELD and A. G. R. SMITH, *Elizabethan People: state and society*, London, 1972, pp. 3, 4, 45; E. H. PHELPS-BROWN and S. V. HOPKINS, 'Wage-rates and Prices: evidence of population pressure in the 16th century', *Economics*, n.s., XXIV, 1957, pp. 289 sqq.; J. CORNWALL, 'English Population in the early 16th century', *Economic History Review*, 2nd ser., XXIII, 1970, pp. 32 sqq.; W. K. JORDAN, *Edward VI: the threshold of power; the dominance of the Duke of Northumberland*, London, 1970, p. 482; *Edward VI: the protectorship of the Duke of Somerset*, London, 1968, pp. 401–2.

276 J. A. SCHUMPETER, *History of Economic Analysis*, London, 1954, esp. pp. 180, 219, 251–2, 254, 257–8; D. P. O'BRIEN, *J. R. McCulloch: a study in classical economics*, London, 1970, pp. 316–19.

277 J. A. SCHUMPETER, *Business Cylces: a theoretical, historical and statistical analysis of the capitalist process*, 2 vols., New York and London, 1939, p. 74; A. MARSHALL, *Elements of the Economics of Industry*, London, 1949, pp. 103 sqq.; L. VON MISES, *Socialism: an economic and sociological analysis*, London, 1936, pp. 197–8; and see his *Human Action: a treatise on economics*, Chicago, 1963 and his *Money and Credit*; also SCHUMPETER, *History of Economic Analysis* and *Capitalism, Socialism and Democracy*, New York, 1975.

278 G. N. CLARK, *Wealth of England*, London, 1946, pp. 2, 41, 92; P. RAMSEY, *Tudor Economic Problems*, London, 1963, p. 15; A. L. ROWSE, *England of Elizabeth: the structure of society*, London, 1973, p. 244; J. CLAPHAM, *Concise Economic History of Britain from the earliest times to 1750*, Cambridge, 1949, p. 186; J. N. L. BAKER, 'England in the Seventeenth Century' in H. C. DARBY, *op. cit.*, 435–7; CORNWALL, 'English Population', 32, 44.

279 E. A. WRIGLEY and R. S. SCHOFIELD, *Population History of England, 1541–1871*, London, 1981, pp. 528, 531–2 and M. W. FLINN'S review of same in *Economic History Review*, 2nd ser., XXXV, 1982, pp. 443 sqq. (quot. 457); *Cambridge Economic History*, vol. IV, pp. 13, 32, 52–4.

280 ROWSE, *op. cit.*, 243 sqq.; CORNWALL, loc. cit., 44; WRIGLEY and SCHOFIELD, *op. cit.*, 419, 435, 531.

281 TH. HARDY, *Mayor of Casterbridge*, London, 1975, pp. 199 (quot.) sqq.

282 *Cambridge Econ. Hist.* IV, 483; PHELPS-BROWN and HOPKINS, 'Prices of Consumables', 183, 194–5.

283 Institute of Historical Research, London, Beveridge Price and Wage History Research MSS, ser. J. 35.

284 *Capitalism, Socialism and Democracy*, 31–2, 67–8; and see his *Business Cycles*.

285 *Ibid.*, 87 sqq., 231 sqq. (quot. 232); and see VON MISES, *Human Action*, 552 sqq., 585–6; USHER, *Early History*, 17, 18.

286 For a discussion, see my 'Landowners and Farmers'.

287 VON MISES, *Money and Credit*, 315 sqq.

288 CHALLIS, *Tudor Coinage*, 246–7; GOULD, 'Royal Mint', 240, 248; DEFOE, *Complete English Tradesman*, 47; Corp. of London R.O., Ct of Orphans, invs Francis Meynell alderman, cit. and goldsmith 1666–7; Sir Martin Noell knt, cit. and scrivener 1666; Chas Everard esq., cit. and goldsmith 1665.

289 KENNEDY, CASH, HAVINDEN, REED, J. S. MOORE, VAISEY, BREARS, BESTALL and FOWKES – *op. cit.*; Lancs. R.O., Cons. Ct Cestr., Liverpool invs.

290 REED, *op. cit.*, 35–6, 80–1; CASH, *op. cit.*, 61–2; J. S. MOORE, *op. cit.*, 66; BESTALL and FOWKES, *op. cit.*, 86, 143 sqq., 219 sqq., 231 sqq.; HAVINDEN, *op. cit.*, 101, 141–2, 254; Lancs. R.O., Cons. Ct Cestr. inv. Geo. Ackers gent. 1588 Liverpool.

291 Leics. R.O., Arch. inv. 1638/290.

292 Lancs. R.O., Cons. Ct Cestr., wills and invs Robt Wolfall 1578 linen draper, Ann Hughson 1583 wid., Jn Naile 1584, Wm Syme als Tristram 1609 hooper, Eliz. Formby 1622 wid., Hugh Sturzaker 1623 saddler – all Liverpool; BESTALL and FOWKES, *op. cit.*, 149; BREARS, *op. cit.*, 107, 109.

293 Lancs. R.O., Cons. Ct Cestr.

294 J. R. T. HUGHES, *Fluctuations in Trade, Industry and Finance: studies in British economic development 1850–1860*, Oxford, 1960, pp. 265, 267; VANE, *Ledger*, 237; CLAPHAM, *Bank of England*, I, 130; T. S. ASHTON, *Economic History of England: The Eighteenth Century*, London, 1972, pp. 185 sqq.; *Industrial Revolution*, London, 1948, pp. 101–2; ANDERSON and COTTRELL, *op. cit.*, 220.

295 Generally, probate invs as listed in A. J. CAMP, *Wills and their Whereabouts*, Bridge Place, Canterbury, 1963, and others in family archives. Cf. B. A. HOLDERNESS, 'Credit in English Rural Society before the 19th century', *Agricultural History Review*, XXIV, 1976, pp. 101–2; 'Credit in a Rural Community, 1660–1800: some neglected aspects of probate invs', *Midland History*, III, 1975–6, pp. 95, 98, 100, 103, 108.

Refs for cash/credit ratios: (a) printed: J. H. WILSON, *Wymondham Invs 1590–1641*, Norwich, 1983, pp. 5 sqq., 24–7, 29, 30; RAINE, *op. cit.*, 35, 243 sqq.; *Wills and Admons fr. Knaresborough Ct Rolls*, pt II, 220 sqq.;

Wills and Invs fr. Reg. at Durh., pt II, 62−4; pt IV, 268−9; EMMISON, *Jac. Invs*, 57−8, 73−4, 91, 130−1; CASH, *op. cit.*, 4, 5, 7, 22−3, 35 sqq., 46, 49, 57−9, 61−3, 70−1, 73, 75−7, 83, 115 sqq.; HAVINDEN, *op. cit.*, 150 sqq., 233−4; BANKES and KERRIDGE, *op. cit.*, 43−6; E. BATESON, *History of Northumberland*, 15 vols., London, 1893−1940, V, 403−4; REED, *op. cit.*, 35−6, 82−5, 90, 93 sqq., 101−3; KENNEDY, *op. cit.*, 14−16, 55−6, 63−6, 76−7, 85 sqq., 108−9, 117, 120−1, 126−8; D. WOODWARD, *op. cit.*, 229 sqq., 253; BESTALL and FOWKES, *op. cit.*, 36−7, 120−2, 148−9, 170−1, 188−9, 201 sqq., 241−2, 247 sqq., 277−9, 288; EARWAKER, *op. cit.*, (III), 15 sqq.; J. O. HALLIWELL, *Anc. Invs. of Furniture, Pictures, Tapestry, Plate etc. illustrative of domestic manners of the English in the 16th and 17th cents*, London, 1854, pp. 1 sqq., 15 sqq.; H. HALL, *op. cit.*, 153−4; MELLING, *op. cit.*, 110−12; J. S. MOORE, *op. cit.*, 43−4, 51, 54−5, 63, 68 sqq., 79; PICCOPE, *op. cit.*, pt III, 201 sqq.; W. E. PRESTON, *Wills proved in Ct of Manor of Crosley, Bingley, Cottingley and Pudsey*, Bradford Hist. and Antiq. S., Loc. Rec. Ser., I, 1929, pp. 64−5, 140−2; F. R. TWEMLOW, *The Twemlows: their wives and their homes*, Wolverhampton, 1910, p. 235; VAISEY, *op. cit.*, 60, 62−4, 75−6, 88 sqq., 105 sqq., 115 sqq.; *Miscellanea*, Thoresby Soc., IV, 1895, pp. 163−6; BREARS, *op. cit.*, 9 sqq., 14 sqq., 37 sqq., 57−8, 67−70, 74−5, 89−92, 96 sqq., 106 sqq.

(b) MSS: − P.R.O., P.C.C., Invs ser. I no 212; parchmt invs p. 1660 nos 572, 2887, 3665, 3672; B.L., Add. Chs 54108, 55455; Add. MS 36582 fos 6−8, 86, 88−90, 107−8, 112, 130; Add. Rolls 18517, 30064, 32860; Beds. R.O., ABP/W/1607/98; 1616/54; FN 1094; GA 1732; PA 180; Birm. Ref. Lib., Gen. Coll. nos 252320, 281292, 350253, 350255, 395525, 468177; Bodleian Lib., Cons. and Arch Cts Oxf. O.W. etc. 30/4/11; Brist. R.O.; Cons. Ct inv. 1628/59; Devizes Mus., cat no 233, invs Jn and Jas Filkes 1629 and 1637; Hants. R.O., Arch. Ct Winton, O.W. and Invs, Hy Watridge 1650 Alton; Cons. Ct Winton, O.W. and Invs, Jn Woodman 1637 Fetcham; Herts. R.O., Cashiobury and Gape Coll. 8780; Halsey Coll. 12434, 12448, 14594; Kent R.O., Arch. Ct Cant., Inv. Reg. 61 no 12; Inv. Ppr, Jn Plummer 1660 Minster; Cons. Ct Cant., Regs Accts and Invs, 9 fo. 307; 14 fo. 312; Inv. Regs, 14 fo. 588, 20 fo. 369; Inv. Pprs, 6/76, 9/81, 12/31, 16/77.

Lancs. R.O., Cons. Ct Cestr. invs, Nic. Ogden 1635 Spotland; Ric. Melling 1571, Wm Goodacre 1602, Pet. Tarbock 1613, Alice Eccleston 1615, Ric. Bolton and Th. Sergeant 1618, Ric. Cross 1619, Eliz. Formby and Th. Johnson 1622, Jn˙Ryecroft and Hugh Sturzaker 1623, Ric. Barrowclough 1625, Jn Seddon and Jn Haughton 1627, Ralph Sandiford 1632, Brian Blundell and Ric. Holmes 1633, Wm Pendleton 1634, Judith Ulster and Wm Tarleton 1635, Cath. Hall 1636, Geo. Gilberthorpe and Wm Higginson 1639, Gilbert Holt 1640, Sam. Williamson 1641, Hy Robinson 1642, Anne Moore 1645 − all Liverpool; DD/B1. 24/13.

Leics. R.O., Arch. O.W. and Invs: Jn Coke 1580, Wm Winterscale 1591, Th. and Ellen Ramsdale als Ramsden 1593, Ric. Swan 1595, Chris. Needham and Jn Rodes 1603, Wm Gregory 1614 − all Leicester; Ric. Bonner 1641 Lindridge; Invs: 1599/40, 1599−1600/18; 1602/7, 181; 1603/105, 109; 1608/51, 112; 1612/170; 1614/99, 155, 175; 1616/54, 97; 1625/10, 18, 120; 1626/141, 169, 194; 1627/56, 78, 111, 130, 197; 1628/75, 158, 167, 205;

1630/122; 1631/25, 42, 64, 100, 104, 124; 1632/60, 107, 109, 116, 124, 148–9, 161, 194; 1633/31, 74, 312; 1635/215; 1636/23, 49, 62, 75, 78, 164–5, 194; 1636–7/159, 170; 1637/36, 92; 1638/203, 205, 222, 301, 309; 1639/22, 64, 101, 116, 125, 130, 143; 1640/16; 1641/70, 146; 1641–2/31; 1644/2; 1645/7, 10; 1646/8; 1647/29, 43, 81; 1648/21; 1658/221; 1659/28, 56, 314; 1660/75, 90, 107; 1660 (Commy) 30; 1671/37 (1658); Commy Ct Manor of Evington no 112; Commy Ct Manor of Rothley nos 7, 32; Beaumanor Coll. DG9/2049.; Lindenhall MSS 94, 109–10.

Lichfield Jt R.O., invs Ric. Saunders 1595, Jn Foxley 1635, both Coventry; Lincs. R.O., Cons. Ct invs 1632–3/75, 217; Nfk R.O., Cons. Ct invs 1617/51; 1630/174; 1632/10, 16, 56, 62; 1633/149, 180, 308; 1637–68/118; 1639/247; 1642/171; Northants. R.O., Cons. Ct Petr., Hunts. Inv K 1613–87 Abraham King of Toseland; Fitzwilliam (Milton) Coll., Misc., nos 907, 913, 918, 920; Sfk R.O. (Bury) Commy Ct Bury St Edm.'s 1647–8/46 (1641); (Ips.) Arch. invs 1583/16; 1590/24, 41, 128; GB 1/2/14/33; Wilts. R.O., Ex-Dioc. Reg. Sarum, unclass. invs: Jas Mayhu c. 1540 Fonthill, Jn Nott er 1585 Bps Cannings, Wm Rundell c. 1600 N. Bradley, Roger Brabant 1619 Calne, Th. Mapson 1622 Sevenhampton, Th. Eyres 1631 New Sarum, Nic. Erby 1632 Chisbury, Joan Bigges 1632 Gt Bedwyn, Wm Vennard 1633 Calne, Matt. Browne 1634 L. Bedwyn, Jos. White 1638 Calne, Nic. Stokes 1640 Warminster, Ed. Oddell 1641 New Sarum, Jn Cooke 1643 Wilton; Arch. Ct Wilts., Jn Gleede 1631 Purton Pevenhill; Arch. Ct Sarum, Jn Bitham 1632 Gt Amesbury, Wm Kent 1633 Boscombe, Hy Moggeridge 1637 Dinton; Cons. Ct Sarum, Th. Lyte 1627 Easton Pierce, Nic. Bishop 1634 Nettleton, Ric. Hulberte 1635 Imber, Hy White er 1642 Langley Burrell; Pec. Ct Hurstbourne and Burbage, O.W. etc. bdl. 1 no 10; Acc. 122 Chittoe Ct Bk 1616; Worcs. R.O. (Hereford and Worcester), Cons. Ct O.W. etc. 1614/169.

296 J. COX, *Records of the Borough of Northampton*, vol. II, Northampton, 1898, pp. 211–12; WILLAN, *Inland Trade*, 83–5, 104; F. J. BAIGENT and F. E. MILLARD, *History of the Ancient Town and Manor of Basingstoke*, London, 1889, pp. 562–4; G. H. TUPLING, *Economic History of Rossendale*, Chetham Soc., n.s., LXXXVI, 1927, p. 176; J. R. S. WHITING, *Trade Tokens: a social and economic history*, Newton Abbot, n.d., pp. 13 sqq., 19, 20, 34 sqq.; Aberystwyth, Nat. Lib., St Asaph probate invs (Denbighs.) Th. Platt jun. 1667 Wrexham.

Select bibliography
of printed and typescript books and journals

(Place of publication, except for society series, is London, unless otherwise stated)

Anonymous and various:

Acts of the Privy Council of England new series, ed. J. L. Dasent, 32 vols., 1890–1907.
—— 14 vols., 1921–64.
Calendar of Treasury Papers 1697–1701/2, Rolls series, 1871.
Calendar of Wynne (of Gwydir) Papers 1515–1690, London, Aberystwyth and Cardiff, 1926.
Case of John Littlebales, against the pretended petition of the waggoners travelling the northern roads of England, The, sine loco nec data.
Case of Richard Fielden, in relation to the petition of the waggoners, The, sine loco nec data.
'Commercial Bills', *Bank of England Quarterly Bulletin*, vol. I, no 5, 1961.
Dawn of Modern Banking, The, Center for Medieval and Renaissance Studies, University of California, New Haven and London, 1979.
Essays in Modern English History in Honor of W. C. Abbott, Cambridge, Mass., 1941.
Is not the Hand of Joab in all this? or an inquiry into the grounds of a late pamphlet intituled The Mystery of the New-Fashioned Goldsmiths or Bankers, 1676.
Journals of the House of Commons.
Journals of the House of Lords.
Letters and Papers, foreign and domestic of the reign of Henry VIII, preserved in the Public Record Office, the British Museum and elsewhere in England, Public Record Office, 23 vols., 1862–1932.
Modern Reports, or select cases adjudged in the courts of King's Bench, Chancery, Common Pleas and Exchequer from the restoration of Charles II to the twenty-eighth year of George II, ed. T. Leach, 12 vols., 1793–6 and various editions.
'Natural History of Dorking', *Gentleman's Magazine*, vol. xxxiii, 1763.
Reasons for Setling Admiralty Jurisdiction ... offered to the Two Houses of Parliament, sine loco, 1690.
Reasons Humbly Offered to the Honorable House of Commons, Why Wagoners ought not to be obliged to a certain Weight, sine loco nec data.
Studi in Onore di Amintore Fanfani, vol. iv, Milan, 1962.

Victoria History of the Counties of England.

Wills and Administrations from the Knaresborough Court Rolls, Surtees Society, vols. civ, cx, 1902–5

Wills and Inventories from the Registry at Durham, parts ii, iii, iv, Surtees Society, vols. xxxviii, cxii, cxlii, 1860, 1906, 1929.

Wills and Inventories illustrative of the history, manners, language, statistics etc. of the Northern Counties of England from the eleventh century downwards, part i, Surtees Society, 1835.

Acaster, E. J. T., 'Joint Stock Innovation: Joplin, Gilbert and George Pollard', *Three Banks Review*, no cxxvi, 1980.

Aerts, E., 'Prof. R. De Roover and Medieval Banking History', *Revue de la Banque*, cahier 8/9, 1980.

Albert, W., 'The Justices' Rates for Land Carriage 1748–1827', *Transport History*, vol. i, 1968.

—— *The Turnpike Road System in England 1663–1840*, Cambridge, 1972.

Allison, K. J., 'Flock Management in the Sixteenth and Seventeenth Centuries', *Economic History Review*, 2nd series, vol. xi, 1958.

—— 'The Wool Supply and the Worsted Cloth Industry in Norfolk in the Sixteenth and Seventeenth Centuries', typescript thesis, Ph.D., Leeds University, 1955.

Anderson, B. L. and Cottrell, P. L., *Money and Banking in England: the development of the banking system 1694–1914*, 1974.

Anderson, B. L. and Latham, A. J. H. (eds), *The Market in History*, 1986.

Anderson, E., *Les Reports du treserudite Edmund Anderson*, 2 pts, 1664 and various editions.

Anderton, B., 'Selections from the Delaval Papers in the Public Library of Newcastle on Tyne' in *A Volume of Miscellanea*, Publications of the Newcastle on Tyne Records Committee, vol. ix, 1930.

Andrews, J. H., 'Thanet Seaports 1650–1750' in Roake and Whyman, q.v.

—— 'The Trade of the Port of Faversham 1650–1750' in Roake and Whyman, q.v.

Apperson, G. L., *Gleanings after Time*, 1907.

Armour, C., 'The Trade of Chester and the State of the Dee Navigation 1600–1800', typescript thesis, Ph.D., London University, 1956.

Ashton, R., *The Crown and the Money Market 1603–1640*, Oxford, 1960.

Ashton, T. S., 'The Bill of Exchange and Private Banks in Lancashire 1790–1830' in Ashton and Sayers, q.v.

Ashton, T. S., and Sayers, R. S., *Papers in English Monetary History*, Oxford, 1953.

Åström, S.-E., *From Cloth to Iron: the Anglo–Baltic trade in the late seventeenth century*, Societas Scientiarum Fennica, Commentationes Humanum Litterarum, tomus xxxiii, no 1, Helsinfors (Helsinki), 1963.

Attwell, G., *The Faithfull Surveyour*, Cambridge, 1662.

Aubrey, J., *The Natural History and Antiquities of the County of Surrey*, 5 vols., 1719.

—— *The Natural History of Wiltshire*, edited by J. Britton, 1847.

—— *Wiltshire: the topographical collections of John Aubrey, F.R.S., A.D. 1659–70*, edited by J. E. Jackson, Devizes, 1862.

Austen, B., *English Provincial Posts 1633–1840: a study based on Kent examples*, London and Chichester, 1978.

Austin, M. M. and Vidal-Naquet, P., *Economic and Social History of Ancient Greece*, 1977.

B., I(J)., see Brown, J.

Bacon, F., *Essays*, various editions.

Bacon, N., *The Annalls of Ipswiche*, edited by W. H. Richardson, Ipswich, 1884.

Bagehot, W., *Lombard Street*, 1873.

Baker, J. H., 'The Law Merchant and the Common Law before 1700', *Cambridge Law Journal*, 1979.

Baker, J. N. L., 'England in the Seventeenth Century' in Darby, q.v.

Bankes, J. and Kerridge, E. (eds), *The Early Records of the Bankes Family at Winstanley*, Chetham Society, 3rd series, vol. xxi, 1973.

Barley, M. W., *Lincolnshire and the Fens*, 1952.

Barnes, D. G., *A History of the English Corn Laws from 1660 to 1846*, 1930.

Baster, A. S. J., *The Imperial Banks*, 1929.

—— *The International Banks*, 1935.

Bates, E. H. (ed.), *Quarter Sessions Records for the County of Somerset, vol. i: James I, 1607–1625*, Somerset Record Society, vol. xxiii, 1907.

Bateson, M. (ed.), *Records of the Borough of Leicester, 3 vols., Cambridge, 1899–1905*.

Batho, G. R. (ed.), *The Household Papers of Henry Percy, ninth Earl of Northumberland*, Royal Historical Society, Camden 3rd series, vol. cxiii, 1962.

Bax, A. R., 'Notes and Extracts from the Account Book of Richard Bax, a Surrey yeoman', *The Antiquary*, vol. vi, 1882.

Baxter, R., 'The Poor Husbandman's Advocate', *Bulletin of the John Rylands Library*, vol. x, 1926.

Beaumont, W. (ed.), 'Some Instructions given by William Booth esq. to his stewards John Carrington and William Rowcrofte upon the purchase of Warrington by Sir George Booth bart. and William Booth his son, A.D. 1628' in *Miscellanies relating to Lancashire and Cheshire, vol. iii*, Chetham Society, vol. lvii, 1862.

Beckett, J. V., *Coal and Tobacco: the Lowthers and the economic development of West Cumberland 1660–1760*, Cambridge, 1981.

Beckwith, I. S., 'The River Trade of Gainsborough 1500–1850', *Lincolnshire History and Archaeology*, no ii, 1967.

Beloff, M., 'Humphrey Shalcrosse and the Great Civil War', *English Historical Review*, vol. liv, 1939.

Bennett, J. H. E. (ed.), *The Rolls of Freemen of the City of Chester*, 2 pts, Record Society for Lancashire and Cheshire, vols. li, lv, 1906–8.

Bergier, J. F., 'Taux de l'Interêt et Crédit à Court Terme à Genève dans la seconde moitié du XVIe siècle' in *Studi in Onore di Amintore Fanfani*, vol. iv, Milan, 1962.

Best, H., see Woodward, D.

Bestall, J. M. and Fowkes, D. V. (eds), *Chesterfield Wills and Inventories 1521–1603*, Derbyshire Record Society, vol. i, 1977.

Bettey, J. H., 'The Marketing of Agricultural Produce in Dorset in the Seventeenth Century', *Dorset Natural History and Archaeological Society's Proceedings*, vol. ix (xcix), 1977.

Bidwell, W. H., *Annals of an East Anglian Bank*, 1900.

Biéler, A., *La Pensée Economique et Social de Calvin*, Geneva, 1959.

Billingsley, J., *A General View of the Agriculture of the County of Somerset*, 1798.

Bindoff, S. T., 'The Greatness of Antwerp' in *New Cambridge Modern History*, vol. i, edited by G. R. Elton, Cambridge, 1958.

Bisschop, W. R., *The Rise of the London Money Market 1640–1826*, 1910.

Blaxton, J., *The English Usurer, or usury condemned*, 1634.

Blencowe, R. W., 'Extracts from the Journal and Account Book of the Reverend Giles Moore', *Sussex Archaeological Collections*, vol. i, 1848.

Blith, W., *The English Improver Improved*, 1652.

Blome, R., *Britannia*, 1673.

Blomquist, T. W., 'The Dawn of Banking in an Italian Commune: thirteenth century Lucca' in *The Dawn of Modern Banking*, Center for Medieval and Renaissance Studies, q.v.

—— 'The Early History of European Banking: merchants, bankers and Lombards of thirteenth-century Lucca in the county of Champagne', *Journal of European Economic History*, vol. xiv, 1985.

Bonser, K. J., *The Drovers*, 1970.

Bowden, P. J., *The Wool Trade in Tudor and Stuart England*, 1962.

Boyd, W. K. (ed.), 'Chancery Proceedings *tempore* Elizabeth, A.D. 1560 – A.D. 1570', *Collections for the History of Staffordshire*, new ser., vol. x, pt 1, 1907.

Boys, J., *A General View of the Agriculture of the County of Kent*, 1796.

Bradney, J. (Sir), *A History of Monmouthshire*, 4 vols., 1904–34.

Braudel, F. (F. P.), *Civilization and Capitalism: 15th–18th century*, 3 vols., 1982–4.

Braudel, F. P. and Spooner, F., 'Prices in Europe from 1450 to 1750' in Postan, Rich and Habakkuk, q.v.

Brears, P. C. D., *Yorkshire Probate Inventories 1541–1689*, Yorkshire Archaeological Society, Record Series, vol. cxxxiv, 1972.

Brentnall, H. C. (ed.), 'A Document from Great Cheverell', *Wiltshire Archaeological Magazine*, vol. liii, 1950.

Brereton, W., *Travels in Holland, the United Provinces, England, Scotland and Ireland 1634–5*, Chetham Society, vol. i, 1844.

B[rown], I.[J.], *The Marchants Avizo*, 1607.

Brownlow, R., *Reports (A Second Part) of Diverse Famous Cases in Law*, 1652 and various editions.

Buelow, G. (ed.), 'Journey through England and Scotland made by Lupold von Wedel in the years 1584 and 1585', *Transactions of the Royal Historical Society*, new ser., vol. ix, 1895.

Bulstrode, E., *Reports of Divers Resolutions and Judgements*, 3 pts, 1657–9 and various editions.

Burgon, J. W., *The Life and Times of Sir Thomas Gresham*, 2 vols., [1839].

Burke, P. (ed.), *Economy and Society in Early Modern Europe*, New York and London, 1972.

Burley, K. H., 'The Economic Development of Essex in the later Seventeenth and early Eighteenth Centuries', typescript thesis, Ph.D., London University, 1957.

Butlin, S. J., *Australia and New Zealand Bank: the Bank of Australasia and the Union Bank of Australia Ltd., 1829–1951*, 1961.

C., J., see C[hild], J.

Camden, W., *Britannia*, edited by Gibson, 1695.

Camp, A. J., *Wills and their Whereabouts*, Bridge Place, near Canterbury, 1963.

Campbell, M., *The English Yeoman under Elizabeth and the early Stuarts*, New Haven, 1942.

Campling, A., *The History of the Family of Drury*, sine data.

Cannan, E., *The Paper Pound of 1797–1821*, 1919.

Carew, R., *The Survey of Cornwall* (1602), 1769.

Carthew, T., *Reports of Cases adjudged in the Court of King's Bench from the third year of King James the Second to the twelfth of King William the Third*, 1741 and various editions.

Carus-Wilson, E. M. (ed.), *Essays in Economic History*, 3 vols., 1954–62.

Cash, M. (ed.), *Devon Inventories in the Sixteenth and Seventeenth Centuries*, Devon and Cornwall Record Society, new ser., vol. xi, 1966.

Cave, C. H., *A History of Banking in Bristol from 1750 to 1899*, Bristol, 1899.

Cave, T. and Wilson, R. A. (eds), *The Parliamentary Survey of the Lands and Possessions of the Dean and Chapter of Worcester*, Worcestershire Historical Society, 1924.

Chabert, R. E., 'More about the Sixteenth Century Price Revolution' in P. Burke, q.v.

Chalklin, C. W., *Seventeenth-Century Kent: a social and economic history*, 1965.

Challis, C. E., 'The Circulating Medium and the Movement of Prices in Mid-Tudor England' in P. H. Ramsey, q.v.

—— *The Tudor Coinage*, Manchester, 1978.

Charles, B. G. (ed.), *Calendar of the Records of the Borough of Haverfordwest 1539–1660*, Cardiff, 1967.

Charlesworth, J. (ed.), *Wakefield Manor Book 1709*, Yorkshire Archaeological Society Record Series, vol. ci, 1939.

Chartres, J. A., *Internal Trade in England 1500–1700*, 1977.

—— 'The Marketing of Agricultural Produce' in Finberg and Thirsk, q.v., vol. v, pt 2.

—— 'Road Carrying in England in the Seventeenth Century: myth and reality', *Economic History Review*, 2nd ser., vol. xxx, 1977.

C[hild], J., *A New Discourse of Trade*, 1693.

—— *A Tract against Usurie presented to the High Court of Parliament*, 1621.

Churchyard, T., *The Worthines of Wales* (1587), 1776.

Cipolla, C. M., 'The So-called "Price Revolution": reflections on the Italian situation' in P. Burke, q.v.

Clapham, J., Sir, *The Bank of England: a history*, 2 vols., Cambridge, 1944.

Clark, D. K., 'A Restoration Goldsmith-Banking House: the Vine on Lombard Street' in *Essays in Modern English History in Honor of W. C. Abbot*, Cambridge, Mass., 1941.

—— 'Edward Backwell as Royal Agent', *Economic History Review*, vol. ix, 1938.

Clay, C., *Public Finance and Private Wealth: the career of Sir Stephen Fox 1627–1716*, Oxford, 1978.

Cliffe, J. T., *The Yorkshire Gentry from the Reformation to the Civil War*, 1969.

Cockburn, J. (ed.), *Western Circuit Assize Orders 1629–1648: a calendar*, Royal Historical Society, Camden 4th ser., vol. xvii, 1976.

Coke, E., *Institutes of the Lawes of England*, 4 pts, 1628, 1629, 1642–4 and various editions.

—— *The Reports*, 13 pts, 1777 and various editions.

Coker, [J.], *A Survey of Dorsetshire*, 1732.

Coleman, D. C., 'London Scriveners and the Estate Market in the later Seventeenth Century', *Economic History Review*, 2nd ser., vol. iv, 1951.

Coleman, D. C. and John, A. H. (eds), *Trade, Government and Economy in Pre-Industrial England*, 1976.

Colyer, R. J., *The Welsh Cattle Drovers: agriculture and the Welsh cattle trade before and during the nineteenth century*, Cardiff, 1976.

Cooper, J. P. (ed.), *Wentworth Papers 1597–1628*, Royal Historical Society, Camden 4th ser., vol. xii, 1973.

Cornwall, J. C. K., 'English Population in the early Sixteenth Century', *Economic History Review*, 2nd ser., vol. xxiii, 1970.

—— 'The Agrarian History of Sussex 1560–1640', typescript thesis, M.A., London University, 1953.

Court, W. H. B., *The Rise of the Midland Industries, 1600–1838*, 1953.

Cowper, J. M., 'Tudor Prices in Kent, chiefly in 1577', *Transactions of the Royal Historical Society*, vol. i, 1875.

Cox, J. (ed.), *The Records of the Borough of Northampton*, vol. ii, Northampton, 1896.

Cox, R. H., *The Green Roads of England*, 1927.

Crick, W. F. and Wadsworth, J. E., *A Hundred Years of Joint Stock Banking*, 1930.

Crofts, J., *Packhorse, Waggon and Post*, 1967.

Croke, G., *The Reports of Sir George Croke knt during the reigns of Queen Elizabeth, James I and Charles I*, 3 pts, 1661–7 and various editions.

Cullen, L. M., *Anglo–Irish Trade 1660–1800*, Manchester, 1968.

—— *An Economic History of Ireland since 1660*, 1972.

Cullen, L. M. and Smout, T. C. (eds), *Comparative Aspects of Scottish and Irish Social and Economic History 1600–1900*, Edinburgh, sine data.

Culley, G., *Observations on Livestock*, 1786.

Cunnington, B. H. (ed.), *Records of the County of Wiltshire: extracts from quarter sessions rolls*, Devizes, 1932.

Dalison, W., *Les Reports des divers Special Cases*, 1689 and various editions.
Darby, H. C. (ed.), *An Historical Geography of England before 1800*, Cambridge, 1948.
Davies, C. S. L., 'Provision for Armies, 1509–50', *Economic History Review*, 2nd ser., vol. xvii, 1964.
Davies, M. G., 'Country Gentry and Payments to London, 1650–1714', *Economic History Review*, 2nd ser., vol. xxiv, 1971.
—— *The Enforcement of English Apprenticeship: a study in applied mercantilism*, Cambridge, Mass., 1956.
Davies, R. (ed.), *The Life of Marmaduke Rawdon of York*, Camden Society, vol. lxxxv, 1863.
Davis, D., *A History of Shopping*, London and Toronto, 1966.
Davis, R., *The Rise of the British Shipping Industry*, 1962.
Davis, T., *A General View of the Agriculture of the County of Wiltshire*, 1794.
Dawe, D., *Skilbecks: drysalters 1650–1950*, 1950.
D'Ewes, S., *Compleat Journal of the House of Lords and House of Commons throughout the whole reign of Queen Elizabeth*, 1693.
Defoe, D., *A Plan of the English Commerce*, 1738.
—— *A Tour through England and Wales*, 2 vols., 1928.
—— *The Complete English Tradesman*, Edinburgh, 1839.
Dempsey, B. W., *Interest and Usury*, 1948.
De Roover, R., *Business, Banking and Economic Thought in late medieval and early modern Europe: selected studies*, edited with introduction by J. Kirshner, and introduction by R. A. Goldthwaite, Chicago and London, 1974.
—— (ed.), *Gresham on Foreign Exchange*, Cambridge, Mass. and London, 1949.
—— *L'Evolution de la Lettre de Change XIVe–XVIIe siècle*, Paris, 1953.
—— *Money, Banking and Credit in Medieval Bruges*, Cambridge, Mass., 1958.
—— *The Rise and Decline of the Medici Bank 1397–1494*, Cambridge, Mass., 1968.
Duckham, B. F., 'The Fitzwilliams and the Navigation of the Yorkshire Derwent', *Northern History*, vol. ii, 1967.
—— *The Inland Waterways of East Yorkshire 1700–1900*, East Yorkshire Local History Society, vol. xxix, 1973.
—— *The Yorkshire Ouse: the history of a river navigation*, Newton Abbot, 1967.
Dyer, A. D., *The City of Worcester in the Sixteenth Century*, Leicester, 1973.
—— 'The Market Towns of Southern England 1500–1700', *Southern History*, vol. i, 1979.

Earwaker, J., *Lancashire and Cheshire Wills and Inventories at Chester*, Chetham Society, new series, vol. iii, 1884.

—— *Lancashire and Cheshire Wills and Inventories 1572–1696*, Chetham Society, new series, vol. xxviii, 1893.

Edwards, P. R., 'The Horse Trade in the Midlands in the Seventeenth Century', *Agricultural History Review*, vol. xxvii, 1979.

Ehrenberg, R., *Capital and Finance in the Age of the Renaissance: a study of the Fuggers and their connections*, 1928.

Eland, G. (ed.), *Shardeloes Papers of the 17th and 18th centuries*, 1947.

Ellis, H. (ed.), *Original Letters Illustrative of English History*, 3rd ser., vol. i, 1846.

Ellis, W., *A Compleat System of Experienced Improvements made on Sheep, Grass-lambs and House-lambs*, 1749.

Emerson, W. R., 'The Economic Development of the Estates of the Petre Family in Essex in the 16th and 17th centuries', typescript thesis, D.Phil., Oxford University, 1951.

Emmison, F. G., *Elizabethan Life: morals and the church courts*, Chelmsford, 1973.

—— (ed.), *Jacobean Household Inventories*, Bedfordshire Historical Record Society, vol. xx, 1938.

Evans, E. J. and Beckett, J. V., 'Cumberland, Westmorland and Furness' in Finberg and Thirsk, q.v., vol. v, pt 1.

Everitt, A., 'The Marketing of Agricultural Produce' in Finberg and Thirsk, q.v., vol. iv.

Farey, J., *A General View of the Agriculture and Minerals of Derbyshire*, 3 vols., 1811–17.

Feavearyear, A. E., *The Pound Sterling*, Oxford, 1931.

Fedorowicz, J. K., *England's Baltic Trade in the early Seventeenth Century*, Cambridge, 1980.

Felix, D., 'Profit Inflation and Industrial Growth', *Quarterly Journal of Economics*, vol. lxx, 1956.

Fenton, G., *A Treatise of Usurie*, 1611.

Fiennes, C., *Journeys*, edited by C. Morris, 1947.

Fifoot, C. H. S., *Lord Mansfield*, 1936.

Finberg, H. P. R. and Thirsk, J. (eds), *The Agrarian History of England and Wales*, 8 vols., Cambridge, 1967– in progress.

Firth, C. H. and Rait, R. S. (eds), *Acts and Ordinances of the Interregnum*, 3 vols., 1911.

Fisher, F. J., 'The Development of the London Food Market 1540–1640' in Carus-Wilson, q.v., vol. [i].

Fishwick, H. (ed.), *The Survey of the Manor of Rochdale 1626*, Chetham Society, new ser., vol. lxxi, 1913.

Fitzherbert, *The Boke of Husbandrie*, 1523.

—— *The Boke of Surveyinge and Improvementes*, 1535.

Folkingham, W., *Feudigraphia: the synopsis or epitome of surveying*, 1610.

Forbes, W., *A Methodical Treatise concerning Bills of Exchange*, Edinburgh, 1703.

Frank, T., *An Economic History of Rome*, Baltimore, 1927.

—— (ed.), *An Economic Survey of Ancient Rome*, 6 vols., Baltimore, 1933–40.

Franklin, T. B., *British Grasslands*, 1953.

Freeman, C. E. (ed.), 'Elizabethan Inventories' in *Harrold Priory: a twelfth century dispute; and other articles*, Publications of the Bedfordshire Historical Record Society, vol. xxxii, 1952.

Fry, C. B., *Hannington: the records of a Wiltshire parish*, Gloucester, 1935.

Fryde, E. B., 'The Deposits of Hugh Despenser the younger with Italian Bankers', *Economic History Review*, 2nd ser., vol. iii, 1951.

Fuller, T., *The History of the Worthies of England* (1662), edited by P. A. Nuttall, 3 vols., 1840.

Gardiner, D. (ed.), *Oxinden Letters 1607–1642*, 1933.

Gardiner, S. R. (ed.), *Reports of Cases in the Courts of Star Chamber and High Commission*, Camden Society, new ser., vol. xxxix, 1886.

Gaut, R. C., *A History of Worcestershire Agriculture and Rural Evolution*, Worcester, 1939.

Gay, E. F., 'The Temples of Stowe and their Debts: Sir Thomas Temple and Sir Peter Temple, 1603–1653', *Huntington Library Quarterly*, vol. ii, 1938–9.

Gerard, T., *The Particular Description of the County of Somerset* (1633), edited by E. H. Bates, Somerset Record Society, vol. xv, 1900.

Gerrard, C. M., 'Taunton Fair in the Seventeenth Century: an archaeological approach to historical data', *Somerset Archaeology and Natural History* (Proc. Soms. Archaeol. and Nat. Hist. S.), vol. cxxviii, 1984.

Giles, J. A., *History of the Town and Parish of Bampton*, 1848.

Gill, H. and Guilford, E. L. (eds), *The Rector's Book of Clayworth 1672–1701*, Nottingham, 1910.

Gill, M. A. V., 'The Newcastle Goldsmiths and the Capital', *Archaeologia Aeliana*, 5th ser., vol. viii, 1980.

Godfrey, E. S., *The Development of English Glassmaking 1560–1640*, Oxford, 1975.

Goldthwaite, R. A., 'Local Banking in Renaissance Florence', *Journal of European Economic History*, vol. xiv, 1985.

Gonner, E. C. K., *Common Land and Inclosure*, 1912.

Gough, R., *The History of Myddle*, Sunninghill, Ascot, Berks., 1979.

Gould, J. G., *The Great Debasement: currency and the economy in Mid-Tudor England*, Oxford, 1970.

—— 'The Great Debasement and the Supply of Money', *Australian Economic History Review*, vol. xiii, 1973.

—— 'The Royal Mint in the early Seventeenth Century', *Economic History Review*, 2nd ser., vol. v, 1952.

Gouldesborough, J., *Reports of that learned and judicious clerk John Gouldesborough*, 1653 and various editions.

Gras, N. S. B., *A History of Agriculture in Europe and America*, sine data.

—— *The Evolution of the English Corn Market from the Twelfth to the Eighteenth Century*, Cambridge, Mass., 1915.

Grice-Hutchinson, M., *Early Economic Thought in Spain 1177–1740*, 1978.

Gurney, D., *The Record of the House of Gournay*, 1848.

H., S.H.A. (ed.), *Letter-Books of John Hervey, First Earl of Bristol 1651–1750*, 3 vols., Wells, 1894.

—— *The Diary of John Hervey, First Earl of Bristol*, Wells, 1894.

Hainsworth, D. R. (ed), *The Commercial Papers of Sir Christopher Lowther 1611–1644*, Surtees Society, vol. clxxxix, 1977 (1974).

—— *The Correspondence of Sir John Lowther of Whitehaven 1693–1698: a provincial community in wartime*, British Academy, 1983.

Hall, H., *Society in the Elizabethan Age*, 1887.

Hall, M. W., 'Early Bankers in Genoan Notarial Archives', *Economic History Review*, vol. vi, 1936.

Hamer, J. H., 'Trading at Saint White Down Fair, 1637–1649', *Somerset Archaeology and Natural History* (Proc. Soms. Archaeol. and Nat. Hist. S.), vol. cxii, 1968.

Hamilton, A. H. A. (ed.), *Quarter Sessions from Queen Elizabeth to Queen Anne*, 1878.

Hamilton, E. J., 'American Treasure and Andalusian Prices, 1503–1660', *Journal of Economic and Business History*, vol. i, 1928.

—— *American Treasure and the Price Revolution in Spain, 1501–1650*, Cambridge, Mass., 1934.

—— 'American Treasure and the Rise of Capitalism (1500–1700)', *Economica*, new ser., vol. ix, 1929.

—— 'Prices as a Factor in Economic Growth', *Journal of Economic History*, vol. xii, 1952.

Harbin, E. H. Bates (ed.), *Quarter Sessions Records for the County of Somerset, vol. ii: Charles I, 1625–1639*, Somerset Record Society, vol. xxiv, 1908.

Hardy, W. J. (ed.), *Hertford County Records: notes and extracts from the sessions rolls 1581–1698*, vol. i, Hertford, 1905.

Hardy, W. Le and Reckitt, G. L., *County of Buckingham: calendar of the sessions records*, vol. iii, Aylesbury, 1939.

Harland, J. (ed.), *The House and Farm Accounts of the Shuttleworths of Gawthorpe Hall*, Chetham Society, vols. xxxv, xli, xliii, xlvi, 1856–8.

Harper, L. A., *The English Navigation Laws: a seventeenth-century experiment in social engineering*, New York, 1939.

Harrison, W., 'The Description of England' in Holinshed *et al.*, q.v., vol. i.

Havinden, M. A. (ed.), *Household and Farm Inventories in Oxfordshire, 1550–1590*, Historical Manuscripts Commission, Joint Publication no x, Oxford Record Society, vol. xliv, 1965.

Heal, A., *The London Goldsmiths 1200–1800*, Cambridge, 1935.

Henry, J. A., *The First Hundred Years of Standard Bank*, edited by H. A. Siepmann, 1963.

Henstock, A., 'Cheese Manufacture and Marketing in Derbyshire and North Staffordshire 1670–1870', *Derbyshire Archaeological Journal*, vol. lxxxix, 1969.

Hessels, J. H. (ed.), *Ecclesiae Londino-Batavae Archivum*, 3 vols., Cambridge, 1887–97.

Hetley, T., *Reports and Cases*, 1657 and various editions.

Hewett, W., *The History and Antiquities of the Hundred of Compton*, Reading, 1844.

Hey, D., *Packmen, Carriers and Packhorse Roads: trade and communication in North Derbyshire and South Yorkshire*, Leicester, 1980.

Hibbert, T. D. (ed.), 'Letters relating to Lancashire and Cheshire *tempore* James I, Charles I and Charles II', *Historic Society of Lancashire and Cheshire: Proceedings and Papers*, session iv, 1852.

Higonnet, R. P., 'Bank Deposits in the United Kingdom 1870–1914', *Quarterly Journal of Economics*, vol. lxxi, 1957.

Hinton, R. W. K. (ed.), *The Port Books of Boston 1601–1640*, Lincolnshire Record Society Publications, vol. 1, 1956.

Historical Manuscripts Commission, *Twelfth Report*, 1890, Appendix, pts i, iv.

—— *Thirteenth Report*, 1892, Appendices i, ii.

—— *Calendar of the Manuscripts of the Marquess (Marquis) of Bath at Longleat House*, 5 vols., 1904–80.

—— *Calendar of the Manuscripts of the Marquess (Marquis) of Salisbury at Hatfield House* (Appendix to *Twelfth Report*) several parts, 1883– in progress.

—— *The Manuscripts of His Grace the Duke of Portland at Welbeck Abbey* (Appendices to *Thirteenth, Fourteenth and Fifteenth Reports*), 4 vols., 1891–7.

—— *Report on the Manuscripts of His Grace the Duke of Buccleuch and Queensberry at Montagu House*, 3 vols. in 4 pts, 1899–1926.

—— *Report on Manuscripts in Various Collections*, 8 vols., 1901–14.

—— and see under Havinden, Vanes.

Holden, J. M., 'The Bill of Exchange during the Seventeenth Century', *Law Quarterly Review*, 1951.

—— *The History of Negotiable Instruments in English Law*, 1955.

Holderness, B. A., 'Credit in English Rural Life before the Nineteenth Century, with special reference to the period 1650–1720', *Agricultural History Review*, vol. xxiv, 1976.

—— 'Credit in a Rural Community 1660–1800: some neglected aspects of probate inventories', *Midland History*, vol. iii, 1975–6.

Holdsworth, W., *A History of English Law*, vol. i, 1956; vol. iii, 1935; vol. viii, 1937.

Holinshed, H. and Harrison, W., augmented by J. Hooker, *Chronicles*, 3 vols., 1587.

Horrocks, J. W. (ed.), *The Assembly Books of Southampton*, 4 vols., 1917–25.

Horsefield, J. K., 'The Bank of England as Mentor', *Economic History Review*, 2nd ser., vol. ii, 1949.

—— 'The Beginnings of Paper Money in England', *Journal of European Economic History*, vol. vi, 1977.

—— 'The "Stop of the Exchequer" Revisited', *Economic History Review*, 2nd ser., vol. xxxv, 1982.

Houghton, J. (ed.), *Husbandry and Trade Improv'd, being a collection of many valuable materials*, 4 vols., 1692 and various editions.

Hudleston, C. R. (ed.), *Naworth Estate and Household Accounts 1648–1660*, Surtees Society, vol. clxviii, 1958 (1953).

Hughes, E., *Studies in Administration and Finance 1558–1825*, Manchester, 1934.

—— *North Country Life in the Eighteenth Century*, 2 vols., 1952–65.

Hughes, J. R. T., *Fluctuations in Trade, Industry and Finance: studies in British economic development 1850–1860*, Oxford, 1960.

Hunt, R. C., *The Development of the Business Corporation in England 1800–1867*, Cambridge, Mass., 1936.

Ibbetson, D., 'Assumpsit and Debt in the early Sixteenth Century: the origins of the indebitatus count', *Cambridge Law Journal*, 1982.

Jackman, W. T., *The Development of Transportation in Modern England*, 1962.

James, M. E. (ed.), *The Estate Accounts of the Earl of Northumberland 1562–1637*, Surtees Society, vol. clxiii, 1955.

Jenkins, D. (ed.), *Legal History Studies*, Cardiff, 1972.

Jewell, H. M., *English Local Administration in the Middle Ages*, Newton Abbot and New York, 1972.

John, A. H., 'English Agricultural Improvements and Grain Exports 1660–1765' in Coleman and John, q.v.

Johnson, A. C., 'Roman Egypt', in Frank, *Economic Survey*, q.v.

Johnson, H. C. (ed.), *Minutes of Proceedings in Sessions 1563 and 1574–1592*, Wiltshire Record Society, Devizes, 1949.

Jones, G. P., 'Some Sources of Loans and Credit in Cumbria before the Rise of Banks', *Transactions of the Cumberland and Westmorland Antiquarian and Archaeological Society*, new ser., vol. lxxv, 1975.

Joslin, D. M., *Central Banking in Latin America*, 1963.

—— 'London Private Bankers 1720–1785' in Carus-Wilson, q.v., vol. ii.

Judges, A. V., 'Philip Burlamachi: financier of the Thirty Years War', *Economica*, vol. vi, 1926.

—— 'The Origins of English Banking', *History*, vol. xvi, 1931.

Kaeuper, R. W., *Bankers to the Crown: the Riccardi of Lucca and Edward I*, Princeton, N.J., 1973.

Kalm, P., *Kalm's Account of his Visit to England*, 1892.

Keble, J., *Reports in the Court of King's Bench from XII to XXX King Charles II*, 2 pts, 1685 and various editions.

Kennedy, P. A., *Nottinghamshire Household Inventories*, Thoroton Society, Record Series, vol. xxii, 1963.

Kepler, J. S., *The Exchange of Christendom: the international entrepôt at Dover 1622–51*, Leicester, 1976.
Kerridge, E., 'Early Modern English Markets' in Anderson and Latham, q.v.
—— 'Landowners and Farmers in England during the "Price Revolution" in the 16th and 17th centuries' in *Agricoltura e Transformazione dell' Ambiente secoli XIII – XVIII*, ed. A. Guarducci, Prato, [1984].
—— *Textile Manufactures in Early Modern England*, Manchester, 1985.
—— *The Agricultural Revolution*, 1967.
—— 'The Movement of Rent, 1540–1640' in Carus-Wilson, q.v., vol. ii.
Keynes, J. M., *Treatise on Money*, 2 vols., 1930.
King, W. T. C., *History of the London Discount Market*, 1936.
Kirby, J., *The Suffolk Traveller*, 1764.
Kirk, R. E. G. and E. F. (eds.), *Returns of Aliens dwelling in the City and Suburbs of London from the reign of Henry VIII to that of James I*, Publications of the Huguenot Society of London, vol. x, in 4 pts, 1900–8.
Knappen, M. M., *Tudor Puritanism*, Chicago and London, 1970.
Kneisel, E., 'The Evolution of the English Corn Market', *Journal of Economic History*, vol. xiv, 1954.

L., J., *A Discourse concerning the great Benefit of Drayning and Imbanking and of Transportation by Water within the Country*, sine loco, 1641.
Lane, F. C., *Venice and History*, Baltimore, 1966.
Larkin, J. F. (ed.), *Stuart Royal Proclamations*, vol. ii, Oxford, 1983.
Larkin, J. F. and Hughes, P. L. (eds), *Stuart Royal Proclamations*, vol. i, Oxford, 1973.
Lattes, E., *La Libertà della Banche a Venezia del secolo XIII al XVII*, Milan, 1869.
Laurence, J., *A New System of Agriculture*, 1726.
Le Cheminant, K., *Colonial and Foreign Banking Systems*, 1931.
Leigh, E., *England Described*, 1659.
Leighton-Boyce, J. A. S. L., *Smiths the Bankers, 1658–1958*, 1958.
Leland, J., *The Itinerary*, edited by L. T. Smith, 5 vols., 1906–10.
Lennard, R. V., 'English Agriculture under Charles II: the evidence of the Royal Society's "Enquiries"', *Economic History Review*, vol. iv, 1932–4; and reprinted in W. E. Minchinton, *Essays in Agrarian History*, q.v., vol. i.
Leonard, W., *Reports and Cases of Law*, 2 vols., 1658 and various editions.
Lewis, E. A. (ed.), *The Welsh Port Books (1550–1603)*, Hon. Cymmrodorion Society, Cymmrodorion Record Series, vol. xii, 1927.
Lisle, E., *Observations in Husbandry*, 1757.
Lodge, E. (ed.), *Illustrations of British History*, 3 vols., 1838.
Lodge, E. C. (ed.), *The Account Book of a Kentish Estate 1616–1704*, British Academy, 1927.
Longfield, A. K., *Anglo-Irish Trade in the Sixteenth Century*, 1929.
Lopez, R. S., *The Commercial Revolution of the Middle Ages 950–1350*, Englefield Cliffs, N.J., 1970.
—— 'The Trade of Medieval Europe: the South' in Postan and Rich, q.v.
Lopez, R. S. and Raymond, I. W., *Medieval Trade in the Mediterranean World*, New York, 1935.

Lowe, N., *The Lancashire Textile Industry in the Sixteenth Century*, Chetham Society, 3rd ser., vol. xx, 1972.

Lupton, D., *London and the Country Carbonadoed and Quatred into severall Characters*, 1632.

Lutwyche, E., *Un Livre des Entries*, 2 vols., 1704 and various editions.

MacCaffrey, W. T., *Exeter, 1540–1640*, Cambridge, Mass. and London, 1975.

McGrath, P. (V.) (ed.), *Merchants and Merchandise in Seventeenth-Century Bristol*, Bristol Record Society, vol. xix, 1955.

—— 'The Marketing of Food, Fodder and Livestock in the London area in the Seventeenth Century', typescript thesis, M.A., London University, 1948.

Malynes, G., *Consuetudo vel Lex Mercatoria*, 1622, 1655, 1656.

—— *The Maintenance of Free Trade*, 1622.

Mann, J. de L., 'Clothiers and Weavers in Wiltshire during the Eighteenth Century' in Pressnell, *Studies in the Industrial Revolution*, q.v.

—— (ed.), *Documents Illustrating the Wiltshire Textile Trades in the Eighteenth Century*, Wiltshire Record Society, vol. xix, 1963.

—— *The Cloth Industry in the West of England from 1660 to 1880*, Oxford, 1971.

Marcham, W. M. and F. (eds), *Court Rolls of the Bishop of London's Manor of Hornsey 1603–1701*, 1929.

Marius, J., *Advice concerning Bils of Exchange*, 1651; and in Malynes, *Consuetudo*, 1655, 1656, q.v.

Marsden, R. G. (ed.), *Select Pleas in the Court of Admiralty, vol. ii: 1547–1602*, Selden Society, vol. xi, 1897.

Martin, J. B., *'The Grasshopper' in Lombard Street*, 1892.

Marshall, J. D., 'Kendal in the late Seventeenth and Eighteenth Centuries', *Transactions of the Cumberland and Westmorland Antiquarian and Archaeological Society*, new ser., vol. lxxv, 1975.

Marshall, W., *A Review (and Complete Abstract) of the Reports to the Board of Agriculture from the Midland Department of England*, 1815.

—— *A Review of the Reports to the Board of Agriculture from the Northern Department of England*, 1808.

—— *A Review (and Complete Abstract) of the Reports to the Board of Agriculture from the Southern and Peninsular Departments of England*, 1817.

—— *A Review of the Reports to the Board of Agriculture from the Western Department of England*, 1810.

—— *Minutes, Experiments, Observations and General Remarks on Agriculture in the Southern Counties*, 2 vols., 1799.

—— *The Rural Economy of Glocestershire*, 2 vols., Gloucester, 1789.

—— *The Rural Economy of the Midland Counties*, 2 vols., 1790.

—— *The Rural Economy of Norfolk*, 2 vols., 1787.

—— *The Rural Economy of the Southern Counties*, 2 vols., 1798.

—— *The Rural Economy of the West of England*, 2 vols., 1796.

—— *The Rural Economy of Yorkshire*, 2 vols., 1788.

Mather, W., *Of Repairing and Mending the Highways*, 1696.

Melling, E. (ed.), *Kentish Sources iii: aspects of agriculture and industry*, Maidstone, 1961.

Melton, F. T., *Sir Robert Clayton and the Origins of English Deposit Banking 1658–1685*, Cambridge, 1986.

Mendenhall, T. C., *The Shrewsbury Drapers and the Welsh Wool Trade in the XVI and XVII Centuries*, 1953.

Millican, P., *A History of Horstead and Stallinghall*, Norwich, 1937.

Mimardière, A. M., 'The Warwickshire Gentry, 1660–1730', typescript thesis, M.A., Birmingham University, 1963.

Minchinton, W. E., 'Bristol – Metropolis of the West in the Eighteenth Century', *Transactions of the Royal Historical Society*, 5th ser., vol. iv, 1954.

—— (ed.), *Essays in Agrarian History*, 2 vols., Newton Abbot, 1968.

Mises, L. von, *Human Action*, Chicago, 1966.

—— *Theory and History*, 1958.

—— *The Theory of Money and Credit*, Indianapolis, 1981.

Moore, F., *Cases Collect & Report*, 1663 and various editions.

Moore, J., *The History or Narrative of the Great Level of the Fenns called the Bedford Level*, 1685.

Moore, J. S., *The Goods and Chattels of our Forefathers: Frampton Cotterell and District Probate Inventories 1539–1804*, London and Chichester, 1976.

Morton, J., *The Natural History of Northamptonshire*, 1712.

Mosse, M., *The Arraignment and Conviction of Usurie: that is the iniquities and unlawfulness of usurie displayed in sixe sermons preached at St Edmunds Burie in Suffolke, upon Prov. 28.8*, 1595.

Munday, R., 'A Legal History of the Factor', *Anglo-American Law Review*, vol. vi, 1977.

Munro, J. H., 'Bullionism and the Bill of Exchange in England 1272–1663' in *Dawn of Modern Banking*, q.v.

Nef, J. U., 'Prices and Industrial Capitalism in France and England, 1540–1640' in Carus-Wilson q.v., vol. [i].

—— *The Conquest of the Material World*, Chicago and London, 1964.

—— *The Rise of the British Coal Industry*, 2 vols., 1932.

Nelson, B., *The Idea of Usury*, Chicago, 1969.

Noonan, J. T., *The Scholastic Analysis of Usury*, Cambridge, Mass., 1957.

Norden, J., *Speculi Britanniae Pars: The Description of Hartfordshire*, 1598.

—— *The Surveiors Dialogue*, 1618.

North, D., *Discourses upon Trade, principally directed to the cases of interest, coynage, clipping, increase of money*, 1691.

North, J., *The Lives of the Rt Hon. Francis North, Baron Guilford; the Hon. Sir Dudley North; and the Hon. and Rev. Dr John North*, edited by A. Jessop, 3 vols., 1890.

Notestein, W., Relf, F. H. and Simpson, H. (eds), *Commons Debates 1621*, 7 vols., New Haven, 1935.

Ogilby, J., *Britannia*, 1675.

Origo, I., *The Merchant of Prato: Francesco di Marco Datini*, 1957.

Owen, C. C., 'The Early History of the Upper Trent Navigation', *Transport History*, vol. i, 1968.

Parkes, J., *Travel in England in the Seventeenth Century*, Oxford, 1925.

Pawson, E., *Transport and Economy: the turnpike roads of eighteenth century Britain*, London and New York, 1977.

Pearce, B., 'Elizabethan Food Policy and the Armed Forces', *Economic History Review*, vol. xii, 1949.

Phelps-Brown, E. H. and Hopkins, S. V., 'Seven Centuries of Building Wages' in Carus-Wilson, q.v., vol. ii.

—— 'Seven Centuries of the Prices of Consumables compared with Builders' Wage-rates' in Carus-Wilson, q.v., vol. ii, and in Ramsey, q.v.

—— 'Wage-rates and Prices: the evidence for population pressure in the sixteenth century', *Economica*, new ser., vol. xxiv, 1957.

Phillimore, W. P. W. and Fry, G. S. (eds), *Abstracts of Gloucestershire Inquisitiones Post Mortem in the reign of King Charles the First*, Index Library, British Record Society, 3 pts (vols.), 1893–9.

Piccope, G. J. (ed.), *Lancashire and Cheshire Wills and Inventories from the Ecclesiastical Court Chester*, Chetham Society, 3 portions, vols xxxiii, li, liv, 1857–61.

Pitt, W., *A General View of the Agriculture of the County of Leicester*, 1809.

—— *A General View of the Agriculture of the County of Northampton*, 1809.

Plot, R., *The Natural History of Oxfordshire*, Oxford, 1677.

—— *The Natural History of Staffordshire*, Oxford, 1686.

Plucknett, T. F. T., *A Concise History of the Common Law*, 1956.

Pococke, R., *The Travels through England of Dr Richard Pococke, successively bishop of Meath and Ossory, during 1750, 1751 and later years*, Camden Society, new ser., vols xlii, xliv, 1888–9.

Postan, M. M., 'Private Financial Instruments in Medieval England', *Vierteljahrschrift fuer Sozial-und-Wirtschaftsgeschichte*, vol. xxiii, 1930.

Postan, M. M., Rich, E. E. and H. J. Habakkuk (eds), *The Cambridge Economic History of Europe*, vol. ii, 1952; vol. iv, 1967.

Postlethwayt, M., *The Universal Dictionary of Trade and Commerce, translated from the French of M. Savary, with large additions and improvements*, 2 vols., 1757.

Powell, E., 'Pryce (Newtown Hall) Correspondence, Etc.', *Collections Historical and Archaeological relating to Montgomeryshire*, vol. xxxi, 1900.

Powell, E. T., *The Evolution of the Money Market 1385–1915*, 1966.

P[owell], R., *Depopulation Arraigned*, 1636.

Pressnell, L. S., *Country Banking in the Industrial Revolution*, Oxford, 1956.

—— (ed.), *Studies in the Industrial Revolution presented to T. S. Ashton*, 1960.

Prestwich, M., 'Italian Merchants in late Thirteenth and early Fourteenth Century England' in *Dawn of Modern Banking*, q.v.

Prideaux, W. S. (ed.), *Memorials of the Goldsmiths' Company, being gleanings from their records between the years 1335 and 1815*, 2 vols., sine loco nec data.

Procter, T., *A Profitable Worke to this Whole Kingdome*, 1610.

Prynne, W., *Brief Animadversions on Amendments of, and Additional*

Explanatory Records to, the Fourth Part of the Institutes of the Lawes of England, 1669.

Purvis, J. S., 'A Note on XVI Century Farming in Yorkshire', *Yorkshire Archaeological Journal*, vol. xxvi, 1944–7.

—— (ed.), *Select XVI Century Causes in Tithe from the York Diocesan Registry*, Yorkshire Archaeological Society Record Series, vol. cxiv, 1949 (1947).

R., J., *The Mystery of the New-fashioned Goldsmiths and Bankers*, 1676.

Raine, J. (ed.), *Wills and Inventories from the Register of the Archdeacon of Richmond*, Surtees Society, vol. xxvi, 1853.

Raleigh, W., *Observations touching Trade and Commerce with the Hollander and other Nations, as it was presented to King James*, 1653.

Ramsay, G. D., *The End of the Antwerp Mart, vol. ii: The Queen's Merchants and the Revolt of the Netherlands*, Manchester, 1986.

—— 'The Smugglers' Trade: neglected aspects of English commercial development', *Transactions of the Royal Historical Society*, 5th ser., vol. ii, 1952.

Ramsey, P. H. (ed.), *The Price Revolution in Sixteenth Century England*, 1971.

Ray, J., *Historia Plantarum*, 3 vols., 1686–1704.

Raymond, R., Lord, *Reports of Cases*, 1696 and various editions.

Reddaway, T. F., 'The London Goldsmiths *circa* 1500', *Transactions of the Royal Historical Society*, 5th ser., vol. xii, 1962.

Reddaway, T. F. and Walker, L. E. M., *The Early History of the Goldsmith's Company 1327–1509*, 1975.

Reed, M. (ed.), *The Ipswich Probate Inventories 1583–1631*, Suffolk Record Society, vol. xxii, 1981.

Reyce, R., *The Breviary of Suffolk*, (1618), edited by Lord F. Hervey, 1902.

Rhodes, W. E., 'Italian Bankers in England and their Loans to Edward I and Edward II' in Tout and Tait, q.v.

Richards, R. D., 'A Pre-Bank of England Banker – Edward Backwell', *Economic History*, vol. i, 1929.

—— *The Early History of Banking in England*, 1929.

—— 'The First Fifty Years of the Bank of England' in Van Dillen, q.v.

—— 'The Pioneers of Banking in England', *Economic History*, vol. i, 1929.

Riden, P. (ed.), *George Sitwell's Letterbook 1662–66*, Derbyshire Record Society, vol. x, 1985.

Risdon, T., *The Chorographical Description or Survey of the County of Devon*, 1723.

Ritchie, J. (ed.), *Reports of Cases decided by Francis Bacon in the High Court of Chancery (1617–1621)*, 1932.

Roake, M. and Whyman, J. (eds), *Essays in Kentish History*, 1973.

Robinson, H., *The British Post Office: a history*, Princeton, N.J., 1948.

Robinson, T., *An Essay towards a Natural History of Westmorland and Cumberland*, 1709.

Rostovtzeff, M., *Social and Economic History of the Hellenistic World*, 3 vols., Oxford, 1941.

—— *Social and Economic History of the Roman Empire*, 2 vols., Oxford, 1947.

Rowlands, M. B., *Masters and Men in the West Midlands Metalware Trades before the Industrial Revolution*, Manchester, 1975.

Rowse, A. L., *The England of Elizabeth: the structure of society*, 1973.

Runciman, S., 'Byzantine Trade and Industry' in Postan, Rich and Habakkuk, q.v., vol. ii.

Russell, E., 'The Societies of the Bardi and Peruzzi and their dealings with Edward III' in Unwin, q.v.

Rutherford, J. (ed.), *The Miscellaneous Papers of Captain Thomas Stockwell 1590–1611*, Southampton Record Society, 2 vols. 1932–3.

Samuel, E. R., 'Sir Francis Child's Jewellery Business', *Three Banks Review*, no 113, 1977.

Sayers, R. S., *Central Banking after Bagehot*, Oxford, 1957.

—— *Gilletts in the London Money Market 1867–1967*, Oxford, 1968.

—— *The Bank of England 1891–1944*, 2 vols., Cambridge, 1976.

Scarlett, J., *The Stile of Exchanges*, 1682.

Schumpeter, J. A., *Business Cycles: a theoretical, historical and statistical analysis of the capitalist process*, 2 vols., New York and London, 1939.

—— *Capitalism, Socialism and Democracy*, New York, 1975.

—— *History of Economic Analysis*, 1954.

Serjeant, W. R. and R. K., *Index of the Probate Records of the Archdeaconry of Suffolk, 1444–1700*, Index Library, British Record Society, vols cx, cxi, 1979–80.

Seyer, S., *Memoirs of Bristol*, 2 vols., 1821.

Sharrock, R., *History of the Propagation and Improvement of Vegetables by the Concurrence of Art and Nature*, Oxford, 1660.

Sheppard, W., *The Touchstone of Common Assurances*, 1648.

Shower, B., *Reports of Cases in the King's Bench during the reigns of Charles the 2nd, James the 2nd and William the 3rd*, 2 vols., 1794 and various editions.

Skeel, C., 'The Cattle Trade between England and Wales from the Fifteenth to the Nineteenth Centuries', *Transactions of the Royal Historical Society*, 4th ser., vol. ix, 1926.

Smith, A., *The Wealth of Nations*, edited by W. Cannan, 2 vols., 1961.

Smith, R., *Sea-Coal for London: history of the coal factors in the London market*, 1961.

Smith, T., *De Republica Anglorum*, 1583.

Smith, W., *The Particular Description of England, 1588*, edited by H. B. Wheatley and E. W. Ashbee, 1879.

Smith, W. and Webb, W., *The Vale Royall of England*, 1656.

Smith, W. J. (ed.), *Herbert Correspondence: the sixteenth and seventeenth century letters of the Herberts of Chirbury, Powis Castle and Dolgnog, formerly at Powis Castle in Montgomeryshire*, Cardiff and Dublin, 1963.

Smout, T. C., *Scottish Trade on the Eve of Union 1660–1707*, Edinburgh and London, 1963.

Smyth, J., *A Description of the Hundred of Berkeley*, Berkeley Manuscripts, vol. iii, edited by J. Maclean, Gloucester, 1885.

—— *The Names and Surnames of all the able and sufficient Men fit for His Majesty's Service in the Wars within the County of Gloucester*, 1902.

Sneyd, C. A. (ed.), *A Relation, or rather a True Account, of the Island of England; with sundry particulars of the customs of these people, and of the royal revenues under King Henry the Seventh, about the year 1500*, Camden Society, vol. xxxvii, 1847.

Spratt, J., 'Agrarian Conditions in Norfolk and Suffolk, 1600–1650', typescript thesis, M.A., London University, 1935.

Steele, R., *A Bibliography of the Royal Proclamations of the Tudor and Stuart Sovereigns*, 2 vols., Oxford, 1910.

Stenton, F. M., 'The Road Systems of Medieval England', *Economic History Review*, vol. vii, 1936.

Stephens, W. B., *Seventeenth Century Exeter: a study of industrial and commercial development*, Exeter, 1958.

Stern, W. M., 'Cheese shipped coastwise to London towards the middle of the eighteenth century', *Guildhall Miscellany*, vol. iv, 1973.

—— 'Fish Marketing in London in the first half of the eighteenth century' in Coleman and John, q.v.

Stewart, H., *History of the Worshipful Company of Gold and Silver Wyre-drawers*, 1891.

Stocks, H. (ed.), *Records of the Borough of Leicester 1603–1688*, Cambridge, 1923.

Stone, G. and Meston, D., *Law relating to Money-lenders*, 1927.

Stone, L., *An Elizabethan: Horatio Palavicino*, Oxford, 1956.

—— *The Crisis of the Aristocracy 1558–1641*, Oxford, 1965.

Stow, J., *Survey of London*, edited by H. B. Wheatley, 1956.

Stradling, J., *Storie of the Lower Borowes of Merthyrmawr*, edited by H. J. Randall and W. Rees, South Wales and Monmouthshire Record Society, vol. i, sine data.

Strieder, J., *Aus Antwerpener Notariatsarchiven*, Stuttgart, Berlin and Leipzig, 1930.

Sutherland, L. S., 'The Law Merchant in England in the Seventeenth and Eighteenth Centuries', *Transactions of the Royal Historical Society*, 4th ser., vol. xvii, 1934.

Sykes, J., *The Amalgamation Movement in English Banks, 1825–1924*, 1926.

Tawney, R. H. and Power, E. (eds), *Tudor Economic Documents*, 3 vols., 1924.

Taylor, A. M., *Gilletts: bankers at Banbury and Oxford*, Oxford, 1964.

Taylor, E. G. R., 'Leland's England' in Darby, q.v.

Taylor, J., *A New Discovery by Sea*, reprinted in *Miscellanea Antiqua Anglicana*, vol. iii, 1873.

—— *The Carriers Cosmographie*, 1637.

Te Lintum, C., *De Merchant Adventurers in de Nederlanden*, The Hague, 1905.

Temple, R. C., Sir (ed.), *The Travels of Peter Mundy in Europe and Asia*

1608–1667, vol. iv: Travels in Europe 1639–1647, Hakluyt Society, ser. 2, vol. lv, 1925.

Thirsk, J., *English Peasant Farming: the agrarian history of Lincolnshire from Tudor to recent times*, 1957.

—— 'The Sales of Royalist Land during the Interregnum', *Economic History Review*, 2nd ser., vol. v, 1952.

Thirsk, J. and Cooper, J. P. (eds), *Seventeenth Century Economic Documents*, Oxford 1972.

Thomas, J. H., 'A Seventeenth-century Merchant's Account Book' in Webb, Yates and Peacock, q.v.

Thomas, S. E., *The Rise and Growth of Joint Stock Banking*, vol. i, 1934.

Thomson, G. S., *Life in a Noble Household 1641–1700*, 1937.

Thomson, J., *History of Leicester*, Leicester, 1849.

Thornton, G. A., *A History of Clare, Suffolk*, Cambridge, 1930.

Tout, T. F. and Tait, J. (eds), *Historical Essays by Members of Owens College*, Manchester, 1902.

Tupling, G. H., *The Economic History of Rossendale*, Chetham Society, new ser., vol. lxxxvi, 1927.

Turnbull, G. L., 'Provincial Road Carrying in the Eighteenth Century', *Journal of Transport History*, vol. iv, 1977.

—— *Traffic and Transport: an economic history of Pickfords*, 1979.

Unwin, G. (ed.), *Finance and Trade under Edward III*, Manchester, 1918.

Upton, A. F., *Sir Arthur Ingram, c. 1565–1642: a study of the origins of an English landed family*, 1961.

Usher, A. P., *The History of the Grain Trade in France 1400–1710*, Cambridge, Mass., 1913.

—— *The Early History of Deposit Banking in Mediterranean Europe*, vol. i, Cambridge, Mass., 1943.

—— 'The Origins of Banking: primitive banks of deposit 1200–1600', *Economic History Review*, vol. iv, 1934.

Vaisey, D. G. (ed.), *Probate Inventories of Lichfield and District 1568–1680*, Collections for a History of Staffordshire, 4th series, Staffordshire Record Society, vol. v, 1969.

Van Der Wee, H., 'Anvers et les Innovations de la Technique financière aux XVIe et XVIIe siècles', *Annales: économies, sociétés, civilisations*, vol. xxii, 1967.

—— 'Sporen van Disconto te Antwerpen tijdens de XVIe eeuw', *Bijdragen tot de Geschiedenis der Nederlanden*, vol. x, 1955.

—— *The Growth of Antwerp and the European Economy, 14th to 16th centuries*, 3 vols., The Hague, 1963.

Van Dillen, J. G. (ed.), *History of the Principal Public Banks*, 1964.

Vanes, J. (ed.), *The Ledger of John Smythe 1538–1550*, H.M.C. Joint Publication 19, and Bristol Record Society, vol. xxviii, 1974.

Ventris, P., *The Reports of Sir Peyton Ventris*, 2 pts, 1726.

Verney, F. (ed.), *Memoirs of the Verney Family during the Civil War*, 3 vols., 1892.

Vives, J. V., *An Economic History of Spain*, Princeton, N.J., 1969.

Wadsworth, A. P. and Mann, J. de L., *The Cotton Trade and Industrial Lancashire 1600–1780*, Manchester, 1931.
Ward, W. R., *The English Land Tax in the Eighteenth Century*, 1953.
Waylen, J., *A History Military and Municipal of the Town ... Marlborough*, 1844.
Webb, J., *Memorials of the Civil War between King Charles I and the Parliament of England, as it affected Herefordshire and the adjacent counties*, 2 vols., 1879.
Webb, J., Yates, N. and Peacock, S. (eds), *Hampshire Studies presented to D. Dymond*, Portsmouth, 1981.
Webb, S. and B., *The Story of the King's Highway*, 1963.
West, W., *The First Part of Simboleography*, 1615.
Westerfield, R. B., *Middlemen in English Business 1660–1760* in *Transactions of the Connecticut Academy of Arts and Sciences*, vol. xix, New Haven, 1915.
Whitwell, R. J., 'Italian Bankers and the English Crown', *Transactions of the Royal Historical Society*, vol. xvii, 1893.
Willan, T. S., *Elizabethan Manchester*, Chetham Society, 3rd ser., vol. xxvii, 1980.
—— *River Navigation in England 1600–1750*, 1964.
—— *The English Coasting Trade*, Manchester, 1938.
—— *The Inland Trade*, Manchester, 1976.
Willcox, W. B., *Gloucestershire: a study in local government*, New Haven, 1940.
Williams, C. (ed.), *Thomas Platter's Travels in England, 1599*, 1937.
Williams, M. I., 'Some Aspects of Glamorgan Farming in Pre-Industrial Times' in S. Williams' *Glamorgan Historian*, vol. ii, Cowbridge, 1965.
Williams, N. J., *Contraband Cargoes: seven centuries of smuggling*, 1959.
—— 'Francis Shaxton and the Elizabethan Port Books', *English Historical Review*, vol. lxvi, 1951.
—— 'The Maritime Trade of the East Anglian Ports 1550–1590', typescript thesis, D.Phil., Oxford University, 1952.
—— *Tradesmen in Early Stuart Wiltshire*, Wiltshire Records Society, vol. xv, 1960 (1959).
Williams, W. O., 'The Anglesey Gentry in Tudor and Stuart Times', *Anglesey Antiquarian Society and Field Club*, 1948.
Willson, D. H. (ed.), *The Parliamentary Diary of Robert Bowyer 1606–1607*, Minneapolis, 1931.
Winch, H., *The Reports of Sir Humphrey Winch*, 1657 and various editions.
Winchester, B., *Tudor Family Portrait*, 1655.
Woodward, D. (ed.), *The Farming and Memorandum Books of Henry Best of Elmswell 1642*, British Academy, 1984.
Woodward, D. M., *The Trade of Elizabethan Chester*, Hull, 1970.
—— 'A Comparative Study of the Irish and Scottish Livestock Trades in the Seventeenth Century' in Cullen and Smout, q.v.

Wright, T. W., *Queen Elizabeth and Her Times*, 2 vols., 1838.
Wrigley, E. A. and Schofield, R. S., *The Population History of England, 1541–1871*, 1981.
Wyatt, T. G., 'The Part Played by Aliens in the Social and Economic Life of England during the reign of Henry VIII', typescript thesis, M.A., London University, 1951.

Yale, D. E. C., 'A View of the Admiralty Jurisdiction: Sir Matthew Hale and the Civilians' in D. Jenkins, q.v.
—— (ed.), *Lord Nottingham's Chancery Cases*, Selden Society, 2 vols., vols lxxiii, lxxix, 1957–61.
Yelverton, H., *The Reports of Sir Henry Yelverton*, 1674 and various editions.
Youings, J., *The Dissolution of the Monasteries*, 1971.

Summary of select manuscript sources

Public Record Office

Court of Chancery:
  Proceedings, series i, ii
  Judicial Proceedings (Common Law side), Rolls Chapel series
Court of Exchequer:
  Augmentation Office: – Miscellaneous Books; Parliamentary Surveys;
  Particulars of Grants, Leases, etc.
  King's Remembrancer: – Depositions by Commission; Memoranda,
  Recorda; Miscellaneous Books; Special Commissions
  Treasury of Receipt: – Books
Court of Requests: Proceedings
Court of Star Chamber: Proceedings
Duchy of Lancaster: Pleadings
Prerogative Court of Canterbury:
  Inventories: Series I; 1718–82; Paper 1660–circa 1725;
  Parchment post 1660
Privy Council Registers
State Papers: Domestic, Ireland

British Library

Additional Charters, Manuscripts and Rolls
Egerton Manuscripts
Harleian Manuscripts
Lansdowne Manuscripts
Sloane Manuscripts

Aberystwyth, National Library

Episcopal Consistory Court of Hereford: Original Wills, Administrations
  and Inventories
Episcopal Consistory Court of St Asaph: Original Wills, Administrations
  and Inventories

Basset Down House
Neville Maskelyne's Account Book

Bedfordshire Record Office
ABP/W; FN 1094; GA 1732; PA 180

Berkshire Record Office
Archdeaconry Court of Berkshire, Original Wills etc.

Birmingham Reference Library
General Collection

Bodleian Library, Department of Western Manuscripts
Aubrey Manuscripts
Consistory and Archdeaconry Courts of Oxford: Original Wills etc.
English History: Herrick Papers
Hearne's Diaries
Topographical Manuscripts

Bradford City Library
Cunliffe-Lister Manuscripts

Bristol Record Office
Consistory Court of the Bishop of Bristol with the Deanery of Bristol:
    Inventories

Bristol University Library
Shrewton Manuscripts

Cheshire Record Office
Cholmondeley Collection
Court of the Vicar-General of the Chancellor of the Diocese in the Episcopal
    Consistory of Chester and the Rural Deaneries of the Archdeaconry:
    Original Wills and Administrations, with Inventories
Quarter Sessions Records: Lists of Informations etc.; Quarter Sessions Books

Chester Record Office
Town Clerk's Records: Protested Bills etc.

Deene House

Brudenell Manuscripts

Denbighshire Record Office (Clwyd Record Office)

Denbigh Borough Records

Devizes Museum (Wiltshire Natural History and Archaeological Society)

William Gaby His Booke 1656
Catalogue no 233

Devon Record Office

Brookings-Rowe Bequest
Exeter City Library Manuscripts
Huntsham Manuscripts
Marwood Tucker Collection

Essex Record Office

Archbishopric of Canterbury: Peculiar Court of the Archbishop in the
    Peculiar Deanery of Bocking: Inventories, Original Wills
Petre Manuscripts
D/DYW.17.

Friends' House, London (Society of Friends Library)

James Dix's Manuscripts

Gloucestershire Record Office

Marcham Collection
D.36/N.19; D.326/E.1

Hampshire Record Office

Archeaconry Court of Winchester: Original Wills and Inventories
Consistory Court of Winchester: Original wills and Inventories
Winchester City Records: Chamberlain's Accounts

Hertfordshire Record Office

Cashiobury and Gape Collection; Halsey Collection; Lytton Collection

House of Lords Record Office

House of Lords Papers

Institute of Historical Research, University of London

Beveridge Price and Wage History Research Manuscripts

Kent Archives Office

Archdeaconry Court of Canterbury: Inventory Papers; Inventory Registers
Consistory Court of Canterbury: Inventory Papers; Inventory Registers;
   Registers of Accounts and Inventories

Lancashire Record Office

Cavendish of Holker Collection
Court of the Vicar-General of the Chancellor of the Diocese in the Episcopal
   Consistory of Chester and in the Rural Deaneries of the Archdeaconry:
   Original Wills and Administrations, with Inventories
Hopwood Collection
Kenyon of Peel Collection
Knowsley Manuscripts
Petre of Dunkenhalgh Collection
Towneley of Towneley Manuscripts

Leicester Museum

City Records: Hall Papers
35/29/378; 4D.51/1

Leicester Town Hall

Quarter Sessions Records

Leicestershire Record Office

Beaumanor Collection
Commissary of the Bishop of Lincoln in the Archdeaconry of Leicester and
   the Court of the Archdeacon: Inventories; Wills and Administrations,
   with Inventories
DE 23/2/45

Lincolnshire Archives Office

Massingberd-Mundy Deposit

Liverpool Record Office

Norris Papers
Sir Willoughby Aston's Diary (920 MD 172)

Manchester Record Office

M.91/M1/26 (Rodes of Rochdale Accounts)

Middlesex Record Office

Archdeaconry Court of Middlesex (Middlesex Division): Inventories

Norfolk Record Office

Business Records
City Records: Books of Minutes of the Court of Assembly Proceedings;
    Books of Minutes of the Mayor's Court
Diocesan Records: Archdeaconry Court of Norfolk, Inventories; Arch-
    deaconry Court of Norwich, Inventories; Episcopal Consistory Court
    of Norwich, Inventories; Peculiar Court of the Dean and Chapter of
    Norwich, Inventories
Yarmouth Library Manuscripts: Pengelly Letters

Northamptonshire Record Office

Finch-Hatton Collection
Fitzwilliam (Milton) Collection
Miscellaneous Ledgers
Westmorland Collection
Young (Orlingbury) Collection

Nottinghamshire Record Office

Manorial Court of Mansfield: Original Wills etc.

Shakespeare's Birthplace Library, Stratford-on-Avon

Willoughby de Broke Collection

Somerset Record Office

Somerset County Documents
Strachey Collection (DD/SH)

Suffolk Record Office (Bury St Edmunds)

Episcopal Commissary Court for Bury St Edmunds with the Archdeaconry
    of Sudbury: Inventories

Suffolk Record Office (Ipswich)

Archdeaconry of Suffolk: Inventories; Original Wills and Inventories
Blois Family Archives

William Salt Library, Stafford

Paget of Beaudesert Manuscripts

Wiltshire Record Office

Archdeaconry Court of Sarum: Original Wills, Administrations and Inventories

Archdeaconry Court of Wiltshire: Original Wills, Administrations and Inventories

Charlton Estate Papers (Accession 88)

Episcopal Consistory Court of Salisbury: Original Wills, Administrations and Inventories

Ex Diocesan Registry of Salisbury: Unclassified Original Wills, Administrations and Inventories

Peculiar Court of Hurstbourne and Burbage: Original Wills, Administrations and Inventories

Worcestershire Record Office (Hereford and Worcester)

Episcopal Consistory Court of Worcester: Original Wills, Administrations and Inventories

705:85 (Bulk Accession 950), parcel 9

705:128 (Bulk Accession 1188), parcel i.

Index of persons

Acciaiuoli fam., 2, 3
Ackton, Jn, 49
Alberti fam., 2
Allet, Lady, 54
Anthony, Ed., 70
Arkwright, Sir Ric., 81
Ashby, Wm, 54
Aston, Sir Roger and Mrs, 54

Backwell, Ed., 70, 76–7, 79–81
Bacon, Sir Francis, 37, 67
Bagehot, W., 79
Baker, Jn, 49, 61, 63
Bankes, Jas, 55, 66–7
Bardi fam., 2, 3
Barron, Mr, 49
Bartlet(t), Wm, 44, 56
Barwell, Ric., 52–3
Beccaria, Cesare Bonesana,
    Marchese di, 88
Bedford, Wm Russell, Earl of, 55,
    57
Benham, Mr, 49
Bennet, Mr (London), 63
Best, Hy, 40, 42
Betts, Mr, 54
Binley, Mr, 54
Blande, Mr (Bristol), 48
Blaxton, J., 34
Blois, Hy, 46, 48–9, 56, 61, 63
Blumfyld, Mr, 56
Bole, Paul, 70
Bolton, Jn, 97

Bond, Jn, 48
Botero, Giovanni, 87–8
Boulton, Th., 97
Boyle, Mr, 54
Bradshaw, Ric., 47
—, Th., 60, 70
Bramwell, Lord, 39
Bridgwater, Francis Egerton,
    Duke of, 81
Brook, Jn, 49
Broughton, Mr, 63
Brown, Ric., 43, 45
Brownbrygg, Matt., 49
Browne, Jn, 50
—, Rachel, 42–3
—, Th., 58, 64
—, Wm, 50
Browning, fam., 46, 54–5
Bruce, Ed., Lord, 55
Bufken, Jacob, 48
Burghley, Wm Cecil, Lord, 56
Burlamachi, Philip, 3, 4, 54
Burnell, Mr, 49

Calvin, Jn, 37
Cantillon, Ric., 88
Cardinall, Mr (Stoke by Nayland),
    44
Carmichell, Sir Hugh, 54
Carr, Robt, E. of Somerset, 54
Cavendish, Sir Wm, 50
—, Wm, D. of Devonshire, 79
Cecil, Wm, Ld Burghley, 56

Student, Geo., 58
Sullom, Th., 61
Sydnam, Humph., 63
Symons, Ric., 44

Temple, Sir Th., 46, 63
—, Sir Ric., 63–4
Thomas, Mr, 53
Treswell, Mr, 67
Trewlanes, Robt, 63
Trobridge, Jn, 56
Turner, Francis, 48

Van Kasteren, Johan, 68
Vanlore, Pet., 4, 54, 66
Van Soldt, Jan, 62
Verney, Sir Ralph, 58, 60, 64–5
Vyner, Sir Robt, 79
—, Th., 66

Wadden, Mrs Alice, 63
Walker, Mrs (Hull), 48

Wallington, Hy, 50
Walton, Th., 45, 58–9, 64
Wansborough, Robt, 19
Warburton, Lady, 66
Warren, Ric., 70
Watson, Mr, 54
Watts, Mr, 54
Welser fam., 3
Wheeler (Whiller), Sir Edm., 54
Whitehall, Gilbert, 70, 77, 79, 81
Wilkinson, Th., 55
Wilson, Matt., 96
William III, 79
Winterfloode, Jn, 43
Wither, Geo., 38
Woode, Th., 44
Woolrich, Mr, 54
Worall, Mr, 47
Wormeley, Wm, 48
Wren, Mr, 54
Wright fam., 81
Wrigley, E. A., 89–91
—, Mr, 64

Index of places

Index of subjects

acceptance, 43, 59, 61, 72–4
agriculture, 16 sqq., 82, 86–7, 93, 97
ale, 23, 25
ancient demesne, 7
annuities, 48, 55–6, 66
apprentices, 52, 69
arbitrage, 4, 6, 16
Arkwright and Co., 81
armies, 26, 64, 69, 79, 80
assignment, 40, 46, 48–50, 52, 54, 56, 58–9, 67 sqq., 73–4, 76, 79
assumpsit, 72–3
attorneys, 41–2, 44

bacon, 25–6, 28, 32
Bacon, Cobbold and Co., 81
badgers, 5, 10, 29
bailees, 10
bailiffs, 53, 55
baizes, 17, 48
bakers, 29, 31, 98
bankers, 1–4, 42, 46 sqq., 98–9
bank-notes, 2, 42, 71, 76 sqq., 82, 97
Bank of England, 77 sqq.
Banks of Amsterdam, Delft, Hamburg, Rotterdam, Stockholm, 2
barges, 12, 30
barley, 19, 22 sqq., 29, 30
bearer bills, 41–2, 67–8, 74, 81
beef, 19, 24, 29, 50

beer, 22–3, 25, 32
bigg, 22
Bill on London, 47, 51, 60, 76 sqq.
bills obligatory, 2, 39 sqq., 45–7, 49, 59, 67, 69, 71–2, 74 sqq., 84, 94 sqq.
bills of exchange, 2, 14, 35, 38–9, 43, 45 sqq., 76 sqq., 94, 97–9
bills of lading, 14
Blackheath Country, 25
Blackmoors, 20, 22, 24
blanketmakers, 17
boats, 7, 11, 12
bonds, 39, 40, 44, 54, 67, 78, 94 sqq.
book debts, 33, 94 sqq.
booksellers, 12
boroughs, 7, 8, 11, 13, 26, 36, 64
bottled ale, 25
Brass Wire Co., 80
bread, 22
Breckland, 17, 20, 28
breweries, 27, 29
bridges, 7, 8, 11
brokers, 67, 78, 83
bullion, 2, 69, 80
bulls, 19
burgesses, 7, 52
business cycles, 37–8, 50–1, 77, 81–3, 87, 91–3, 97, 99

cadgers, 9
canals, 11

factors, 6, 15, 17, 18, 29–31, 33,
40, 42 sqq., 50–2, 55–6, 58,
61, 63–5, 68–9, 76–7
fairs, 5–7, 15, 20, 48, 51
fallow wool, 17
farmers, 7, 18, 22, 29, 30, 86,
97–8
farriers, 10
fat stock, 6, 7, 19–21, 24 sqq., 50
fellmongers, 17, 98
Fen Country, 11, 12, 17, 19, 20,
22–5, 27–8, 30, 32
fertilisers, 22, 25
fish, 7, 25, 28, 31–2, 49, 63
fishmongers, 33, 48–9
flax, 25
Flemings, 79
floating, 25
fodder, 22
forbearance, 34–5, 67
fowl, 25, 28
fractional reserves, 1, 2, 67, 69,
76–8
fruit, 25–6, 28, 30–1, 86
fulling, 15
fustian dealers, 77

geese, 25
Germans, 3, 4
glass, 9, 26
glaziers, 63
Gloucester cheese, 23, 27
glovers, 17, 98
gold, *see* precious metals
Goldney's bank, 81
goldsmith-bankers and Goldsmiths' Co., 42, 52–5, 65 sqq.,
76 sqq.
graziers, 19–21, 32, 46, 52, 62, 98
grazing butchers, 20, 27, 30, 33,
52
Great Fire, 99
Greeks, 1
grocers, 58, 98
Gurney's bank, 46, 54–5, 77, 82

haberdashers, 44, 98
hackneymen, 13

hardware, 6, 12, 14, 52, 97–8
hares, 25, 28
hatters, 97
hay, 22, 27–8
hemp, 25
Herries' Bank, 78
higglers, 9, 29
High Suffolk, 19–21, 23 sqq.,
30–2
highwaymen, 10
High Weald, 21–2, 24
Hoare's Bank, 76
hops, 19, 23, 28, 30, 32, 56
horses, 7, 13, 20, 24, 28, 32
hosiers, hosiery, 6, 14–17, 48, 52,
63, 76–7
hospitals, 79
Hudson's Bay Co., 80

imperial banks, 83
Industrial Revolution, 81–2, 93
inflation, 35–7, 82, 85, 87
inland bills of exchange, 45 sqq.,
76 sqq., 97–9
inland navigation, 7, 10–12, 31
innkeepers, 10, 86, 98
inns, 10, 13, 14, 29
Inns of Court, 73
insurance, 6, 34, 77, 80, 84
intelligence, 14, 15, 51
interest, 34 sqq., 46, 49, 66, 68–9,
79
international banks, 83
ironmongers, ironmongery, 6, 12,
14, 52, 97–8
Irish, 13
Italians, 1–4

jersey, 17
jewellers, jewellery, 54, 78, 86
Jews, 4
jobbers, 22, 30
joint-stock banks, 80–4
joint-stock companies, 77, 80–4
Jones and Co., 82
judgment debts, 40, 44
justices of peace, 29

solicitors, 53
soot, 22
Southdown Country, 19, 21, 25−7
South Seacoast Country, 21, 24, 27
sovereign debts, 3, 76, 79, 80
Spanish wool, 17, 18
stables, 27
steers, 19
stock (capital), 3, 18, 49, 76−8, 80, 82, 93
stockbreeders, 19−21, 23, 62
'Stop' of the Exchequer, 79
store animals, 6, 20−1, 24, 31−2, 62
streets, 8, 20
Suffolk Bank, 77
Sugarhouse Co., 49
swalers, 29, 31
swedes, 19
Swiss, 79

tailors, 97−8
tax collectors, taxes, 2, 55, 57, 64−5, 70, 76−7, 79−81
textile manufacturers, 14, 16, 17, 33, 42−4, 47, 49, 55, 67, 70, 77, 98
textiles, 6, 7, 10, 14−17, 41−2, 48−50, 76−7, 93
timber, 11, 12
tobacco, 25, 86
tokens, 99
tolls, 7
Town banks, 76−8
transaction cost, 34
transport, 7sqq., 47, 93
tranters, 29
travellers' cheques, 52, 78
travelling salesmen, 15
turkeys, 25, 28
turnips, 19, 24, 28
turnpikes, 7, 8
Tuscans, 2, 3

'Unicorn' Bank, 77, 80
union cloths, 17
universities, 13

usance, 45, 49, 57sqq., 63−5, 69, 74, 81, 83, 97
usurers, usury, 3, 34sqq., 41, 46−7, 49, 67, 80, 97, 99

Vale of Berkeley, 21, 23−4, 27−8, 30, 32
Vale of Evesham, 21sqq., 27, 32
Vale of London, 21, 24, 27−8, 30−2
Vale of Pickering, 19, 23−6, 28, 32, 52
Vale of Taunton Deane, 17, 19, 22, 24, 26−7
Vales of Hereford, 17, 19, 20, 22−5, 28
veal, 24, 28
vintners, 48

wages, wage-workers, 8, 85−6, 93, 95, 98
wagoners, 8, 9
wagons, 7sqq., 13
Wales, 17, 21sqq., 51
warehouses, 27
watches, 9, 86
Wealden Vales, 20sqq., 27−8
weavers, 33, 98
weld, 25
West Country, 10, 16, 17, 21sqq., 44, 52, 55
West End banks, 77−8
Western Waterlands, 17, 19sqq., 27−8
West-of-England textile district, 10, 16, 26
wharves, 10, 11, 29
wheat, 19, 22−4, 26−7, 29−31
whittawers, 17, 98
widows, 67, 86, 95, 97
woad, 25, 32
womenfolk, 17, 30, 40, 42−3, 48, 50, 54, 62−3, 66−7, 79, 86−7, 95−7
Woodland, the, 10, 17, 19sqq., 26−8
wool, 6, 11, 12, 16−18, 24−5, 50
woolcombers, 17, 18